THE DIVE SITES OF
SOUTH AFRICA

ANTON KOORNHOF

PASSPORT BOOKS
NTC/Contemporary Publishing Company

This edition published in 1997 by
Passport Books
An imprint of NTC/Contemporary Publishing Company
4255 West Touhy Avenue, Lincolnwood (Chicago), Illinois, 60646-1975
U.S.A.

International Standard Book Number: 0-8442-4853-3
Library of Congress Catalog Card Number: 97-67402

First published in South Africa by Struik Timmins Publishers (Pty) Ltd in 1991
Revised edition published in the UK by New Holland (Publishers) Ltd in 1995

Revised by Jennifer Stern
Managing editor: Annlerie van Rooyen
Editor: Glynn Williamson
Design concept: Philip Mann
Design and DTP: Julie Farquhar
Cover design: Peter Bosman
Map DTP: Bill Smuts
Medical consultant: Dr. Cleeve Robertson

Reproduction by Unifoto (Pty) Ltd, Cape Town
Printed and bound by Tien Wah Press (Pte) Ltd, Singapore

Photographic Acknowledgements:
page 134 S Adey; pages 74 (top), 75 (top), 82, 92, 96, 103, 104, 105 A Bannister; pages 11, 74 (bottom left), 77, 81, 102, 109, 116, 118, 119 J Brazendale; pages 43, 55 (bottom) G Cliff; front cover inset, pages 16, 88 Colour Lab/Struik Image Library; page 28 R de la Harpe; page 10 C Didcott; pages 141, 151 G Dreyer; page 122 J du Plessis; page 158 A Grey; page 153 L Hoffman (Struik Image Library); page 97 P Joubert (ABPL Photo Library); pages 17, 23, 29, 34, 36, 37, 51, 55 (top), 56, 63, 66 D King; pages 156, 157, 160 P Lambert; page 93 B J Maarsingh; pages 76, 83 (top), 111, 115, 136, 147, 149, 159 C Maxwell; pages 84, 139, 142 C Mostert; title page, pages 46, 49, 71, 101 (right) A Mountain; spine, page 31 M Nelson; page 144 P Pickford (Struik Image Library); cover, back cover inset, pages 15, 35, 39, 40, 41, 42, 45, 53, 54, 67, 75 (bottom left), 162, 174 P Pinnock; page 60 H Potgieter; pages 52, 129, 135, 143 C Roberson; pages 4, 22, 83 (bottom left and right), 101 (left), 125, 131, 146 J Seier; pages 61, 72, 75 (center left and right) P Southwood; pages 100, 117, 123, 128, 133, 152 G Spilby; page 74 (bottom right) D Steele (Photo Access); pages 12, 13, 19 E Thiel (Struik Image Library); pages 73, 89, 95, 98 J van der Walt; pages 25, 75 (bottom right), 145 P Wagner (Photo Access); page 108 K Young (Photo Access).

Author's Acknowledgements

Writing a guide book of this nature requires the help and goodwill of local experts, dive operators and divemasters who contribute their time and knowledge. Of the many people who helped me with my diving and research, I would like to give special thanks and appreciation to the sponsors of the first edition of this book:

Toyota South Africa; Protea Hotels; Ocean Divers International; Sun International; Sodwana Bay Lodge; J R Diving (Sodwana); Beekman Fibreglass; M&J Stores; and to **Malcolm Turner** who provided much of the information on wrecks (author of *Shipwrecks and Salvage, 1505 to the Present*, Struik 1988); **Dr Allan Kayle**, who checked the First Aid section in the first edition of this book; and to my brother, **Philip Koornhof**, who made it possible.

Publishers' Acknowledgements

The publishers gratefully acknowledge the invaluable assistance which the following people, and the organizations they represent, provided in updating this book:

Dr Cleeve Robertson, principal of the Ambulance Training College, Cape Town, for revising and updating *Health and Safety for Divers*; **Gavin Manning** and **Trevor Krull**, African Dive Adventures; **Christopher Sharpe**, Fotokino; **Jose Vieira**, Dive Africa Tours; **Grant Jameson**, Professional Diving Centre; **Andy Cobb**, Andy Cobb Ecodiving; **Roux le Noury**, Dive Nautique; **Gregg Horn**, Waterfront Divers; **Dennis Croukamp**, Kowie Dive School; **Michele Smit**, Mossel Bay Divers; **Boetie Scheun**, BS divers; **Aaron De Gouveia** and **Anita Els**, Scuba Africa; **John Piers**, Kenilworth-on-Sea; **Drew Grey**, BOING; **André Botha**; **Jaco Smit**, Scuba Venture; **Penny Krone**, Oceanography Library, UCT; **Charles Maxwell**, Underwater Video Services; **Mike Klee**, Mike's Dive Shop; **Duncan Pattenden**, Orca Industries; **Gregg Mathews**, Blue Water Divers; **Denise Coetzee**, SA Underwater Union; **Quinten Swanepoel**, NAUI (Africa Branch); **Johnny van der Walt**; **Peter Southwood**; **Anton van der Walt**; **Jaco Boshoff**, SA Maritime Museum; **Geremy Cliff**, Natal Sharks Board; **Paul Williams**, Sea Fisheries Research Institute; **Tony McEwan**, Two Oceans Aquarium; and **Kim Kruyshaar** who supplied the information on the proposed Simon's Town wreck trail.

CONTENTS

HOW TO USE THIS BOOK

THE REGIONS

The dive sites included in this book are arranged within six main geographical areas, or regions of South Africa: KwaZulu-Natal, the Eastern Cape, the Garden Route, the Southern Cape, the South-Western Cape, and Inland. An introduction to the individual regions describes the key characteristics and features of these main areas, as well as the general diving conditions that prevail.

THE SUBREGIONS

The larger geographical regions are divided into smaller subregions. Background information on climate, environment, points of interest and advantages or disadvantages to diving in the locality are provided.

THE MAPS

A detailed map is included near the front of each regional or subregional section. The purpose of the map is to easily identify the location of the dive sites described: this is achieved by repeating the number in the dive sites section, and on the map. For example:

1 will cross-reference to both the map and the dive site.

The map legend illustrated below pertains to all maps used in this book. Please note that the border around the map is not a scale bar.

N2	Motorways	7	Dive site numbers		Restricted diving area
N2	National road	Lighthouse			Nature reserve
tarred untarred	Main road	Wreck site			
tarred untarred	Minor road	⊕	Hospital		Marine reserve
N2 M4	Route numbers	O	City		
Rivers / Dam	Water features	o	Town & village		Marine sanctuary
TABLE MOUNTAIN	Mountain range	●	Place of interest		Built-up area

THE DIVE SITE DESCRIPTIONS

Each region's or subregion's premier dive sites are listed and begin with a number corresponding to the relevant map, a star rating, and symbols indicating key information (*see* below) pertaining to that site. Critical practical details (i.e. location, access, conditions and average and maximum depths) precede the description of the site, its marine life and special points of interest.

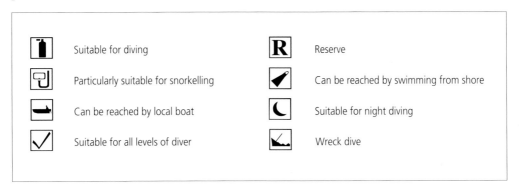

Suitable for diving   R   Reserve

Particularly suitable for snorkelling   Can be reached by swimming from shore

Can be reached by local boat   C   Suitable for night diving

Suitable for all levels of diver   Wreck dive

THE STAR-RATING SYSTEM

Each site has been awarded a rating, with a maximum of five and a minimum of one star.

★ pertains to scuba diving, and

★ to snorkelling, as follows:

★★★★★	first class
★★★★	highly recommended
★★★	good
★★	average
★	poor

THE REGIONAL DIRECTORIES

At the end of each region in the dive sites section is a regional directory with helpful telephone numbers and addresses. Here you will find practical information on how to get to an area, where to stay and eat, dive facilities, regional highlights and emergency measures.

OTHER FEATURES OF THIS BOOK

• Each section of the book is colour coded for ease of reference, as per the contents page.
• A general introduction to South Africa will fill you in on historical details of the country, and tell you a bit about the people and the economy of the country. This is followed by travelling tips – how to get to South Africa and how to get around the country once you are there. There is a wealth of information on diving and snorkelling in each region.
• Boxes containing interesting tips and concise information on marine reserves and certain species of marine life exist throughout the text.
• Feature spreads on special items of interest, such as the wreck of the HMS *Birkenhead* and ragged-tooth sharks, are combined in the dive site text to make this a wholly informative and interesting book which no diver should be without.

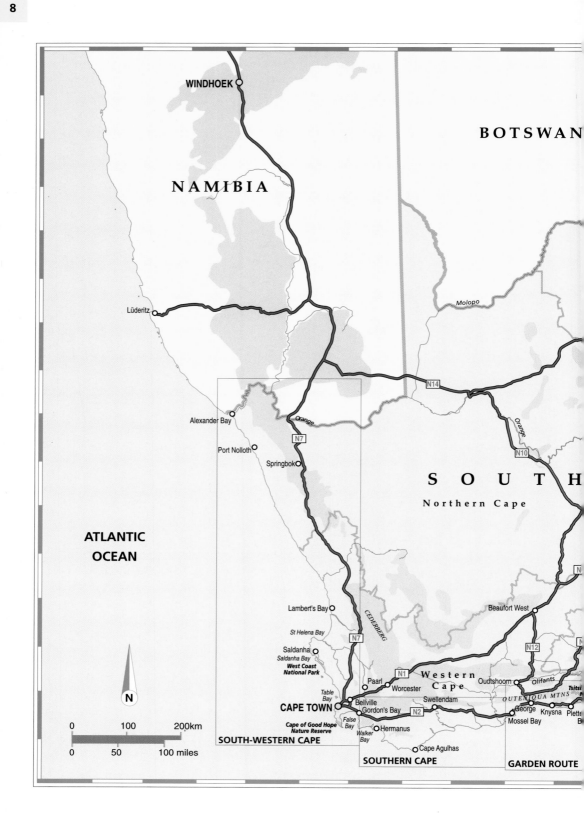

WINDHOEK

BOTSWAN

NAMIBIA

Molopo

Lüderitz

N14

Alexander Bay

Orange

Orange

N7

N10

Port Nolloth

Springbok

S O U T H

Northern Cape

ATLANTIC
OCEAN

Lambert's Bay

Beaufort West

St Helena Bay

CEDERBERG

N7

N12

Saldanha
Saldanha Bay
West Coast
National Park

Paarl

N1

Western
Cape

Oudtshoorn

Olifants

N

Worcester

OUTENIQUA MTNS

Tsitsi

Table
Bay

CAPE TOWN

Bellville
Gordon's Bay

Swellendam

George

Knysna

Plette

N2

Mossel Bay

B

Cape of Good Hope
Nature Reserve

False
Bay

Hermanus

Walker
Bay

Cape Agulhas

SOUTH-WESTERN CAPE

N

0   100   200km

0   50   100 miles

SOUTHERN CAPE

GARDEN ROUTE

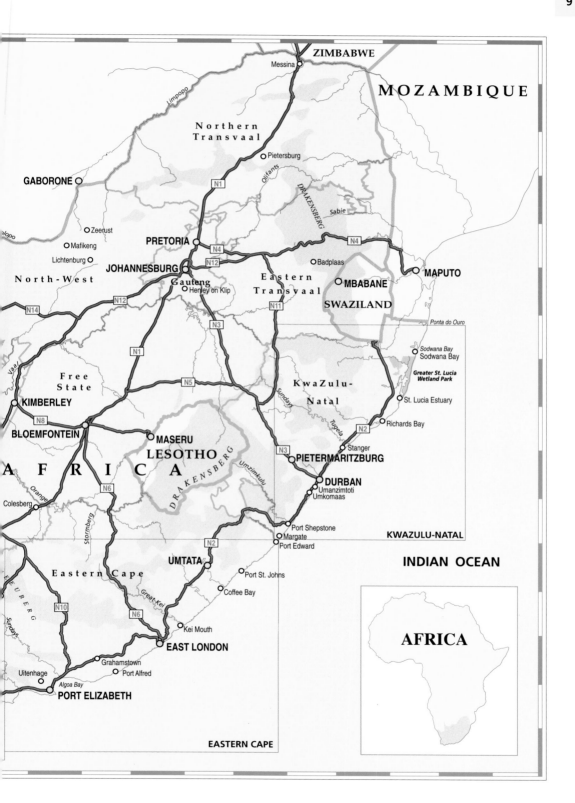

INTRODUCING SOUTH AFRICA

With the new dispensation in South Africa, more and more people are travelling to this captivating country and discovering just how much it has to offer. This is as much due to its interesting history and fascinating cultural mix as it is to the spectacular scenery and extensive tourism and adventure infrastructure.

THE NATURAL ENVIRONMENT

South Africa has a long and varied coastline and straddles the dividing line between the Indian and Atlantic oceans. The east coast is washed by the warm, southward-moving Mozambique, or Agulhas, Current which influences the prevailing temperatures, so that sub-tropical conditions prevail, despite the fact that the entire country (from about 27–34°S) falls outside the tropics. The Benguela Current flows northward along the west coast, but as it carries icy water from the polar regions, it does not bring rainfall to this arid area.

Coupled with the great range in altitude and latitude, the very different natures of these two oceans contribute to the vast range of climatic and vegetational conditions in this 'world in one country'.

Most of the country lies on a high central plateau (over 1500m (5000ft)) bounded by narrow coastal plains. The east coast is characterized by a high summer rainfall and, especially towards the north, high temperatures and humidity, while the West Coast is exceptionally dry with hot days and freezing-cold nights. The central plateau also experiences summer rainfall which decreases towards the west. Due to its altitude and distance from the sea, the interior shows a wide annual and daily temperature range.

The Western Cape experiences a heavy winter rainfall while the summer climate is hot and dry (unlike the east coast), while the Southern Cape is subject to rain all-year round, with most of the rain falling in winter.

The loggerhead turtle (above), which breeds in Maputaland, is the most common turtle found in southern Africa.
Coffee Bay (left) is on the spectacular Wild Coast, famed for its lonely beaches, sheer cliffs and thundering waves.

Not surprisingly, the weather and rainfall patterns are reflected in the dominant vegetation types in the various regions, with subtropical forests on the northern east coast, savanna grasslands in the interior and semidesert conditions on the west coast. The Southern Cape is characterized by temperate forests and the Western Cape shows a classic Mediterranean climate and vegetation, and is home to thousands of species of flowering plants. Small areas of montane grassland occur along the escarpment, most notably in the Drakensberg.

WHAT TO SEE AND DO

South Africa is one destination where non-diving companions have absolutely no reason to be bored, and even the most enthusiastic divers will be sorely tempted to spend at least a few days exploring this fascinating country.

Probably the first thing that springs to mind is a game-viewing safari. These range from relatively inexpensive self-drive, self-catering options in one of the excellent national parks, such as Umfolozi-Hluhluwe (not too far from the very popular dive resort of Sodwana Bay), or the world-renowned Kruger National Park in the Eastern Transvaal, to the somewhat more pricey, fully catered luxury safaris in one of the many private game reserves. Whichever option you choose, you are likely to see spectacular bushveld scenery and a wide variety of game, possibly even the 'big five' (lion, rhino, elephant, leopard and buffalo).

The best time of year for game-watching is very early summer (late September to early November), as there is very little grass or tree cover and standing water is found only in permanent water-holes or perennial rivers. The animals gather around these water-sources and can be easily seen through the scant vegetation. Once the rains fall, usually sometime in November, the animals become more difficult to spot through the new growth and even more difficult to find, as there are convenient pools of water all over and they are not bound to the regular water-holes. More adventurous visitors may wish to join a guided walking safari for a period ranging from a few hours to a few days.

Cape Point, a dramatic end to the Cape Peninsula.

For a wild experience of a different kind, white water rafting on the Tugela River in KwaZulu-Natal takes place in summer, and in winter, on the Doring River in the Western Cape. Less strenuous trips are run on the Orange, Breede and Vaal rivers all year.

Horse trails operate in the mountainous Drakensberg, on the beaches of the Western Cape and through the temperate forests of the Garden Route in the Southern Cape. There is good surfing along most of the coast, a vast network of hiking trails, and some excellent sport and natural climbing venues. South Africa's only ski-resort, at Rhodes in the Eastern Cape, relies on a snow machine to guarantee snow in June and July.

Those who wish to can take to the sky with one of the local gliding clubs or launch from a convenient hill with one of the many paragliding or hang-gliding schools. There are sky-diving clubs near most cities. On a

An artificial reef, formed by a number of wrecks in Smitswinkel Bay, is popular with more adventurous divers.

more relaxing note, hot-air ballooning trips are a superb way to view areas previously unvisited country, and trips are run over the Magaliesberg near Johannesburg, the Cape Winelands, the Drakensberg and the Pilanesberg Nature Reserve near Sun City.

Less energetic travellers need not fear. You will find, scattered along the coast and further inland, a number of rather sophisticated resorts with casinos, theatres and the like. The cities offer almost every urban attraction you could wish for, ranging from theatre, operas and symphony concerts to nightclubs, pubs and restaurants, and shopping malls, walking trails up mountains and through botanical gardens.

There is plenty of opportunity to indulge in the more usual tourist activities such as visiting gold mines, museums, or general sight-seeing. The Cape, particularly, is a traveller's delight, offering spectacular scenery, picturesque wine farms with world-class wines for sale and tasting, incredible wildflowers in spring (August to September), and magnificent beaches. The many museums and reconstructed rural and urban settlements should enable you to learn a little of the history and culture of this interesting country.

LIVING IN SOUTH AFRICA

South Africa has some familiarity (possibly notoriety) as it has been in the news for many years; firstly as the country which coined the phrase 'apartheid' and enshrined this policy in its constitution, and secondly, as the latest democracy in Africa. Many visitors, therefore, have certain preconceptions when they arrive and most are surprised to find that the country seems to function perfectly well with most people seeming to get on with their daily lives.

The cities are vibrant and cosmopolitan with informal street trading contrasting with established businesses and a sophisticated infrastructure. Of course, many people still live in 'traditional' settlements but these are all in the rural areas and, like elsewhere in the world, many of the younger people are moving to the cities to be educated or to seek employment. As in almost every African country, many of these people live in abject poverty and do not have access to proper housing, sanitation, health care or education.

Since the elections and smooth hand-over of power in April 1994 all has not been plain sailing, but despite the intermittent conflict and the continuing economic problems, the mood has been one of constant optimism. The new government has pledged to redress the inequalities inherited from the previous regime and is trying to find ways of financing the Reconstruction and Development Programme (RDP) which, it is hoped, will give all South Africans access to employment, housing and all essential services. Most of the funding for this will have to be siphoned off from other areas of government spending, obtained from increased taxes or borrowed.

Much foreign exchange, of course, can be obtained from tourism, so if you decide to travel to this country, try to support local businesses rather than buy prepaid packages in your home country. If you look around you will also find many small businesses, ranging from the local basket-sellers at Sodwana Bay and street-food vendors in the cities, to small shops and restaurants. Supporting these local entrepreneurs ensures that the benefits of tourism go directly to the people, and can only be for the good of the country as a whole.

HIGHLIGHTS OF NEIGHBOURING COUNTRIES

It would be a shame to travel all the way to South Africa and not at least be aware of some of the attractions of its neighbours. What follows is just some of the highlights and more details can be obtained from your travel agent:

Lesotho lies entirely within South Africa's borders, and is a mountainous country with miles of tracks suitable for long hikes, mountain-bike trails and pony-trekking which can be organized at many of the small resorts or villages. Trout fishing is rewarding in the many picturesque streams and experienced hang- or paragliders can bring their gliders and enjoy some superb ridge-soaring here.

Swaziland, on the border of South Africa and Mozambique, is less than a day's drive from Sodwana Bay, and offers magnificent hiking in Malalotja Nature Reserve and a very good value-for-money big-game safari experience at Mkhaya Wildlife Refuge. One day white water rafting trips on the Great Usutu River are run in summer.

Mozambique is only just recovering from 20 years of civil war and has a very undeveloped and haphazard infrastructure but is blessed with a long and glorious tropical coastline. There are a few dive operators scattered along the coast but the most dependable operations can be found in the Bazaruto Archipelago.

Botswana is a huge, underpopulated country, most of which falls within the somewhat desolate but beautiful Kalahari Thirstland. The Okavango Delta, one of the world's most spectacular wetland areas with miles of limpid, reed-fringed channels and huge game-filled plains, is renowned for well organised dugout canoe safaris. Horse trails, bird-watching, and quad-bike safaris can also be arranged.

Namibia offers superb desert scenery, long horse trails, strenuous hikes, excellent bird-watching and magnificent game-viewing in Etosha National Park. The only perennial rivers are those forming its borders, the Orange in the south and the Kunene and Kavango in the north. Interesting, well organized commercial canoeing and rafting trips of between half a day and six days are run on these rivers.

Zimbabwe offers good game-viewing in Hwange and Mana Pools national parks. The fascinating remains of the city state of Great Zimbabwe and, of course, the spectacular Victoria Falls, are highlights of this diverse country. Vic Falls, as both the waterfall and the

Sodwana Bay is renowned for its spectacular corals and colourful reefs.

town are affectionately known, offers many exciting activities, the most notable of which is the white water rafting in the Batoka Gorge, reputed to be the best commercially run, one-day white water trip in the world.

Malawi, a little further afield and aptly known as 'the warm heart of Africa', offers interesting freshwater diving in the huge and beautiful Lake Malawi. There are, at the time of writing, four dive operators, and the lake is filled with literally hundreds of species of colourful freshwater tropical fish.

Zambia is a beautiful country with many wilderness areas, lakes and waterfalls. The infrastructure is limited but there are excellent facilities in some of the game parks.

TRAVELLING TO AND IN SOUTH AFRICA

A dive holiday in South Africa need not cost you a fortune. In fact, most of the dive spots are serviced by reasonably priced establishments, or budget hostels. This does not mean you'll have to rough it, as there are also some luxury options available, so with careful planning, you can plan your holiday to suit even the tightest budget and still enjoy great diving.

ENTRY REQUIREMENTS
Holders of the following passports do not need visas to enter South Africa as tourists: United Kingdom, Ireland, Lichtenstein, Germany, Kenya, Malawi, Lesotho, Swaziland and Botswana. All others do and can acquire them free of charge from South African diplomatic representatives or by writing to the Department of Home Affairs, Private Bag X114, Pretoria 0001. If you are travelling from or through an area where yellow fever is endemic, you will need an inoculation certificate.

WHEN TO VISIT
Summer, generally from November to January, is hot and dry in the Western Cape and hot, humid and wet in the rest of the country. Diving at this time of year is best in the Cape (although the water is cold), on the Garden Route Coast and right out in the Mozambique Channel, for example in Protea Banks off the KwaZulu-Natal South Coast. Autumn (February to April) is warm and balmy, becoming decidedly cool by April. Diving over the whole country is variable. Winter (May to July) is cool and dry in KwaZulu-Natal, cold and rainy in the Western Cape and bitterly cold and very dry in the interior. The diving in KwaZulu-Natal is excellent and is enlivened by the presence of migratory ragged-tooth sharks. Spring (August to October) is a good time to visit the Western Cape to see the spectacular flowers, and late September or October is a good time for game-viewing. The

---

*The maypole butterflyfish (**above**) is characterized by curved black lines radiating across the body and fins.*
*Wilderness (**left**), a beautiful resort which forms part of the Garden Route, is the centre of the Cape's lake district.*

diving, as in autumn, is variable, with good conditions interspersed with bad. Tourist pressure, particularly at the coast, is high over school holidays, especially the Easter and Christmas holidays, and the whole of December and most of January. The KwaZulu-Natal Coast is very popular during the winter holidays in July.

PUBLIC HOLIDAYS

1 January	New Year
March/April	Easter weekend
21 March	Human Rights Day
27 April	Freedom Day
1 May	Workers' Day
16 June	Youth Day
9 August	National Women's Day
24 September	Heritage Day
16 December	Day of Reconciliation
25 December	Christmas Day
26 December	Day of Goodwill

TIME ZONE

Central African Standard Time (CAST) is two hours ahead of Greenwich Mean Time and operates throughout southern Africa all year. The only exception is NST (Namibian Standard Time) which is the same as CAST in summer but is one hour behind in winter (from 02:00 on the first Sunday in April to 02:00 on the first Sunday of September).

HEALTH AND SAFETY

Most of South Africa is free from tropical diseases but malaria is endemic in the northern parts of KwaZulu-Natal and the Eastern Transvaal (including the Kruger National Park). This is a life-threatening disease so take all precautions such as using mosquito repellent, sleeping under a net or in an insect-proof room or tent, wearing long pants and a long-sleeved shirt at night, and taking appropriate prophylactic treatment. It is safe to drink tap water but any water obtained from streams or wells should be filtered and purified or boiled, as cholera may be a problem in areas of inadequate sanitation, and bilharzia does occur in some of the rural rivers in the warmer parts of the country. The incidence of HIV infection is high, so take all the recommended precautions.

Be especially aware of the strength of the sun as, at present, some of the highest UV readings in the world are being reached here. Always use a high-factor sunscreen, bring along a wide-brimmed sun hat, good quality sunglasses and a cool, long-sleeved cotton shirt with a collar. A well-fitting peak or peaked cap is essential if you are going to be taking long boat rides to dive sites.

Crime and violence are a risk in the cities where muggings and pick-pocketing are as likely as in any city in the world. Car hijacking is becoming more common, particularly in Johannesburg, and you are advised to drive with your windows closed and doors locked in the cities. If, however, you take sensible precautions such as not walking around alone at night or visiting dubious places of entertainment, you should be quite safe.

The medical services and facilities in South African cities are very sophisticated and equal to the best in the world, but this does not apply to the rural areas, although there are hospitals in all the major cities and most of the larger towns. Expert medical evacuation,

Buffels Bay is a popular recreation and diving spot within the Cape of Good Hope Nature Reserve.

including diver evacuation, is available through Medical Rescue International (MRI) and their subsidiary DivEvac. You can subscribe to one or both of these organizations or, if you already have medical evacuation or dive medical insurance, you can rest securely in the knowledge that there is a sophisticated service close by. Before you leave home check with your insurers that you will be covered in South Africa.

There are medically staffed recompression chambers in Cape Town, East London, Durban and Pretoria and MRI have a portable monoplace chamber.

MONEY
The unit of currency is the rand, divided into one hundred cents. Notes are in denominations of five (being phased out), 10, 20, 50, 100 and 200 rand, and coins in one, two, five, 10, 20 and 50 cents and one, two and five rand. It is quite easy to mistake the old 20 cent and 10 cent coins for the new R2 and R1 coins respectively, so check your change carefully until you are familiar with the coins.

Most towns, and some villages, have banks which are open from 09:00 to 15:00 on weekdays and on Saturday mornings until 11:00, and will change traveller's cheques or do credit card transactions. Most hotels, restaurants, car-hire firms, dive operators and some shops will accept all major credit cards and traveller's cheques.

COMMUNICATIONS
Post offices are open from 08:00 to 16:00, Monday to Friday, and 08:00 to 12:00 on Saturdays. Those in small centres and in the suburbs close for lunch between 13:00 and 14:00 on weekdays.

The telephone system is reliable and public 'phones operate on coins or cards which can be purchased from post offices or some shops. Telcom bureaus are a little more expensive than standard public 'phones but are very convenient and can be found in most cities, airports and information bureaus. Cellular phones operate at time of writing only in the major cities and along the main transport networks, but the system is constantly being expanded.

POWER AND ELECTRICITY

Electricity is 220 volt and power points are for round, three-pin 15 amp plugs. Many, but by no means all, caravan parks supply electricity to at least some camp sites. Diesel and petrol are available in even the smallest centres. Liquid Petrolem Gas (LPG) is obtainable at many fuel stations, agricultural co-operatives and, often, at general dealers in small towns. Small butane cannisters (Gaz cannisters) for camping stoves are obtainable at camping and out-door stores in all the cities and in some larger towns. High-tech batteries for cameras and some underwater torches, such as lithium batteries, can be obtained from camera and elec-tronics shops in the major cities.

MAJOR ENTRY POINTS

There are three international airports in South Africa; one in Johannesburg, one in Cape Town and one in Durban. All the major airports have a reasonably priced bus service into town, usually to the railway station or some other central point. Most backpackers' hostels will pick up guests from airports or stations, as will most hotels will do the same if you arrange this in advance. If you are entering South Africa from Botswana, Namibia, Mozambique or Zimbabwe by bus or train, you will arrive at the Rotunda in Johannesburg where you will find a Tourist Information Centre. From there you can arrange transport to your hotel or backpackers' hostel.

LANGUAGE AND CUSTOMS

South Africa has 11 official languages. They are (in alphabetical order): Afrikaans, English, Ndebele, North Sotho, South Sotho, Swati, Tsonga, Tswana, Venda, Xhosa and Zulu. English is the official first language, but Zulu, Xhosa and Afrikaans are widely spoken and understood.

GETTING AROUND BY AIR

There are airports in all the cities and most of the major towns, and there are numerous flights between them. SAA flies between all the major centres, and other airlines such as Comair and Airlink, fly the routes between smaller centres. Check with travel agents as the routes and tariffs change regularly. Comair, SAA and Sunair all offer significant discounts on each of their flights.

GETTING AROUND BY RAIL

The long distance rail service is reliable and very comfortable and offers a good alternative to flying. There are regular services between Johannesburg and Port Elizabeth, and Johannesburg and East London, and daily services between Cape Town, Johannesburg and Durban. The Blue Train between Johannesburg and Cape Town is rather pricey, but is very luxurious and well worth the extra cost.

GETTING AROUND BY ROAD

There are car rental agencies in the cities and most of the larger towns. The larger agencies will allow one-way rentals but, if you don't intend travelling far, there are smaller, usually cheaper, agencies scattered around the suburbs of the major cities, and it is worth making a few enquiries. The road network is extensive and in excellent condition but distances are great, and if you are not used to long-distance driving, it may be safer to take a bus than to rent or borrow a car. Long-distance buses, most of which can be booked through travel agencies, Computicket (a computerized theatre and transport booking network) or Tourist

Information Centres, operate in major centres. Crowded, cheap, and not-too-comfortable, mini-buses operate between even the most unlikely little towns. To get information about these, enquire at backpackers' hostels or at the crowded parts of the major train and bus stations; you will need patience and a sense of humour if you choose this mode of transport!

HOTELS, GUEST HOUSES AND RESORTS
Hotels are graded on a star system with a five-star hotel offering a wide range of services including 24-hour room-service, air-conditioning, heating, bar service and à la carte menu, while hotels of two stars or less are not required to offer room-service, although many do. The grading system does not give any indication of value-for-money as many one- or two-star hotels offer very comfortable accommodation and excellent food at a good price. There are a number of RCI-affiliated (Resort Condomunium International) resorts, many close to some of the better diving spots, so time-share owners would do well to consider a swop. Guest houses are not graded and offer a smaller range of services, but usually provide very good value for money.

CAMPING
Caravanning and camping are very popular activities in South Africa and there are caravan parks in almost every centre. Many of these offer camping facilities as well, but some are rather sticky about non-permeable ground-sheets; so, if you intend camping in one spot for a considerable time, you would do well to enquire in advance. Most parks offer hot and cold water in communal ablutions, power points and hand-washing laundry facilities. Other than fireplaces, very few offer cooking facilities or refrigerators.

Fully equipped caravans or camper vans can be hired in South Africa. Contact CI Leisure Rentals, P O Box 4300, Kempton Park 1620, tel. (011) 396 1860, or Knysna Camper Hire, P O Box 1286, Knysna 6570, tel. (0445) 22 444.

YOUTH HOSTELS AND BACKPACKERS' INFRASTRUCTURE
Budget travel is booming in South Africa and there are backpackers' hostels in almost every centre. The Hostel Association of South Africa has offices in Cape Town at the Tourist Information Centre, tel: (021) 419 1853, and offers a wealth of information on budget accommodation and travel. A very useful publication is *BUG (Backpackers' Up-to-date Guide)* published by Kirk Hall, Port St Johns. It is an inexpensive booklet listing budget accommodation and is updated every six months. It can be bought at most backpackers' hostels. Most hostels offer some form of 'grapevine' system and many offer regular transport between centres and some even have reciprocal arrangements with local dive operators.

RECOMMENDED READING
Backpacker's Up-to-date Guide (BUG), 1994. Kirk Hall. Kirk Hall, Port St Johns. (updated twice-yearly)
Southern Africa on a Budget, Stern, J. 1994. Struik, Cape Town.
Guide to South African Game and Nature Reserves, 1994. C and T Stuart. Struik Publishers, Cape Town.
A Guide to Bed and Breakfast and Guest Houses in South Africa, 1994. Struik, Cape Town.
A Guide to Caravan Parks in Southern Africa, Struik, 1995. Cape Town.
A Guide to Guest Farms and Country Lodges in Southern Africa, 1994. Struik, Cape Town.
A Guide to Holiday Cottages and Flats in Southern Africa, 1995. Struik, Cape Town.
A Guide to Hotels in Southern Africa, 1995. Struik, Cape Town.

DIVING AND SNORKELLING IN SOUTH AFRICA

If you are looking for a superb holiday destination with good and varied diving, South Africa is an excellent choice. The diving conditions in most places are not very dependable, but the scenery, game and many other activities should keep you occupied on days when conditions are not up to scratch.

DIVING FACILITIES
The more popular coastal resorts have at least one dive shop, school or club and the main cities, including the inland ones, have many to choose from. The local dive clubs are worth contacting if you are planning to stay for longer than a couple of weeks as they organize inexpensive social dive outings and offer club evenings and air-fills.

The main training agencies are SAUU (South African Underwater Union) which is affiliated to CMAS (World Underwater Federation) and NAUI (National Association of Underwater Instructors). PADI (Professional Association of Dive Instructors), SSI (Scuba Schools International) and PDIC (Professional Dive Instructors Corporation) are also represented, but to a lesser extent.

DIVING CONDITIONS
The diving conditions vary greatly and, although the sea life is spectacular, some sections of the coast do not offer dependable diving conditions.

The Maputaland coast of KwaZulu-Natal offers the only true tropical coral reef diving in the country with water temperatures in excess of 20°C (68°F) and, particularly in the winter, visibility averaging between 10 and 40m (33 to 130ft). Although the reefs are all about 1km (⅝ mile) offshore and can be accessed by boat only, snorkelling is possible from the shore. All launches are off the beach and the ride through the surf is quite exhilarating. Due to the

*The distinctive powder-blue surgeonfish (**above**) is common on tropical reefs, and is easily identifiable.*

*Divers delight in exploring the dense and plentiful kelp forests (**left**) in the South-Western Cape.*

delicate nature of the reefs and the intensity with which the more popular sites are dived, no anchoring is allowed, so drift diving is the norm. This is also the case further down the coast, near Durban and particularly on the South Coast, where strong currents flow over the offshore reefs. Those who don't fancy the idea of surf launches can still enjoy some excellent diving in Durban Bay. Trident Diving is situated right on Maydon Wharf and has a state-of- the-art walk-on dive boat which does regular charters in Durban Bay.

The Protea Banks, off the South Coast, offer excellent conditions almost all year as they are situated right out in the Mozambique Channel and are not affected by run-off or surge. These reefs are very deep and far out to sea so are only suitable for experienced divers; at least an NAUI Advanced or a CMAS 2-star Certificate is required. They are also accessed by boats launched through the surf. Surf launches are relatively strenuous and divers are expected to assist in pushing the boat out although, if you prefer, you may stay in the boat.

On the whole, the Cape waters are colder and the coastline a little rougher. Diving off the Wild Coast is suitable only for groups of self-sufficient divers or spearfishers as there are virtually no facilities. The coastline from East London to Cape Town is also more dependable in winter but can offer good diving any time of the year with intermittent excellent conditions in summer.

Cape Town, situated on a sharp peninsula with a very sheltered, relatively shallow bay, usually offers a diveable spot somewhere and it is a good idea to liaise with a local operator who can keep track of the wind and let you know where the best conditions are to be found. As a rule, in summer, the south-easterlies blow offshore on the western seaboard of the Cape Peninsula, causing upwelling of crystal-clear, freezing-cold water. Temperatures range from 8–14°C (46–57°F). These superb conditions are often followed by a plankton bloom, which reduces the visibility to less than a few metres. The western shore of False Bay, or the eastern seaboard of the Cape Peninsula (see map on p. 130) experiences strong offshore northwesterly winds in winter. This wind, as well as heralding clean, relatively warm (17–20°C; 63–68°F) water, brings cold, cloudy, rainy weather. For those hardy souls who brave the topside conditions, though, the diving is superb. There are many shore dives along the whole Cape Town coastline and it is not uncommon for local divers to do a shore dive after work in summer and still surface in time for a leisurely sundowner before driving home. Some of the more interesting offshore reefs and wrecks are dived from boats, and most launches are from harbours or sheltered slipways.

Although the crayfishing (diving for rock lobster) is excellent, the West Coast does not offer good scuba diving. The sea is shallow and very exposed with violent wave and surge action, so the water is generally murky. It is also very cold, usually less than 10°C (50°F). The area around Langebaan offers some relatively pleasant spots in the huge, sheltered lagoon which is also usually warmer than the open ocean. No recreational diving is allowed from Lamberts Bay to Alexander Bay as the area is reserved for diamond diving.

RECOMMENDED EQUIPMENT

As mentioned, the water temperature and diving conditions vary considerably along the coast, so the optimum diving equipment for one area may not be suitable for another. In the KwaZulu-Natal region, for example, you could dive quite comfortably with a full 3mm (⅛in) wetsuit, or even a shortie in summer, while anything less than a full 5mm (³⁄₁₆in) wetsuit with hood and bootees is just not adequate in the Western Cape. Further up the coast, most locals use a 7mm (¼in) long-john and jacket with built-in hood. If you intend diving the whole coast and you already own a warm-water suit, such as a 3mm (⅛in) one-piece or long-john and jacket, you can buy or rent a 3 or 5mm (¼ or ³⁄₁₆in) 'chicken vest'.

Launching boats into the surf at Aliwal Shoal on the KwaZulu-Natal South Coast can often be quite treacherous.

This is a sleeveless vest with a built-in hood, and can be worn under a warm-water suit. It reduces flushing and gives extra insulation to the chest and neck area. The optimum wetsuit combination for diving the whole coast would be a long-john (3.5 or 7mm ($\frac{1}{8}$ or $\frac{1}{4}$in), depending on your cold tolerance), a 3 or 5mm ($\frac{1}{8}$ or $\frac{3}{16}$in) jacket for warm water diving and a 7mm ($\frac{1}{4}$in) jacket with a built in hood (and preferably no zips) for the Cape. A 5mm ($\frac{3}{16}$in) long-john and jacket with hood is also a reasonable compromise. Drysuits are suitable for boat dives but can be uncomfortably hot for long surface swims under the hot summer sun.

You will be very uncomfortable diving in the Cape without thermal protection on your feet so you will need to beg, borrow or buy neoprene bootees or 'sockies'. If you intend doing shore dives in the Cape, you will need hard-soled bootees as sockies tend to get shredded on the jagged rocks (sometimes also the feet in the sockies). Of course, if you wear hard-soled bootees, you cannot wear closed-heel fins, so open-heeled fins are the best bet. If you desperately want to wear your closed heel fins and can fit them on over a pair of sockies, take along a cheap pair of plastic or canvas shoes to wear over the rocks. A pair of neoprene gloves will increase comfort and are invaluable if you are doing shore dives, as you could scrape your hands exiting on a rocky shore.

The drift dives in KwaZulu-Natal are very often quite far offshore and in areas where strong currents prevail. For these reasons a **big** surface marker buoy (SMB) is necessary, as a small one could be pulled under the surface of the water or lost to the skipper's sight in the swell or chop. Losing your dive boat 4 or 5km (2½-3 miles) offshore is no joke. The red and white dive flag is known to many divers in South Africa, but means absolutely nothing to most other boaters and has no legal standing as a signal flag. All dive boats and SMBs must therefore display the internationally accepted flag alpha. The two last-mentioned items will be supplied by commercial operators, but if you intend diving independently, please bear this information in mind.

HARVESTING AND COLLECTING

South Africa is famous for its delicious seafood which you can savour in some of the world-class restaurants in the major cities, but if you are sufficiently fit and competent, it is cheaper and more fun to hunt your own. The most popular shellfish are *Haliotis midae*, commonly known as perlemoen (abalone) and crayfish or rock lobster *(Jasus lilandii)* or the Natal crayfish *(Panulirus homarus)*. Spearfishing is also very popular, particularly along the South Cape Coast, the Wild Coast and in KwaZulu-Natal. If you intend harvesting sea-food, please obtain a copy of the latest version of the Sea Fisheries' publication *Do's and Don'ts*. At time of writing, additional regulations were in force in KwaZulu-Natal, details of which can be obtained from the Natal Parks Board or the KwaZulu Department of Nature Conservation. (These are due to be amalgamated and, at the time of wiriting, the new name is not known.) The regulations do change quite regularly and they are likely to change again, so the following guidelines are just that:
• No marine animal may be removed, collected or hunted on scuba.
• No marine organisms may be hunted or collected between sunset and sunrise.
• Crayfish or lobster must be collected **by hand** on snorkel from the shore. Gravid or soft-shelled animals may not be collected. It is not permitted to use bait.
• Perlemoen (abalone) must be collected on snorkel from the shore and must be removed from the rocks by hand or with a blunt, flat instrument of which the front edge measures between 25 and 35mm (approx 1-1.5in) and which has rounded edges.
• Both these animals must be measured in the water (you can buy measuring rings from local dive shops) and released unhurt if they are undersized or, in the case of crayfish, gravid or soft-shelled. A permit is necessary for the collection of these organisms. When you buy your permit, check on the open seasons and current size and bag limits.
• Spearfishing is permitted only on snorkel, either from the shore or from a boat. Speared fish may not be transported on a boat with scuba gear (even if the cylinders are still full). At time of writing, a permit was necessary to spearfish from the shore in KwaZulu-Natal. No tropical reef fish may be speared. Please check species size limits, daily bag limits and closed seasons before setting off. Please also ensure that you can identify the species of fish which you are hunting.
• Before considering any hunting or collecting, familiarize yourself with reserve and conservation areas. The ones outlined on the maps in this book were correct at the time of writing, but they may well have changed. If you are in doubt, err on the conservative side.
• At the time of writing, closed seasons were as follows: rock lobster *(Jasus lilandii)* 31 May to 15 November and perlemoen *(Haliotis midae)* 1 August to 31 October. Certain fish species also enjoy a closed season so be sure to check all regulations.

Red tide, an algal bloom of toxic organisms, occurs on the West Coast (sometimes as far as Cape Town) from time to time, usually in summer. It is very dangerous to eat filter feeders collected during, or even a few months after, a red tide. Crayfish and perlemoen are quite safe to eat but, if you intend collecting mussels, consult with knowledgeable locals first.

WRECKS AND SALVAGE

The South African coast, particularly the Cape Peninsula, is the final resting place of many interesting and historically significant shipwrecks. Until recently, local divers were interested only in salvaging, or, more accurately removing, whatever articles of value they could find. To ensure the preservation and protection of these valuable cultural resources, the National Monuments Council (NMC) issues permits to both archaeologists and the public (with associated archaeological guidelines) for the recovery of materials from shipwrecks which are 50 years old or older. The primary objective of the legislation is to ensure that an adequate record of underwater recovery operations is maintained and that artefact collections are catalogued, conserved and exhibited. It is illegal to destroy, damage, alter, disturb or remove any wreck or portion of a wreck which is, or is generally believed to be, older than 50 years without a permit from the NMC, so unless you want to mount an underwater archaeological expedition, take only photographs and leave only bubbles.

If you would like to survey and salvage a wreck, contact the National Monuments Council, P O Box 4637, Cape Town 8000, for further information. (This information has been adapted from the NMC publication *Historical Shipwrecks and the National Monuments Act.*)

In order to enable interested divers to explore historically relevant wrecks, two wreck routes are in the process of being laid out. The first is in Simon's Bay, near Cape Town, and consists of three wrecks in a sheltered bay and the second will map out details of a number of interesting wrecks along the coast. For details see page 132 and page 147 respectively. Wreck diving is relatively hazardous and the following safety precautions should be taken:
• Do not consider any form of extended penetration, ie entering any area where you do not have a clear exit, either verical or horizontal, unless you are an experienced wreck diver and have planned such a dive.
• Streamline all equipment; tuck octo's and consoles into BC pockets or under a strap and keep your snorkel in your pocket.
• Be very careful of stirring up any sediment in a wreck as this can very quickly reduce visibility to zero.
• Be aware that wrecks may be very unstable and even a gentle nudge can cause the wreck, or part thereof, to shift and possibly trap a diver.
• Remember that your compass will be useless on a steel wreck, so use other forms of orientation and navigation.
Contact the SA Maritime Museum, P O Box 645, Cape Town 8000, tel. (021) 4192505 / 6, for more information.

INLAND DIVING
There are a number of interesting inland dives, mostly caves, quarries and sinkholes. Most of these are real cave dives and are very deep. They should be considered only by very experienced cave divers and require involved expedition planning. Suitably qualified divers who wish to mount or join an expedition should contact one of the following: The Cave Diving Club of South Africa, P O Box 2411, Cresta 2118, or the South African Speleological Association, P O Box 4812, Cape Town 8000.

RECOMMENDED READING
The Living Shores of Southern Africa, 1981. Margo and George Branch and Anthony Bannister. Struik, Cape Town.
Two Oceans, A Guide to the Marine Life of Southern Africa, 1994. George Branch *et al,* David Philip, Cape Town.
Oceans of Life off Southern Africa, 1989. Andrew IL Payne, Robert JM Crawford and Anthony P van Dalsen. Vlaeberg Publishers, Cape Town.
Shipwrecks and Salvage in South Africa, 1505 to the Present, 1988. Malcolm Turner. Struik, Cape Town.
A Guide to the Common Sea Fishes of Southern Africa, 1993. Rudy van der Elst. Struik, Cape Town.

KWAZULU-NATAL

The pleasant all-year-round temperatures, the warm water of the Indian Ocean, and KwaZulu-Natal's proximity to the well-populated interior make this one of the most popular holiday destinations on the South African coast. Lush green hills, covered in sugar-cane and banana plantations rolling down to honey-coloured beaches, are the main features of this subtropical coastline, which encompasses the beautiful regions of Maputaland, the North Coast, Durban and the South Coast.

It is here that the southernmost tropical reefs in the world are found, a fact which can be attributed to the Mozambique Current. The pleasantly warm water, in excess of 21°C (70°F), ensures a prolific growth of coral. This, in turn, offers a habitat to a wide range of inver-tebrates and over 1200 species of fish, many of which are quite docile and therefore easy to observe. The climate is subtropical and during summer, humidity, rainfall and temperatures are very high. The winter climate is pleasant with average temperatures in the low and mid-twenties. The best time of year to dive this coast is from April through to September, when rainfall figures are low and the rivers do not dirty the ocean to any great extent.

A happy concidence is that the winter months are also the time that the migratory spotted ragged-tooth sharks are in residence at Aliwal Shoal in the southern part of the region. Other sharks found in this area which do not pose a big threat to humans are the Java, thresher, hammerhead, lemon, copper and blackfin sharks. Potentially dangerous sharks, such as the great white, mako, Zambezi, dusky and tiger sharks, may be encountered by lucky divers from time to time. No shark attacks on scuba divers have been recorded in KwaZulu-Natal. Shark nets have been installed along the coast to protect bathers and seem to be effective.

The joys of this beautiful underwater environment are not reserved for the qualified scuba diver as there are many shallow coastal pools which are suitable for snorkelling, even for beginners, and the deeper water offshore offers excellent pelagic spearfishing (on permit only) for sufficiently fit and experienced snorkel divers.

*The honeycomb moray eel (**above**) lives in caves and crevices in the reefs and can inflict a nasty bite if harassed.*
*Boats at Jesser Point launch site, Sodwana Bay (**left**), seem insignificant next to the magnificent coastal forest.*

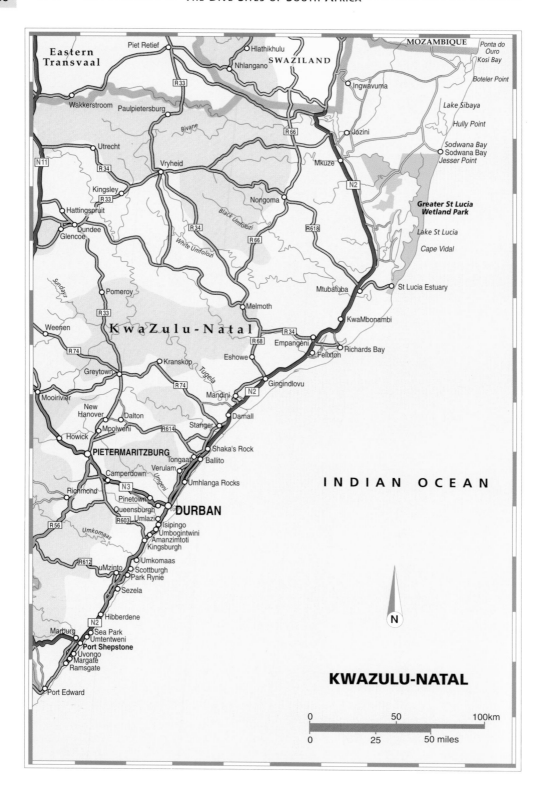

KWAZULU-NATAL

Maputaland

This region stretches from St Lucia in the south to Kosi Bay in the north and is characterized by long, deserted beaches edged by high, forested dunes. Behind the dunes are swamp forests, dominated by magnificent fig trees, and which host a multitude of living things, small and large. Further inland are the vast fresh- and saltwater lakes of St Lucia, Sibaya and Kosi Bay.

The Greater St Lucia Wetland Park, extending from south of the St Lucia Estuary to Sodwana Bay, encompasses the magnificent Lake St Lucia and protects a large marine reserve, game-filled dry savanna, the wetlands of the Mkuze Swamps and ancient coastal dunes with their indigenous forests. It is, in fact, in response to the threatened mining of these dunes that the many smaller parks and reserves in the area were recently consolidated into this more easily administered unit. To the average visitor, though, the various sections still maintain their individual identity, and seem to operate independently.

The best months for diving are from April through to September with the best underwater visibility during May and June. The water temperature is always above 21°C (70°F) with averages of around 24°C (75°F), rising to as high as 28°C (82°F).

It is only recently that scuba diving has overtaken game fishing as the main recreational activity in these waters and, at present, the only spot with good diving infrastructure is Sodwana Bay, widely accepted to be the mecca of diving in South Africa.

Non-diving companions can take leisurely strolls or hikes through the coastal forests, boat trips on the St Lucia or Kosi estuaries or game drives and walking safaris at one of the many nearby private or Parks Board-run reserves, but a little forward planning or a vehicle may be necessary. Less energetic companions can enjoy magnificent stretches of beach and observe birds and small game in some of the camp site or hotel grounds.

The loggerhead and leatherback turtles congregate on these beaches between October and February every year to lay their eggs in the sand. Highly recommended are the guided nocturnal turtle-viewing trips organized by the Natal Parks Board.

The hawksbill turtle, with its distinctive bird-like beak, is usually found in coral reefs of warm, tropical waters.

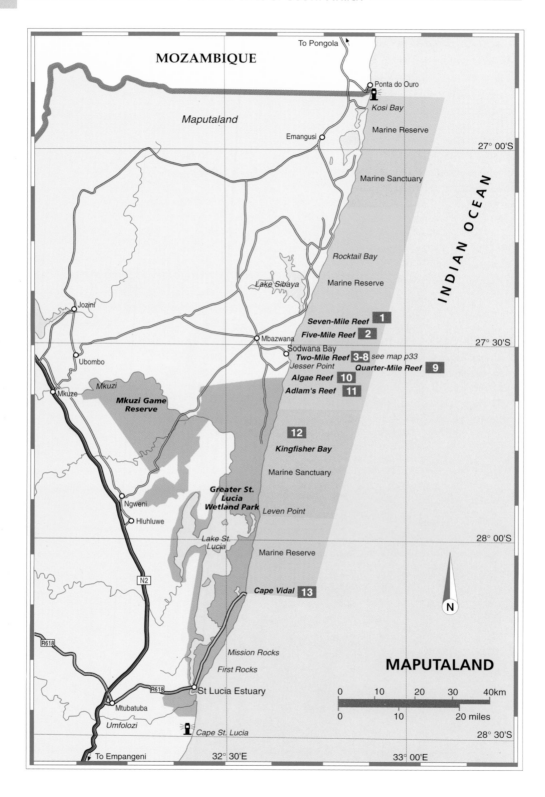

MOZAMBIQUE

Maputaland

To Pongola

Ponta do Ouro

Kosi Bay
Marine Reserve

Emangusi

27° 00'S

Marine Sanctuary

INDIAN OCEAN

Rocktail Bay

Lake Sibaya

Marine Reserve

Jozini

Seven-Mile Reef 1

Mbazwana

Five-Mile Reef 2

27° 30'S

Sodwana Bay

Ubombo

Two-Mile Reef 3-8 see map p33
Jesser Point   Quarter-Mile Reef 9
Algae Reef 10
Adlam's Reef 11

Mkuzi

Mkuze

Mkuzi Game
Reserve

12

Kingfisher Bay

Marine Sanctuary

Greater St.
Lucia
Wetland Park

Leven Point

Ngweni

Hluhluwe

Lake St.
Lucia

28° 00'S

Marine Reserve

N2

Cape Vidal 13

N

Mission Rocks

First Rocks

MAPUTALAND

R618

0   10   20   30   40km

R618

St Lucia Estuary

0   10   20 miles

Mtubatuba

Umfolozi

Cape St. Lucia

28° 30'S

To Empangeni   32° 30'E   33° 00'E

Sodwana Bay

'Sodwana', meaning 'little one on its own' in Zulu, could as well mean 'little paradise on its own', as it is a paradise for anyone with an interest in the great outdoors. Sodwana Bay's coral does not form a continuous reef, but is clearly divided into a number of reefs that run parallel to the shore, each one designated by its distance from the launch site at Jesser Point. The fairly unimaginative names, Quarter-Mile, Two-Mile, Five-Mile and Seven-Mile Reefs, belie the beauty of these popular dive sites.

Two-Mile Reef is the largest of Sodwana's known coral reefs and also the most dived upon. It has afforded many trainees their qualifying dives and therefore holds fond memories for many local divers. The reef is about 1.7km (just over a mile) long and up to 900m (just over a half a mile long) wide and is orientated roughly north-south. Strong currents or surges are rare and it is therefore an excellent site for night dives. The reef life differs in areas and the diver can do a number of varied dives on this accessible reef. The depths vary from a relatively shallow 12m (40ft) to a maximum of 36m (120ft).

The surf launches are a unique and exciting experience. Divers help to push the boat into the shallows, jump in once the engine is started and then hold on tight as the skilled skipper negotiates the waves.

Though every reef hosts its own territorial inhabitants, some of which are very predictable, something new and unexpected often happens: perhaps even a visit from a school of dolphins or an encounter with an enormous and gracefully cruising whale shark.

There is a large Parks Board camp site in which three dive concessionaires operate, all of whom have comfortable, rustic dive camps. There is a small dive shop on the beach which offers air fills, gear rental and sales. All dive charters leave from the launch site at Jesser Point which can be very crowded in season. Many local divers bring their own boats, and sometimes even compressors, and dive completely independently. This has its rewards, but involves a great deal of organization.

1 SEVEN-MILE REEF
★★★★★

Location: 27°26,50'S; 32°43,00'E, some 11km (7 miles) north of Jesser Point and 800m (½ mile) offshore, directly out from the beacon marking the end of the St Lucia reserve. See map p. 32.
Average depth: 18m (60ft)
Maximum depth: 24m (80ft)
The drop-offs and mushroom-shaped pinnacles, characteristic of this wonderful reef with its great diversity of marine life, make it a favourite among divers. Turtles and rays are sighted often and shoals of brightly coloured goldies and other small fish hover above the coral.

HEALTH THREATS

Take the following precautions for malaria:
• wear long-sleeved shirts, long pants and shoes and socks after dark;
• use a mosquito repellant;
• sleep under a mosquito net;
• take appropriate prophylactic treatment.

2 FIVE-MILE REEF
★★★★★

Location: 27°28,20'S; 32°42,10'E, 8km (5 miles) north of Jesser Point and 1km (¾ mile) offshore. See map p. 32.
Maximum depth: 21m (68ft)
This reef is jealously protected by the charter skippers and Natal Parks Board. It is an extremely delicate, large and flat reef with an astounding variety of fine coral, and is remarkably intact. Diving here creates the sensation of diving in an aquarium. In order to preserve it in its pristine state, one dive per day is granted to each concessionaire.

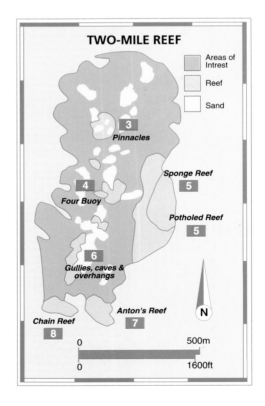

TWO-MILE REEF

Areas of Intrest
Reef
Sand

3 Pinnacles

Sponge Reef
5

4 Four Buoy

Potholed Reef
5

6 Gullies, caves & overhangs

Anton's Reef
7

Chain Reef
8

N

0 — 500m
0 — 1600ft

Well-preserved plate coral, multi-coloured soft corals and clouds of goldies are typical of Seven-Mile Reef.

3 PINNACLES
★★★

Location: On Two-Mile Reef. See map p. 33.
Average depth: 10m (33ft)
Maximum depth: 12m (40ft)
The formation of the corals on this northern section of the reef resembles that of Gullies, Caves and Overhangs (no. 6) further to the south, with sandy gullies flanked by overhangs, walls and swim-throughs. Thousands of fish may be seen, the shallow depths and good light making their colourful patterns even more striking.

4 FOUR BUOY
★★★

Location: On Two-Mile Reef. See map p. 33.
Average depth: 11m (36ft)
Maximum depth: 14m (45ft)
Thousands of divers visited, photographed and handfed the well-known tame moray eel, nicknamed 'Monty', here before it departed, never to be seen again. Maybe the constant supply of frozen pilchards from the bait shop proved a little rich, and it is perhaps better that it now has

a more natural diet. Some other fair-sized morays still occupy the reef, but it is not advisable to try the same antics with them!

The fish life is prolific and varied. Large triggerfish, including the beautiful waistcoasted clown trigger, compete with blue surgeonfish and emperor angelfish for the brighest and weirdest attire. The coral covering is profuse and forms lovely gullies, overhangs and pinnacles.

5 POTHOLED- AND SPONGE REEF
★★★★

Location: On Two-Mile Reef. See map p. 33.
Average depth: 27m (90ft)
Maximum depth: 42m (140ft)
This is a comparatively large and flat section on the eastern and deepest side of Two-Mile Reef. Light penetration is poor because of the depth, so the coral covering is sparse. The north-eastern section is interspersed with large potholed reef structures, huge sponges and red gorgonian sea-fans. Beautiful lilac cup-shaped sponges, gorgonians and black corals are common in the area. The fish life is not as prolific as in most of the other zones.

A gentle but deep drift dive can be enjoyed here, one's weightlessness adding to the sensation of flying slowly and effortlessly over a lunar landscape.

GULLIES, CAVES AND OVERHANGS

★★★★

Location: On Two-Mile Reef. See map p. 33.
Conditions: Because of the shallow depth, there can be surge.
Average depth: 10m (33ft)
Maximum depth: 15m (50ft)

The name indicates what to expect on this longish reef to the north of Anton's Reef (no. 7). A series of sandy gullies cut through the shoreward-facing overhangs, coral arches and pinnacles.

The resident potato bass are big (up to 1.5m (5ft) long) and become quite daring when they sense the possibility of a handout. They make good photographic subjects, with tiny cleaner wrasses darting in and out of their yawning jaws to do a gutsy dental check-up. Sea turtles are often seen here.

The fish are generally bigger than at the previously mentioned sites. A wide range of coral and invertebrates occur in this zone because of the shallow depths and good light penetration.

ANTON'S REEF

★★★★

Location: On Two-Mile Reef. See map p. 33.
Average depth: 15m (50ft)
Maximum depth: 18m (60ft)

This is one of the loveliest and most popular sections of Two-Mile Reef, with a fantastic variety of residential tropical fish and dense shoals of big-eyes, goatfish and snappers which part gently to let the diver through. Scorpionfish, small moray eels, big potato bass, marbled rays and triggerfish are often sighted.

The coral is dense and varied, forming spectacular vistas with small overhangs, walls and swim-throughs. Altogether this is a must for photographers.

CHAIN REEF

★★★★

Location: On Two-Mile Reef. See map p. 33.
Average depth: 15m (50ft)
Maximum depth: 18m (60ft)

This flattish reef is so-called because of the long ship's anchor chain draped around the scattered coral colonies. The fish are mainly small tropicals of every description and cheeky clownfish hiding in their host anemones are often seen. Leaf fish are a common sight on this reef.

SEA SNAKES

These beautiful and graceful animals are usually black and yellow, patterned in stripes or spots, and have a flattened tail which they use rather like an oar or rudder. They are true snakes and, as such, are air breathing, making it necessary for them to return to the surface from time to time. They are extremely venomous but are not considered a major threat as, being backfanged, they are incapable of inflicting a harmful bite to a human unless a diver were to be foolish enough to put his or her finger into its mouth! If you are lucky enough to see one, enjoy the experience and don't frighten it into hiding in a cave as it may drown.

QUARTER-MILE REEF

★★★

Location: 27°32,40'S; 32°41,00'E, approximately 400m (about ¼ mile) north of Jesser Point and the same distance out to sea. See map p. 32.
Access: It can be reached from shore on both scuba and snorkel, but it entails a rather long swim. It is also accessible by boat but very few people go to this expense because the reef is so close to shore.

Spectacular soft corals are prolific off Sodwana Bay.

A two-bar clownfish, secure in its host anemone.

It is not a coral reef, but a rocky one densely overgrown with different species of algae, hence the name. Many brightly coloured tropical fish and invertebrates are found on it. Scorpionfish and rays are often seen.

11 ADLAM'S REEF

★★★★

Location: 27°37,60'S; 32°39,40'E, 10km (6 miles) south of Jesser Point. See map p. 32.
Access: Refer to Algae Reef (no. 10).
Conditions: Very safe and calm with crystal-clear water at low tide.
Average depth: 0.5m (2ft)
Maximum depth: 3m (10ft)
Algae-covered rocks break the surface at low tide, approximately 75m (250ft) out. A kaleidoscope of rainbow-coloured tropical fish hover and dart around the rocks. The bristling spines of poisonous green-black urchins move slowly in the current – beware of the painful sting! Tiny electric-blue juvenile crayfish hide in small holes, with only their long white antennae betraying their presence. Closer inshore shoals of small fish mill aimlessly around in circles, little disturbed by divers.

12 KINGFISHER BAY

★★★★

Location: 27°42,40'S; 32°37,80'E, 20km (12½ miles) south of Jesser Point or 47km (29 miles) north of Cape Vidal. See map p. 32.
Access: Refer Algae Reef (no. 10).
Conditions: It is safe and protected and the water is crystal clear during low tide.
Average depth: 1m (3ft)
Maximum depth: 3m (10ft)
It is a rocky reef that forms a natural barrier to the waves at low tide, about 75m (250ft) out. There are also a

Conditions: There is a strong surge because of its proximity to shore. Great care should be taken when diving here as it may be in the path of ski-boat traffic to and from the launch site and you should take a clearly visible SMB (surface marker buoy) and flag alpha.
Maximum depth: 8m (25ft)
A small reef which is an extension of the rocky platform at Jesser Point, it offers delightful viewing of marine fish and other reef life similar to Algae Reef (no. 10). Gravid ragged-tooth sharks are often found here in summer, as are loggerhead turtles.

10 ALGAE REEF

★★★

  R

Location: 27°35,00'S; 32°40,00'E, 5km (3 miles) south of Jesser Point and 150m (500ft) out to sea. See map p. 32.
Access: Provided you have the nececessary permit, you can drive there along the beach. These can be obtained from the entrance gate at the Sodwana Bay beach as a maximum of 25 vehicles only are allowed onto the beach per day. If you do this beach drive you must remain below the high-water mark and remember to plan your trip so that you travel there and back at low tide.
Average depth: 6m (20ft)
Maximum depth: 8m (25ft)

MARINE RESERVE

The entire area from St Lucia to Cape Vidal is either a reserve or a sanctuary. The area around Sodwana Bay is a marine reserve. No dead or live shells, or reef animals of any kind, may be removed or disturbed. Only fishing and spearfishing of pelagic fish is allowed here. However, shore anglers may catch reef fish.

couple of rocky outcrops in a tidal pool where big octopuses may be found. The tropical fish in the pool are small and colourful, and bigger fish are found behind the breakers. It is well worth the lovely drive along the beach.

St Lucia Estuary

The small fishing haven and popular holiday resort of St Lucia lies on the shores of Lake St Lucia, fed by the waters of the Mkuze River. The mouth of the estuary has a high salinity level and teems with fish. The great number of predators that the fish attract include a vast array of birds such as fish eagles, kingfishers, cormorants, pelicans and flamingoes, while sharks and large game fish also get their fair share. The lake is home to many hippos and crocodiles and hundreds of species of birds.

Fishing is still the foremost recreational activity on the lake and in the ocean and, although it is also a popular spearfishing destination, the reefs are essentially unexplored by scuba divers. There is no organized diving facility in the town so visiting divers have to rely entirely on their own resources.

Crayfish are plentiful in the rocks close to shore and temporary permits can be obtained from the Natal Parks Board. Crayfish may be collected at First Rocks and Mission Rocks to the north of St Lucia village.

13 CAPE VIDAL
★★★★

Location: 28°07,50'S; 32°33,50'E. See map p. 32.
Access: Turn off to St Lucia from the N2 approximately 200km (125 miles) north of Durban. Carry on through St Lucia and take the dirt road to the north to Cape Vidal.

The snorkelling spot is slightly to the right of the entrance to the beach. Four-wheel-drive vehicles are allowed on the beach only after obtaining a permit at the gate.

Conditions: Safe diving in protected, shallow water.
Cape Vidal is a renowned fishing spot which is under the protection of the Natal Parks Board, who offer camping facilities and accommodation in bungalows. There are no real coral reefs in the area and diving is mainly restricted to spearfishing and snorkelling, but the water is almost always clear.

A rocky, crescent-shaped reef forms a protected pool where superb snorkelling can be done in safety at low tide. The reefs are covered with algae and a great variety of small and vividly coloured tropical fish abound in the shallow water, offering divers hours of safe and enjoyable snorkelling.

A school of big-eyes, typically moving as a unit, keeps a cautious distance from this diver.

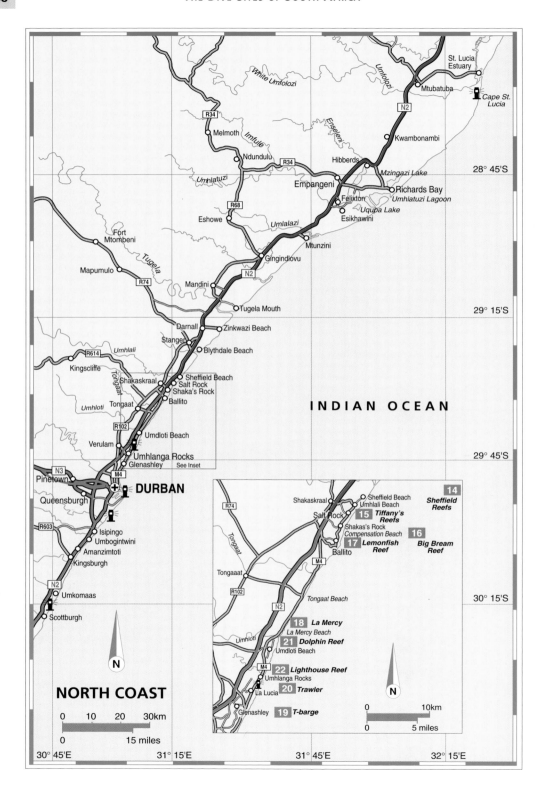

St. Lucia Estuary

White Umfolozi

Umfolozi

Mtubatuba

N2

Cape St. Lucia

R34

Melmoth

Imfule

Enseleni

Kwambonambi

Ndundulu

R34

Hibberds

Mzingazi Lake

28° 45'S

Umhlatuzi

Empangeni

Richards Bay

Umhlatuzi Lagoon

R68

Felixton

Uqupa Lake

Eshowe

Umlalazi

Esikhawini

Fort Mtombeni

Mtunzini

Tugela

Gingindlovu

Mapumulo

R74

Mandini

N2

Tugela Mouth

29° 15'S

Darnall

Zinkwazi Beach

Stanger

R614

Umhlali

Blythdale Beach

Kingscliffe

Sheffield Beach

Shakaskraal

Salt Rock

Tongaat

Shaka's Rock

Umhloti

Tongaat

Ballito

INDIAN OCEAN

R102

Umdloti Beach

Verulam

Umhlanga Rocks

29° 45'S

N3

Glenashley

See Inset

Pinetown

M4

DURBAN

Queensburgh

R603

Isipingo

Umbogintwini

Amanzimtoti

Kingsburgh

N2

Umkomaas

Scottburgh

30° 15'S

Inset map

R74

Shakaskraal

Sheffield Beach

Umhlali Beach

14 *Sheffield Reefs*

Salt Rock

15 *Tiffany's Reefs*

Shakas's Rock

Compensation Beach

17 *Lemonfish Reef*

16 *Big Bream Reef*

Ballito

M4

Tongaaat

R102

N2

Tongaat Beach

18 *La Mercy*

La Mercy Beach

Umhloti

21 *Dolphin Reef*

Umdloti Beach

M4

22 *Lighthouse Reef*

Umhlanga Rocks

20 *Trawler*

La Lucia

Glenashley

19 *T-barge*

N

NORTH COAST

0   10   20   30km

0   15 miles

0   10km

0   5 miles

30° 45'E   31° 15'E   31° 45'E   32° 15'E

The North Coast

This densely populated, beautiful, subtropical stretch of coastline to the north of Durban is a favourite destination for holiday-makers. The summer rainfall is high, and the vegetation is tropical and luxuriant, while the winters are mild and pleasant.

The best-known settlements along this coast are Ballito, Umhlanga Rocks, Durban, Stanger, Empangeni and Richards Bay (an industrial harbour). The diveable reefs in this region are fairly close inshore (generally closer than 600m or 660yds), a fact which has both advantages and disadvantages. The main disadvantage is that the swells can be very big and the water is not as clean as that further out to sea, especially in the summer months when the rain-filled rivers flow into the ocean. The advantages are that a number of good shore dives can be done on scuba, but only by fit and experienced divers as the surf launches can sometimes be quite tricky.

The south-easterly and south-westerly winds clean the seas and ensure good general diving conditions, while the north-easterlies tend to churn up the water, producing poor visibility and big swells. The best months for diving are, therefore, in the winter months of May, June and July – before the August wind sets in.

The North Coast is a well-developed tourist area and non-diving companions will not be bored. The beaches are superb and a visit to the Sharks Board in Umhlanga Rocks is highly recommended for divers and non-divers alike.

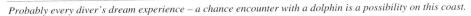

Probably every diver's dream experience – a chance encounter with a dolphin is a possibility on this coast.

Two-bar clownfish live in symbiosis with large sea anemones that have stinging cells harmful to most other fish.

Ballito

It is easy to see why this stretch of coastline has become known as the Dolphin Coast – large shoals of frolicking dolphins are often spotted from shore and have been known to visit divers – a truly unforgettable experience.

14 SHEFFIELD REEFS

★★★★★

Location: 29°28,00'S; 31°16,50'E. See map p. 38.
Access: Pass the Salt Rock Protea Hotel in Salt Rock, turn right into Osborne Drive and right again into Hugh Dent Road. Turn into Sheffield Road and follow the road for 4.3km (6.8 miles), measuring from the Salt Rock Hotel. Park on the right just before the *cul de sac* sign and walk down to the beach. Kit up alongside the road. The fairly long swim requires physical fitness and experience; a less strenuous option is to do a boat dive.
Average depth: 9m (30ft)
Maximum depth: 10m (33ft).
There are two reefs running parallel to shore and each other. Both are approximately 30m (100ft) wide by 100m (330ft) long. The first reef is about 150m (500ft) offshore while the second reef is approximately 200m (660ft) out. A fairly large variety of different fish species is found in the vicinity and crustaceans are plentiful and varied.

15 TIFFANY'S REEF

★★★★★

Location: 29°30,10'S; 31°14,50'E, 500m (⅓ mile) north of the Salt Rock Protea Hotel and about 200m (660ft) out to sea. See map p. 38.
Access: Take Ocean Drive from Ballito past the La Montagne Protea Hotel and start measuring from the hotel. Turn left into Dolphin Road which leads to Salt Rock and turn right into Shrimp Lane, just past the Salt Rock Protea Hotel on the right. Turn left into Hewitt Road and take the first dirt road turn-off to the right, which leads down to a locked boom at the entrance to the beach. Scuba dives from shore are only recommended for experienced divers in good physical shape as they entail rather a long and tiring swim. Boats are launched from either Salmon Bay in Ballito or from George Hulett Place where the locked boom prevents access to the beach, but a key can be obtained from the Town Clerk's office.
Conditions: Visibility can range from as low as 1m (3ft) to as high as 15m (50ft) and shore entries can prove to be very tricky in a big swell.
Average depth: 8m (25ft)
Maximum depth: 20m (65ft)

ENTERING THE SURF

- Never turn your back on the sea.
- Put your fins on behind the beachbreak.
- Maintain neutral buoyancy.
- If in doubt go under, rather than over, a wave.
- Try going out with only snorkel gear and if you struggle, even slightly, don't attempt it on scuba.
- Go out on snorkel but, as a precaution, keep your second stage firmly in your hand.

It is a flattish reef, interrupted by sandy gullies at the outer edge. Game fish occur here in fair numbers and it is, therefore, a popular spot for spearfishing.

Reef fish are found in the deeper areas of Tiffany's Reef. The marine growth is prolific and crayfish occur in large numbers on the edge of the reef.

16 BIG BREAM REEF

★★★★★

Location: 29°31,70'S; 31°13,70'E. See map p. 38.
Access: Take Ocean Drive toward Salt Rock and turn right to the beach just before Martinique flats. The reef is right in front of the Santorini development, approximately 500m (⅓ mile) to the south of Thompson's Bay tidal pool and about 50m (165ft) out to sea.

The coral rockcod preys on tiny fish and crustaceans.

Conditions: There can be surge when large swells break, making this a fair-weather spot.
Average depth: 7m (23ft)
Maximum depth: 8m (25ft)
This is a small reef and is often visited by garrick in winter and queen- and kingfish, as well as queen and king mackerel in summer, so is a popular spearfishing spot. It is also dived on scuba.

17 LEMONFISH REEF
★★★★★

Location: 29°32,22'S; 31°13,34'E. See map p. 38.
Access: Opposite the intersection of Jack Powell Road and Compensation Road, there is an alley between La Mystique and The Bay developments. This leads directly down to the rocks on the beach, from which Lemonfish is approximately 150m (650ft) out to sea. The entry and exit are quite tricky, as they must be done through a gap in the rocks, so a boat dive may be easier.
Average depth: 4m (13ft)
Maximum depth: 8m (25ft)
This is a small but densely populated reef with colourful fish life. According to local divers it is also an excellent

crayfishing spot where you are almost certain to fill your quota. A very interesting and unusual find was made in 1989 by two local divers who discovered a rhino horn in a small cave under the rocks close to shore. A subsequent sweep of the area by Natal Parks Board officials proved fruitless, and the mystery of the solitary horn remains.

18 LA MERCY
★★★★

Location: 29°37,70'S; 33°09,22'E, just behind the shark nets, approximately 600m (¼ mile) out, and some 200-300m (660-1000ft) to the south of an imaginary line straight out from the Sea Belle Restaurant. This is not recommended as a shore dive except for very fit and experienced divers. See map p. 38.
Access: Take the N2 20km (12.5 miles) north of Durban. Turn left to South Beach, carry on for about 3 km (2 miles) to the Sea Belle Restaurant. Park and kit up there.
Average depth: 12m (40ft)
Maximum depth: 16m (52ft)
The reef runs parallel to shore and teems with fish and marine organisms of all descriptions.

The potato bass is one of the largest members of the rockcod family, and the goldies in front are of the smallest.

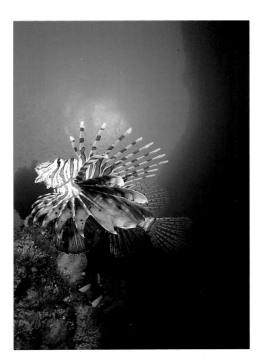

The devil firefish has long, poisonous dorsal spines.

Umhlanga Rocks

Umhlanga Rocks is a very popular holiday resort, just 17km (10 miles) north of Durban.

Umhlanga is also home to the Natal Sharks Board which regularly prepares interesting audio-visuals, lectures, shark dissections and other demonstrations to the public. Booking is advisable (see p. 59).

19 THE T-BARGE
★★★★

Location: Approximately 3km (2 miles) off Virginia Beach. See map p. 38.
Access: By boat launched from Grannies Pool, Umhlanga Rocks; this is an easy launch into a channel.
Conditions: This site is far enough from shore to be reasonably clean when the inshore sites are undiveable.
Average depth: 20m (65ft)
Maximum depth: 27m (90ft)
This barge was sunk to create an artificial reef and has been very successful. The three crane structures at the stern attract lots of fish including coachman, batfish, emperor angelfish and butterflyfish. Bottom dwellers, such as rays and skates, can be seen on the sand around the wreck and pelagic fish, such as daga salmon and giant kingfish or trevally often visit.

20 THE TRAWLER or FONTÃO (1990)
★★★★

Location: 2km (1.5 miles) out to sea, 500m (1650ft) south of the Umhlanga lighthouse. See map p. 38.
Access: Boat from Grannies Pool; this is an easy launch into a channel.
Conditions: Far enough from shore to be reasonably clean when the inshore sites are undiveable.
Average depth: 18m (60ft)
Maximum depth: 27m (90ft)
This old Mozambican trawler was sunk in 1990 to form an artificial reef, and is still largely intact. Large shoals of baitfish swim around the wreck and attract pelagic fish which feed off them.

Lovely tropical fish can also be seen and the rather unusual pineapple fish has been spotted here. This small, plump, yellow-patterned fish hides in crevices by day and ventures out at night, flashing the light-emitting cells located at the angle of its jaws.

21 DOLPHIN REEF
★★★

Location: Approximately 300m (1000ft) off Umdloti Tidal Pool. See map p. 38.
Access: By boat launched from Grannies Pool or from shore through the surf for very fit and experienced divers.
Conditions: Should be dived early in the morning before the north-easterly picks up, especially in summer.
Average depth: 15m (50ft)
Maximum depth: 18m (60ft)
Dolphin Reef is covered in soft corals, mushroom corals and sponges. Skates and rays are often spotted on the sand just off this lovely reef.

22 LIGHTHOUSE REEF
★★

Location: 200m (650ft) to sea, just south of the Umhlanga Rocks Lighthouse. See map p. 38.
Access: By boat from Grannies Pool or as a shore entry for very fit and experienced divers.
Conditions: Should be dived early in the morning before the north-easterly picks up, especially in summer.
Average depth: 10m (33ft)
Maximum depth: 12m (40ft)
This reef is home to a variety of tropical fish and many moray eels, including the honeycomb . Skates and rays are often seen on the sand just off the reef.

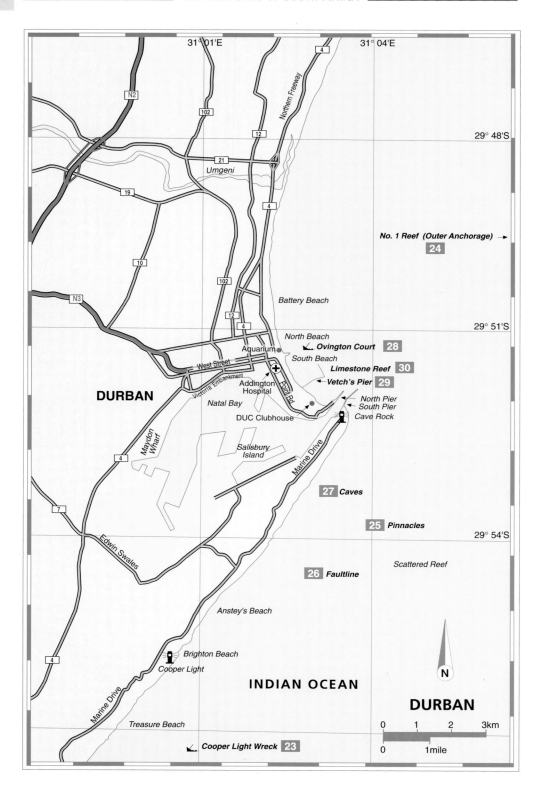

31° 01'E   31° 04'E

N2

102

Northern Freeway

4

29° 48'S

21

Umgeni

19

102

N3

10

No. 1 Reef (Outer Anchorage) →
24

Battery Beach

102

12

4

29° 51'S

North Beach

Aquarium ●   **Ovington Court**   **28**

West Street

South Beach

Limestone Reef   **30**

DURBAN

Victoria Embankment

Addington Hospital

Point Rd

Vetch's Pier   **29**

Natal Bay

← North Pier
← South Pier

DUC Clubhouse

Cave Rock

Maydon Wharf

Salisbury Island

Marine Drive

4

27 *Caves*

7

25 *Pinnacles*

29° 54'S

Edwin Swales

Scattered Reef

26 *Faultline*

Anstey's Beach

4

Brighton Beach

Cooper Light

INDIAN OCEAN

N

DURBAN

Marine Drive

0   1   2   3km

Treasure Beach

0   1mile

Cooper Light Wreck   **23**

Durban

This city is a major tourist destination and offers most of the usual urban delights, as well as standard tourist attractions such as an oceanarium, a snake park, a bird garden, colourful rickshaws and permanent beach front amusement park rides.

The diving in Durban Bay is mostly centred on the two major reefs: No. 1 Reef, otherwise known as Outer Anchorage, and Blood Reef – a rather macabre name which dates back to the days of commercial whaling. Regular charters are run to both these reefs.

The best time to dive is in May, June and July when the rivers are low. A light south-westerly wind usually cleans the water, while the north-easterlies churn up the sea and make it unsafe for diving. The visibility is usually less then 10m (33ft) but can range from zero to as much as 30-40m (100-130ft) when the warm, clean water of the Mozambique Current flows in close to the shore.

Conditions: The *Cooperlight* wreck is best dived during the winter months, though the clean Mozambique water comes in often in summer. Even with clean water, a small ground swell will stir up the silt at the bottom, causing poor or zero visibility.

Average depth: 22m (72ft)
Maximum depth: 33m (110ft)

The identity of the wreck has never been positively confirmed, so it has been named after the Cooper Lighthouse. Even the date of wrecking is not known, but is it thought that it was a whaler scuttled sometime around 1940. The badly rusted hull is about 35m (115ft) long and is covered in plenty of tangled fishing line. Take a knife to cut yourself free, if necessary. It houses a thriving population of stinging hydroids which can give an unwary diver a nasty experience.

Big rays and small, pretty tropical fish, such as goldies, are likely to be encountered. Many beautiful shells can be seen on the sandy floor and around the propeller.

23 THE COOPERLIGHT WRECK
★★

Location: 29°57,40'S; 31°01,10'E, south-east of the Cooper Lighthouse between Brighton Beach and the Umlaas Cutting. See map p. 44.
Access: By boat.

24 NO. 1 REEF OR OUTER ANCHORAGE
★★★

Location: 29°50,20'S; 31°07,40'E, in a direct line due east of the Anchorage beacon. See map p. 44.
Access: It is not easy to pinpoint the better diving spots on this reef as the commercial operators are very

Scorpionfish have developed superb camouflage techniques, as displayed by this one on the reef in the foreground.

protective of their favourite sites but you can find good spots by cruising the reef and looking for pinnacles on an echo-sounder.

Conditions: Best dived in winter, though the clean Mozambique water comes in often in summer.

Average depth: 25m (80ft)

Maximum depth: 30m (100ft)

This unusual name derives from the fact that this was the 'number one' fishing ground in the old days. The reef has many boulders and long pieces of anchor chain can still be found wrapped around the rock pinnacles, forming interesting patterns and nooks and crannies. Big rockcod are present and this is a feeding ground for sharks, so keep a sharp lookout, especially in murky water.

25 THE PINNACLES
★★★

Location: 29°53,80'S; 31°04,40'E, on Blood Reef. See map p. 44.

Access: By boat.

Maximum depth: 18m (60ft)

The Pinnacles derives its name from the rising limestone formations on the reef, and is located at the northern end of the fault line. There is a lot of marine variety and it is a good dive for the more experienced diver. Take a torch.

26 FAULTLINE or DEEP BLOOD
★★★

Location: 29°54,60'S; 31°03,10'E, on Blood Reef. See map p. 44.

Average depth: 18m (60ft)

Maximum depth: 23m (76ft) on the outer side.

This reef lies opposite the water tower further to the south of Blood Reef and derives its name from the natural fault line in the sea bed running parallel to the shore for about 200m (660ft). This fault has formed two huge caves that offer marvellous viewing of all kinds of fish. Many an anchor has come unstuck here and lengths of rusting links can be seen. Behind the fault line and a little deeper at 23m (76ft) are a number of small reefs.

27 THE CAVES
★★★

Location: 29°53,40'S; 31°03,18'E, on Blood Reef. See map p. 44.

Maximum depth: 9m (30ft)

Weathered sandstone formations have collapsed to form caves, holes and gullies making this a memorable dive. A

Slender sweepers are often seen in large schools, hovering around wrecks or over reefs.

feature of this site is the many blowholes. The boiling effect that these create on the surface makes them easy to spot just behind the breakline. The cathedral-like interiors of these caves have been roped by the Durban Underwater Club (DUC) members to aid divers who aren't familiar with the reef.

28 THE OVINGTON COURT (1940)
★★

Location: 29°51,50'S; 31°02,70'E. See map p. 44.
Access: Go south down Gillespie Street and turn left into Rochester Street at the Addington Hospital sign. Carry on to the parking area on the beach. The remains of the engine block and main boiler are visible just behind the breakline, approximately 50m (165ft) out to sea.
Conditions: This site is best dived in winter. The wreck is visible at low tide but the sea is calmer at high tide and it can be very surgy as it lies close to shore.
Average depth: 5m (16ft).
Maximum depth: 7m (23ft).
The *Ovington Court* was a British steel cargo vessel of 6095 tons, carrying a cargo of sugar from Mauritius, when it was driven ashore by a gale-force south-easter during the early hours of the morning of 25 November 1940. Its boilers were shut down to conserve fuel while it was awaiting a berth and the ship was helpless against the force of the wind. Four members of the crew perished. Only the main boiler and engine block remain on the wreck site. The wreck swarms with fish life and huge crayfish can be seen, but no crayfishing is allowed.

29 VETCH'S PIER
★★★★

Location: 29°52,08'S; 31°02,00'E, 800m (0.5 miles) north of the harbour entrance. See map p. 44.
Access: Take Point Road in an easterly direction towards the docks. Turn left into Bell Street and right again onto the dirt road at the bottom. Carry on to the left until you reach the beach, and park there. Kit up and walk down the northerly end of the pipeline and enter there. The remains of the pier are visible during low tide, but at high tide it can be found by swimming slightly to the left of the pipe's end. Start the descent when the depth reaches about 3m (10ft), and swim east along the reef.
Conditions: It is protected by the north and south piers from the south-westerly swells, and is best dived in winter when the water is generally cleaner. Surge can be heavy because of the shallow depth.
Average depth: 3m (10ft)
Maximum depth: 6m (20ft)

This artificial reef was named after Captain James Vetch who attempted to build a breakwater in 1860. Some £160 000, a fortune in those days, was spent on building the pier before the project was abandoned. Most of the building material was subsequently used in the construction of North Pier and other buildings. Consisting mainly of the rubble remains of the old, uncompleted pier, the reef curves in the direction of North Pier and is about 500m (⅓ mile) long by 50m (165ft) wide. The many small holes and crevices are best investigated with a torch.

Characteristic of this reef are the large crayfish that are found in the holes. They seem to know that they are protected (no crayfishing is allowed from North Pier to the Umgeni River mouth) and are not shy at all. There are also eels and octopuses about. Small tropical reef fish dart in and out of their homes, creating a colourful spectacle. Scorpion- and lionfish are common, too, so be careful. The reef ends at the beginning of Limestone Reef.

30 LIMESTONE REEF
★★★★

Location: 21°51,96'S; 31°03,20'E, at the end of Vetch's Pier. See map p. 44.
Access: Swim to the end of Vetch's Pier and swim in a north-easterly direction parallel to the coastline for approximately 400m (¼ mile).
Conditions: Sediment suspends easily in the water and silt entering the area from the harbour can drastically reduce visibility.
Average depth: 6m (20ft)
Maximum depth: 7m (23ft)
This reef, which runs from the tip of Vetch's Pier (no. 29) in a north-easterly direction, is about 400m (¼ mile) long by 40m (130ft) wide. It is a good reef for the learner diver as it is shallow and protected. It consists of a limestone formation, possibly produced by sand outfall from the harbour mouth. Goldies are often found on this reef, together with other tropical fish. A peculiar feature of the reef is that golf balls often wash down the river into the sea from the nearby golf course.

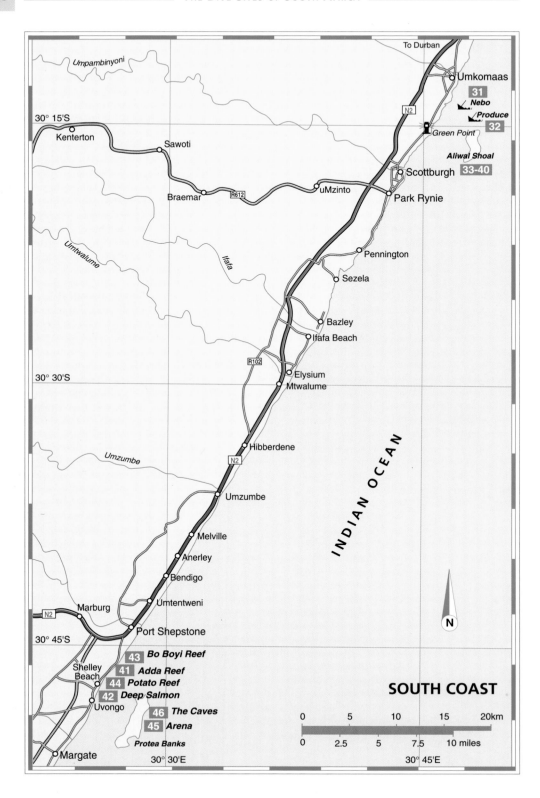

Umpambinyoni

To Durban

Umkomaas

31

Nebo

Produce **32**

N2

30° 15'S

Kenterton

Sawoti

Green Point

Aliwal Shoal

Scottburgh **33-40**

Braemar   R612   uMzinto

Park Rynie

Umtwalume

Ifafa

Pennington

Sezela

Bazley

Ifafa Beach

R102

30° 30'S

Elysium

Mtwalume

Hibberdene

Umzumbe

N2

Umzumbe

Melville

Anerley

Bendigo

INDIAN OCEAN

Marburg

Umtentweni

N2

30° 45'S

Port Shepstone

43 *Bo Boyi Reef*

Shelley   **41** *Adda Reef*
Beach
          44 *Potato Reef*
42 *Deep Salmon*
Uvongo
          46 *The Caves*
45 *Arena*

SOUTH COAST

Protea Banks

Margate

| 0 | 5 | 10 | 15 | 20km |

| 0 | 2.5 | 5 | 7.5 | 10 miles |

30° 30'E   30° 45'E

N

The South Coast

After Sodwana Bay, this is the best-known and most popular dive destination in the country. The diving is most dependable in the winter months, from May to September, when the visibility is usually good and the migratory spotted ragged-tooth sharks are in residence at Aliwal Shoal. There are three main diving areas: Aliwal Shoal, about 5km (3 miles) off Umkomaas, Landers Reef and adjoining reefs, about 9km (5.5 miles) south-west of Aliwal Shoal and approximately 5km (3 miles) off Park Rynie, and Protea Banks, a reef between Margate and Shelley Beach.

The dive sites closer inshore are best dived in winter as the summer rain causes high run-off from the many rivers. The resulting low visibility is exacerbated from time to time by industrial effluent from the nearby SAICCOR pulp-processing plant. Divers have nick-named this scourge the 'purple death'. Protea Banks, about 8km (5 miles) offshore from Shelley Beach, offers year-round diving with visibility ranging from 8m (25ft) to in excess of 40m (130ft), and frequent sightings of game fish and sharks.

The South Coast is an absolute pleasure for non-diving companions as it is a very well-developed tourist area catering mainly for family holidays. Lovely long beaches, comfortable resorts, offering golf, tennis, bowls, horse-riding, and shopping malls and restaurants are major features of the area, and the Wild Coast Sun Casino is a short drive down the coast.

Goldies are one of the commonest reef inhabitants, often found swimming upside down under small overhangs.

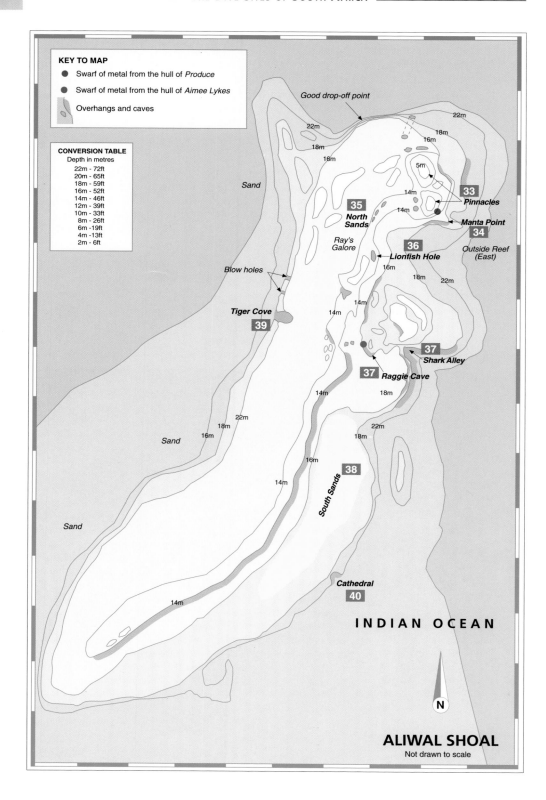

KEY TO MAP
- Swarf of metal from the hull of *Produce*
- Swarf of metal from the hull of *Aimee Lykes*
- Overhangs and caves

CONVERSION TABLE
Depth in metres
22m - 72ft
20m - 65ft
18m - 59ft
16m - 52ft
14m - 46ft
12m - 39ft
10m - 33ft
8m - 26ft
6m - 19ft
4m - 13ft
2m - 6ft

Good drop-off point

22m

Sand

North Sands **35**

Ray's Galore

Blow holes

Tiger Cove **39**

Sand

Sand

Pinnacles **33**

Manta Point **34**

Lionfish Hole **36**

Outside Reef (East)

Shark Alley **37**

Raggie Cave **37**

South Sands **38**

Cathedral **40**

INDIAN OCEAN

N

ALIWAL SHOAL
Not drawn to scale

Umkomaas

Originally known as South Barrow, this is a popular resort at the mouth of the Mkomazi River. The Aliwal Shoal lies 5km (3 miles) offshore, south of Umkomaas.

31 THE NEBO (1884)
★★★

Location: 30°15,20'S; 30°49,00'E, north and shorewards of Aliwal Shoal. See map p. 48.
Access: By boat launched from Umkomaas River mouth.
Conditions: Can be affected by run-off and 'purple death' (see page 51).
Maximum depth: 30m (100ft)
The *Nebo* struck Aliwal Shoal on 20 May 1884 in fair weather and went down immediately with its cargo of railway material. Fortunately, no lives were lost. It lies bottom-up, a rather surreal sight, and is still fairly intact.

32 THE PRODUCE (1974)
★★★

Location: 30°15,00'S; 30°49,30'E, north and shorewards of Aliwal shoal, a little further south and east of the *Nebo* (no. 31). See map p. 48.
Access: By boat launched from Umkomaas River mouth.
Condtions: The wreck has leaked oil from time to time, some even washing up on the beaches. Most of the oil was recently pumped out and the little that remains was sealed in the wreck, although it may still leak.
Maximum depth: 30m (100ft)

The blue Pete lurks among the coral on tropical reefs.

The *Produce* was a Norwegian bulk molasses tanker that struck the north-east pinnacle of the shoal on 11 August 1974, and then drifted off to its present resting place where it lies on its side. No lives were lost. Big game fish, such as daga salmon and kingfish are present, as are most of the usual small tropical fish and many resident brindle bass.

33 THE PINNACLES
★★★

Location: On the north of Aliwal Shoal. See map p. 50.
Access: By boat launched from Umkomaas River mouth.
Conditions: It is best dived when there is little or no surge or current, as the gullies and caves can prove tricky in a strong surge.
Average depth: 12m (40ft)
Maximum depth: 15m (50ft)
Many caves, gullies and overhangs can be explored on this reef, and there are huge shoals of fish everywhere.

34 MANTA POINT
★★★★

Location: North-east of Aliwal Shoal. See map p. 50.
Access: By boat launched from Umkomaas River mouth.
Conditions: This site should be avoided or dived very carefully in a strong surge, as there is a blowhole on the northern edge of the reef.
Average depth: 18m (60ft)
Maximum depth: 24m (80ft)
There are many shoaling fish here as well as the usual small and colourful tropical fish. There is a good chance of spotting a round ribbontail ray.

35 NORTH SANDS
★★★

Location: North-west of Aliwal Shoal. See map p. 50.
Access: By boat launched from Umkomaas River mouth.
Conditions: As this spot is on the northern end of the Aliwal Shoal, it is a good place to start a drift dive in a southerly current.
Average depth: 12m (40ft)
Maximum depth: 15m (50ft)
Rays, skates and sand-sharks of all sizes are often spotted in this flat, sandy section of the reef. There is a large over-hang on the south-east side of this sandy patch where groups of raggies often congregate in winter.

36 LIONFISH HOLE
★★★★

Location: On the northern side of Aliwal Shoal. See map p. 50.
Access: By boat launched from Umkomaas River mouth.
Conditions: This is a good spot to dive if the visibility is good as there is a variety of small marine life to be observed.
Average depth: 12m (40ft)
Maximum depth: 16m (53ft)

Inquisitive potato bass are often encountered.

THE BEAUTIFUL MOORISH IDOL

This exquisitely beautiful and graceful fish is the only member of the family Zanclidae. It is laterally compressed, has distinctive saddle-like markings over its snout and a flowing elongated third dorsal spine. Its specialized mouth shape enables it to feed on algae and tiny crustaceans hiding in small cracks in the reef.

It is most common in the waters off Maputaland, but is often seen on Aliwal Shoal and, when the warm Agulhas Current pushes that far south, has ever been seen off the Eastern Cape coast.

Although its appearance is reminiscent of a coachman, it is far more beautiful and, once seen, will never again be confused with this species.

This is a crater in the pinnacle which almost always has a resident lionfish, hence the name. The invertebrate life and small tropical fish are particularly beautiful.

37 RAGGIE CAVE AND SHARK ALLEY
★★★★

Location: On the eastern edge of Aliwal Shoal. See map p. 50.
Access: By boat launched from Umkomaas River mouth.
Conditions: Must be dived very carefully when surgy.
Average depth: 14m (45ft)
Maximum depth: 16m (48ft)
This section of the reef has a good variety of tropical fish but is best known for housing groups of migratory spot-ted ragged-tooth sharks in winter. This site is in danger of becoming over-dived as careless divers have, in the past, upset the sharks. When sharks are in the cave, they are resting and must not be disturbed. They should be observed from the sides and should never be approached too closely. Although they are not overtly aggressive, do not be fooled by their sleepy appearance. They have been known to chase groups of cheeky divers out of the water and could inflict a serious injury if sufficiently provoked.

38 SOUTH SANDS
★★★★

Location: On the south-eastern side of Aliwal Shoal. See map p. 50.
Access: By boat launched from Umkomaas River mouth.

Blue-banded snappers shoal in large groups and seem totally unperturbed by the photographer's buddy.

Conditions: As this is on the south side of the reef, it is a good place to start a drift dive in a northerly current.
Average depth: 15m (50ft)
Maximum depth: 18m (60ft)
Like North Sands, this site is home to a great number of rays, skates, sand-sharks and guitar-fish. There are some excellent spots on the outer edge of south sands, particularly the two ledges at 18m (60ft) and 22m (72ft) which are seldom dived but are worth exploring.

39 TIGER COVE
★★★★

Location: About midway along the western (inner) edge of Aliwal Shoal. See map p. 50.
Access: By boat launched from Umkomaas River mouth.
Conditions: A good spot to start a northerly drift dive on the inner edge.
Average depth: 14m (45ft)
Maximum depth: 14m (45ft)
This area has lots of caves and overhangs and was named after the large colony of tiger cowries which used to live there but unfortunately fell prey to souvenir-hungry

divers. The inner edge has some pretty ledges at 18m and 22m (60ft and 72ft) and a drift dive along here in a northerly current can be very rewarding.

40 CATHEDRAL
★★★★★

Location: On the eastern (outer) edge of Aliwal Shoal. See map p. 50.
Access: By boat launched from Umkomaas River mouth.
Conditions: Should be dived very cautiously when there is surge.
Average depth: 27m (90ft)
Maximum depth: 28m (93ft)
This is a spectacular hole in the reef and is home to many large stingrays and moray eels. It is often visited by resting spotted ragged-tooth sharks. When the sharks are in the Cathedral, they are enjoying a siesta and are easily disturbed. Even bubbles hitting the top of the archway in front of the cathedral are enough to scare them and they might leave. This would ruin the dive for others who may dive later in the day and is stressful for the sharks, so please take great care not to create undue disturbance.

Margate

This popular seaside resort, which boasts its own airport, offers some of the best diving on the South African coast with vast shoals of game fish and big groups of sharks congregating around Protea Banks.

41 ADDA REEF
★★★

Location: Approximately 1.5m (1 mile) offshore from Shelley Beach. See map p. 48.
Access: A five-minute boat ride from Shelley Beach.
Conditions: Subject to rainy season run-off.
Average depth: 18m (60ft)
Maximum depth: 20ft (65ft)
The reef runs for about 500m (⅓ mile) in a north-south direction. There are some deep caves with soft corals, anemones and many tropical reef fish.

42 DEEP SALMON
★★★

Location: Approximately 1.5km (1 mile) offshore from Shelley Beach. See map p. 48.
Access: A five-minute boat ride from Shelley Beach.
Conditions: As it is close to shore, this reef can be murky in surgy conditions or if the rivers are in flood.
Average depth: 24m (80ft)
Maximum depth: 30m (100ft)
Deep Salmon consists of a large ridge with interesting caves, huge coral trees and colourful tropical reef fish. The rare tiger angelfish has been spotted on this reef.

A close-up of this soft coral shows its feeding polyps.

43 BO BOYI REEF
★★★

Location: Off Shelley Beach. See map p. 48.
Access: This reef is close inshore and is a five-minute boat ride from Shelley Beach.
Conditions: As it is close to shore, this reef can be murky in surgy conditions or if the rivers are in flood.
Average depth: 15m (50ft)
Maximum depth: 18m (60ft)
This reef has many caves and overhangs and large colonies of soft corals. The fish life is prolific and game fish, such as kob or daga salmon, are often seen.

44 POTATO REEF
★★★

Location: Off Shelley Beach. See map p. 48.
Access: This is short (five-minute) boat ride from the Shelley Beach launch site.
Conditions: As it is close to shore, this reef can be murky in surgy conditions or if the rivers are in flood.
Average depth: 20m (65ft)
Maximum depth: 28m (90ft)
This lovely reef has many soft corals and plays host to a great variety of fish life.

45 ARENA
★★★★★

Location: On Protea Banks, about 8km (5 miles) offshore See map p. 48.
Access: It is a boat ride of approximately 15 minutes from Shelley Beach.
Conditions: The Arena is way out in the Mozambique Current and is therefore almost always clear with visibility

Ragged-tooth sharks are known elsewhere as sand tigers (USA) or grey nurse sharks (Australia). They are one of the more easily recognized species of shark, both because of their physical features and their habits. Heavy-bodied with a short, pointed snout, highly distinctive protruding 'ragged' teeth and very small eyes, they are usually light brown in colour with distinct blotches which fade with age. The anal and two dorsal fins are almost the same size.

Unlike most large sharks, they are able to pump water over their gills like bony fishes and they can therefore 'sleep' in caves and gullies, and are capable of controlling their buoyancy by coming to the surface and swallowing air. Slow-moving and usually sluggish, they are not aggressive but some individuals have been known to lose their sense of humour with over-familiar divers. They will, of course, take speared fish, so spearfishers should be wary of them.

Ragged-tooth sharks become sexually mature around the age of seven, at about 220cm (just over 7ft). They gather in the warm waters off the coast of KwaZulu-Natal to mate in the spring, after which the males return to the colder water off the Eastern Cape. A number of eggs are fertilized and the two most successful subsist on their own yolk supply, their less fortunate siblings and unfertilized eggs which the mother produces throughout her pregnancy. After mating, the females migrate further north to Maputaland or Mozambique in order to gestate in the warm, tropical water. They then migrate southwards, following the Agulhas Current, down to the Eastern Cape where they drop their pups in the winter. It seems that the females only mate every second year, although some may make the migration every year.

The young sharks stay in the cooler water in the Cape, sometimes moving as far as the KwaZulu-Natal South Coast in the winter, where they may be seen along with adult males awaiting the spring courtship.

The classic ragged teeth of a raggie are shown here.

A ragged-tooth shark, with distinctive spots and equal-sized anal and dorsal fins, emerges from a cave.

POTENTIAL HAZARDS

• Venomous scorpion-, lion- and stonefish lie in wait for unsuspecting prey and present a serious threat to careless divers who don't watch where they put their hands.
• Moray eels, although not aggressive, may nip any fingers that come into range.
• Groupers seem slow and docile but they are large predators and should be treated with respect.
• Whale sharks, although apparently friendly, are not toys and a flick with their powerful tails will not easily be forgotten.

usually between 15-40m (50-130ft) and never less than 8m (25ft). Be careful as there may be a very strong current. It offers good diving year-round as it is not affected by run-off from the land. The visibility is best from November to May but most of the sharks are more likely to be seen in winter.
Average depth: 28m (90ft)
Maximum depth: 35m (115ft)
Your chances of seeing game fish and sharks on this dive are excellent. Ragged-tooth sharks, hammerhead sharks,

Zambezi sharks, copper sharks or bronze whalers , threshers and even the odd great white shark have been identified in this area. If the current is not too strong, you will be able to explore the reef and marvel at the soft corals and the many beautifully coloured tropical fish. When the current is strong, a fast drift dive can be enjoyed and many game fish, various sharks and rays can be observed.

46 THE CAVES
★★★★★

Location: On Protea Banks, about 8km (5 miles) offshore. See map p. 48.
Access: It is a boat ride of approximately 15 minutes from Shelley Beach.
Conditions: Refer to Arena (no. 45).
Average depth: 28m (90ft)
Maximum depth: 35m (115ft)
This is a big cave filled with hard and soft corals. The fish life is much the same as that at Arena, offering the opportunity to see big game fish and the usual small tropical fish. Like the Arena, your chances of seeing a variety of sharks are excellent. There is also a resident potato bass which local divers have named 'Gavin'.

The yellow-spotted kingfish is just one of the large game fish which divers on Protea Banks are almost sure to see.

HOW TO GET THERE

SODWANA BAY

By road from Durban: Take the N2 north, carry on past Mtubatuba and Hluhluwe to reach the Ngweni / Sodwana Bay turn-off 10km (6 miles) from the Hluhluwe bridge, some 275km (165 miles) from Durban. Turn right over the bridge and left into the dirt road at the signpost 'Sodwana 79km' (50 miles). Pass the Uitspan Café and Garage on the left and turn right after crossing the railway line. After 36km (20 miles), pass the Muzi Traders shop and petrol station on the right. Cross the little bridge into the Sodwana Forest and after a further 26km (16 miles) look out for a Coca Cola sign and turn right at the 'Sodwana Bay / Baai' signpost.

From here it is another 10km (6 miles) to the gate of the Sodwana Bay Lodge on the left and another 7km (4.5 miles) from there to the Natal Parks Board gate. The condition of the dirt road varies from fair to very bad and potholes are common. A four-wheel drive vehicle is not necessary but would be useful in wet weather.

An entrance fee is levied at the first Parks Board gate. Latest check-in time at the main gate to the park is 17:00. If you arrive later than this, you can pay a deposit, which can be collected in the morning when you sign in. During peak season, however, entry may be refused until opening time the next morning. (Yes, you may have to camp next to your car.) The gates remain open, but are guarded throughout the night. The total distance from Durban following this route is 350km (230 miles).

The **Sodwana Shuttle**, tel. (031) 266 9878, runs return trips from Durban or Richards Bay on request for a minimum of four passengers.

By road from Johannesburg: Take the R29 through Ermelo and Piet Retief to Pongola to join the N2 south 25km (15 miles) after Pongola. Turn south and, after 40km (25 miles) turn left into Mkuze. Take the dirt road through Ubombo to Tshongwe and turn right to Mbazwana. After 15km (9.5 miles), take the road to Sodwana and follow the directions as for Durban (above). The total distance from Johannesburg is 590km (350 miles).

By air: The nearest commercial airport is at Richards Bay. There is a small strip at Mbazwana and a grass strip, which can accommodate light aircraft, at Sodwana.

ST LUCIA

Take the N2 from Durban and travel north for about 200km (125 miles) until you reach the St Lucia turn-off.

DURBAN, SOUTH AND NORTH COAST

Durban is served by an international airport, is accessible by train from Johannesburg or Cape Town and can be reached by road from Johannesburg (the N3) and Cape Town (the N2). The North Coast is an hour's drive from Durban on the N2 north and the South Coast about the same going south. Regular buses run these routes; the **Margate Minibus** to the south, tel. (03931) 2 1406, and the **Umhlanga Express**, tel. (031) 561 2860 to the north.

WHERE TO STAY

SODWANA BAY

The Sodwana Bay National Park has a large camp with shady campsites, a few self-contained chalets (for which booking is essential), ablutions with hot and cold water, and a shop and filling station. For chalet bookings contact the Natal Parks Board Central Reservations (see page 59). Campsites are booked directly through the Parks Board office at Sodwana Bay, tel. (035) 571 0051/2/3.

The three dive concessionaires have rustic **self-catering dive camps** within the park and offer accommodation and dive packages. Divers with more sophisticated tastes will be well pampered at the upmarket **Sodwana Bay Lodge**, an RCI-affiliated (Resort Condominium International) time-share resort with all facilities, including a dive shop and training pool. To book, tel. (035) 571 0095.

Phinda Resource Reserve, tel. (011) 803-8421, fax (011) 883 6255, offers very upmarket safari-style accommodation and will be the most popular choice for non-diving companions as escorted game-viewing excursions and other trips can be arranged. They arrange dives through Odysea Diving and will transport divers to and from Sodwana Bay in comfort, even by low-flying plane if tables allow.

ST LUCIA

For those wishing to stay in a comfortable hotel, contact **The Boma** in McKenzie Street, tel. (035) 590 1330. **Saxmere Lodge**, tel. (035) 590 1005, is an unpretentious, inexpensive lodge with large family-sized rooms sleeping anything from four to 10 people. They are near the lagoon. **The Natal Parks Board Camp** is situated near the beach and has shady camping, a swimming pool and boat launching facilities. Campsites should be booked by telephoning (035) 590 1340 or by fax (035) 590 1343, and chalets through Central Reservations (see page 59). The **Cape Vidal Public Resort** is a reserve situated in a dense coastal forest and offers three kinds of self-catering accommodation. Viewing wildlife in the forest, walks, trails, ski-boat and surf fishing, and scuba-diving are just some of the main attractions here. Book through the Natal Parks Board Reservations, P O Box 1750, Pietermaritzburg 3200, or tel. (0331) 47 1981.

NORTH COAST

There is no shortage of hotels and resorts on this coast, although it is close enough to stay in Durban. The five-star **Beverly Hills**, tel. (031) 561 2211, fax (031) 561 2322, is superbly luxurious and has beautiful sea views. Umhlanga visitors could opt for the three-star tranquil **Oyster Box** overlooking the sea, tel. (031) 561 2233, which offers all facilities. The more affordable, self-catering **Umhlanga Beach Mews**, is very close to the launch site at Grannies' Pool and offers dive and accommodation packages in conjunction with Dive Nautique. You can book through Dive Nautique or phone (031) 561 2371 and ask for Beach Mews Reception. **Salt Rock Hotel and Resort**, P O Salt Rock 4391, tel. (0322) 5025, is a three-star hotel resort on the beachfront and also has a caravan park leading onto the beach. To book holiday accommodation in flats and private houses in Ballito, Shaka's Rock, Salt Rock and Sheffield Beach areas, contact **Coastal Living cc**, P O Salt Rock 4391, tel. (0322) 5159.

DURBAN

The four-star **Royal Hotel**, tel. (031) 304 0331, fax 307 6884, is reputedly one of the best hotels in Durban and is priced accordingly. Many more modest hotels are strung out along the beachfront, of which the 'limited service' three-star **Holiday Inn Garden Court**, also on Marine Parade, tel. (031) 37 3341, fax 32 9885, offers good value. Another reasonably priced yet comfortable hotel is the **City Lodge**, tel. (031) 32 1447. They only serve breakfast but other meals and refreshments are available at an adjoining restaurant. The **Tropicana** is conveniently place on Marine Parade, opposite Sea World, tel. (031) 368 1511. **Seaglen Beach Chalets**, 44 Netford Road, Brighton Beach 4052, tel. (031) 466 4136, has nine self-contained cottages overlooking the sea. Also at Brighton Beach is **Ansteys Beach Caravan Park**, 8 Anstey Road, Brighton Beach 4052, tel. (031) 47 4061, which offers caravan stands and tent sites. The beach has shark nets and a tidal pool. For those on a very tight budget, **Tekweni International Youth Hostel**, 169 Ninth Ave, Morningside, tel. (031) 303 1433, offers basic, clean accommodation in a friendly and vibrant atmosphere. 12km (7.5 miles) from the centre of Durban is the **Durban Caravan Park**, 55 Grays-Inn Road, Bluff, tel. (031) 47 3929, which has caravan and tent sites with full ablutions.

THE SOUTH COAST

The Wild Coast Sun, tel. Central Reservations (011) 780 7800, is an upmarket resort and casino in nearby Port Edward. **Kenilworth-on-Sea**, Marine Drive, Margate, tel. (03931) 2 0342, is an attractive and comfortable guest house in a beautiful setting with lovely seaviews. They offer very reasonably priced dinner, bed and breakfast rates with unpretentious, home-style fare. They also offer dive and accommodation packages. **Caravan Cove (Pty) Ltd**, P O Box 42, Park Rynie 4182, tel. (0323) 2 1215, has self-catering chalets and caravan sites. Also in Park Rynie is the **Rocky Bay Caravan Park**, P O Box 198, Park Rynie 4182, tel. (0323) 2 0546. It is situated on the beachfront and has log cabins to hire, as well as caravan and tent sites with full ablutions. Just off *Aliwal Shoal* is **Clansthal Caravan Park**, P O Box 154, Umkomaas 4170, tel. (0323) 3 0211,

which offers self-contained park homes in the caravan park. In the same area is **Widenham Holiday Resort**, P O Box 157, 2 Cheltenham Road, Umkomaas 4170, tel. (0323) 3 0351, about 1km ($^2/_8$ miles) from Umkomaas and which offers self-contained cottages 400m (about ¼ mile) from the beach.

WHERE TO EAT

SODWANA BAY

Your choices are limited. Food can be purchased from the shop in the park; opening times are from 08:00 to 12:00 and 14:00 to 16:00. **Coral Bay and Blueprint Divers** offer optional catered accommodation at their camps. There is, of course, a restaurant and bar at the **Sodwana Bay Lodge**, and accommodation at upmarket **Phinda** includes all meals. For a rather adventurous and authentically African culinary experience take a trip to the rather modest restaurant in **Mbazwana** which caters mainly for the locals.

NORTH COAST

There is no lack of eateries here but try **Razzmatazz**, tel. (031) 561 5847, a somewhat upmarket establishment offering interesting game dishes (like zebra pies and porcupine kebabs) and good seafood. They also have a lovely deck overlooking the sea.

DURBAN

There are plenty of restaurants to choose from in Durban and the following are only a few of the many excellent eateries around. **Langoustine-by-the-Sea** in Durban North, tel. (031) 84 9768, offers excellent seafood, including typical Durban seafood curries. Ask for a seaview when booking. For a real treat, try the **Royal Hotel**, tel. (031) 304 0331, which boasts six different restaurants. **Maitre Per's**, 6 Mona Road, tel. (031) 32 8866, is a small, popular establishment which has the reputation of serving the best Continental food in town. **Elarish on the Bluff**, tel. (031) 466 2086, specializes in spicy Indian food, which is a must when in Durban. For an excellent Greek meal, try **The Greek Taverna**, 213 Musgrave Road, tel. (031) 21 5433, which serves traditional Greek food – take your own wine.

More adventurous eaters should visit **O Cacador Restaurant**, 546 Point Road, tel. (031) 32 5518, which serves excellent, interesting Portuguese meals. **Api Taki Restaurant**, 320 West Street, tel. (031) 305 4451, is well known for its delicious Chinese, Indian and Polynesian cuisine served in a variety of ways. Those who prefer something less exotic should pay a visit to **RJ's Steakhouse**, 36 Gardiner Street, tel. (031) 304 8685, which specializes in steaks and seafood. There are several branches of RJ's around town.

SOUTH COAST

La Cappannina, tel. (03931) 71078, serve good pizza and seafood. **The Teahouse of the Blue Lagoon**, tel. (03931) 4 4149, is right on the beachfront, overlooking the Blue Lagoon. They are open from 08:00 to 17:30, serve breakfast, lunch and teas and operate as a bar in the evenings.

DIVE FACILITIES

SODWANA BAY

The Natal Parks Board have granted concessions to three operators. **Triple 'S'**, tel. (035) 571 0055, runs the Sodwana Dive Retreat in the Park, offering accommodation and dives, and the dive school and shop at the Sodwana Bay Lodge. **Coral Divers**, tel. (0331) 45 3076, offers accommodation and dives as does **Blueprint Diving**, tel. (011)432 2296, who also operate a small dive shop on the beach.

Odysea Diving operate a small, rather more exclusive and flexible charter operation. As they do not hold a concession to operate from within the park, bookings are through their office in Johannesburg, tel. (011) 452 8366.

Air fills are available on the beach. Dives must be booked with the operators the previous day as the boats run a constant shuttle out to the reefs. All the concessionaires offer dive and accommodation packages. Many of the Durban and Johannesburg operators run trips to Sodwana Bay. See page 160 for a list of inland operators.

NORTH COAST

Dive Nautique, 43 Umhlanga Beach Mews, Lagoon Drive, Umhlanga Rocks, tel. (031) 561 1139, runs charters and offers dive and accommodation packages in conjunction with Umhlanga Beach Mews (see p. 59).

DURBAN
Dive Sure, 19 Glenmore Centre, Glenashley, tel. (031) 524-822.

Trident Diving, Maydon Wharf, tel. (031) 305 3081, run regular charters into *Aliwal Shoal*.

Underwater World, 251 Point Road, Durban, tel. (031) 332 5820, offer all facilities. Highly recommended.

Simply Scuba, Cowley Road, Berea, tel. (031) 309-2982.

SOUTH COAST
African Dive Adventures, in the Kenilworth-on-Sea Guest House, tel. (03931) 73 255, run regular dives to *Protea Banks* and the shallower reefs closer inshore.

Andy Cobb Eco Diving, 10 Marion Road, St Winifreds 4126, tel. (031) 96 4239. Andy has dived *Aliwal Shoal* for many years and takes specialized trips to the reef. He also offers a shark diving speciality on *Protea Banks* which he runs in conjunction with African Dive Adventures.

The Whaler Dive Centre, Roland Norris Drive, Umkomaas, tel. (0323) 31562, fax (0323) 73 2253, is very conveniently placed to run trips to *Aliwal Shoal*.

African Watersports, Bisset Road, Umkomaas, tel. (0323) 3 1609, offer regular charters to Mozambique.

Simply Scuba, 8 Moodie Street, Umkomaas, tel. (0323) 73 2233, offers all facilities and trips to Mozambique.

REGIONAL HIGHLIGHTS

THE AREA AROUND MAPUTALAND
The **Hluhluwe-Umfolozi Park** offers spectacular game-viewing, walking safaris and a range of accommodation options. Phone Natal Parks Board Central Reservations (see details this page) for bookings and enquiries.

Boat trips on **Lake St Lucia**, centrepiece of the Greater St Lucia Wetland Park, are run on a regular basis and are a safe and exciting way to view hippos and crocodiles. Enquire and book at the Natal Parks Board camps in St Lucia.

Shakaland, tel. (03546) 912, a reconstructed Zulu village near Ulundi, offers accommodation in pleasantly modernized 'Zulu huts', game viewing, tribal dancing, ethnic food and boat trips on a nearby dam.

The **Maputaland Marine Reserve** lays claims to 20 different ecosystems and is a most interesting visit. Contact the KwaZulu Department of Nature Conservation (see details this page) for more information.

THE AREA AROUND DURBAN
The Natal Sharks Board, in Umhlanga Rocks (North Coast), presents an audiovisual show, followed by a shark dissection, every Tuesday and Thursday at 09:00, Wednesday at 09:00, 11:00 and 14:30, and on the first Sunday of every month at 14:30. It is advisable to book, especially in season. For more information, tel. (031) 561 1017.

Durban Beachfront offers many tourist attractions and some specialised walking and vehicle tours. Contact **Durban Unlimited** (see details this page) for details and booking.

Sea World is one of South Africa's leading marine-research centres and is worth a visit to see the aquarium and dolphinarium, tel. (031) 37 4079.

Fitzimon's Snake Park on Snell Parade, North Beach, tel. (031) 37 6456, is the home to a variety of snakes, crocodiles, leguaans and terrapins. Visitors can watch the snakes and crocodiles being fed over weekends.

The **Amanzimtoti Bird Sanctuary** on the South Coast is a must for bird-lovers. Waterfowl, bird-watching hides and a short walking trail are some of the attractions to be found here.

The **Oribi Gorge Nature Reserve** is close to Port Shepstone and is a rugged expanse of hills, valleys, grassland and a vast canyon. It forms part of the impressive gorge of the Mzimkulwana River and has superb views. It is rich in fauna and various species of antelope live here. There is also comfortable accommodation available in a hutted camp. Contact the Natal Parks Board (see details this page) for more information.

The majestic **Valley of a Thousand Hills** lies between Pietermaritzburg and Durban. The Umgeni River runs through this valley, situated between Natal's Table Mountain and the Indian Ocean. The views are magnificent and the flora beautiful. There are a number of hotels, holiday farms and caravan parks in the vicinity.

The not-too-distant **Drakensberg** Mountains, which includes the spectacular Royal Natal National Park and Giant's Castle Game Reserve, offer excellent hiking, pony trails and bird watching, and is an area not to be missed. Contact Durban Unlimited or Natal Parks Board for informatation (see details this page) or book tours through Kwezintaba Tours, tel. (033) 701 1017.

INFORMATION AND BOOKING

Durban Unlimited Tourist Information, 22 Gardiner St, tel. (031) 304 4934.

KwaZulu Department of Nature Conservation, Private bag X9024 or 367 Loop Street, Pietermaritzburg 3200, tel. (0331) 94 6698

Natal Parks Board Central Reservations, P O Box 662, Pietermaritzburg 3200, tel. (0331) 47 1961

Wildrness Safaris, P O Box 651171, Benmore 2010, tel. (011) 884 1458, fax (011) 883 6255.

National Parks Board, P O Box 787, Pretoria, 0001, tel. (012) 343 1991, or P O Box 7400, Roggebaai 8012, tel. (021) 22 2810.

National Hiking Way Board, Private Bag X447, Pretoria 0001, tel. (012) 310 3839 (for booking hiking trails).

Dolphin Coast Publicity Association, P O Box 534, Ballito 4420, tel. (0322) 61 997.

EMERGENCY NUMBERS

There are **hospitals** in Durban, Port Shepstone and Empangeni:
Durban tel. (031) 32 2111
Port Shepstone tel. (0391) 2 1111
Empangeni tel. (0351) 2 1111
Recompression facilities are available on *SAS Scorpion*, tel. (031) 460 6111. There is a Divevac staff member on duty on the beach at Sodwana Bay during dive operations and one who remains on call for 24 hours.
Divevac Emergency Number: (011) 403 7080 or toll-free (0800) 02 0111
General Emergency Number: 10 111
Ambulance: 10 177

THE EASTERN CAPE COAST

This heterogeneous region includes the two previously nominally independent states of Transkei and Ciskei, which are quite rural in character, and the moderately large cities of East London and Port Elizabeth. The Transkei boasts the breathtaking Wild Coast, famed for its lonely beaches, sheer cliffs and thundering waves, while one of the two official underwater trails in South Africa is to be found at St Croix Island near Port Elizabeth.

The coastline is, in most places, steeply shelving and very exposed to waves rolling in from the open ocean. The northern part of the region has a number of large rivers emptying their considerable load of silt into the sea, creating poor visibility in the summer rainy season. In winter the effects of the cold fronts passing through the western Cape are sometimes felt. The diving in this region is qualitatively different from the almost tropical diving of KwaZulu-Natal. The visibility is usually less than 10m (33ft), although clear water with visibility of over 30m (100ft) does occur from time to time.

When the Agulhas Current move close inshore, divers are treated to clear, warm water and even the appearance of some tropical fish species which come in with the warm flow. Beautiful red, orange and yellow sponges, and small soft and hard corals are typical of the marine life to be found in the Eastern Cape, which also includes gorgonians and small seafans. Sharks, such as ragged-tooths, hammerheads and the occasional Zambezi, are often seen by divers in this area and should be treated with the necessary respect.

Spearfishing and the collecting of seafood are a very popular pastime in this region with many species of game fish available, plentiful crayfish, perlemoen (abalone) at the eastern extreme of its range, oysters in abundance.

Non-diving companions will find plenty to do in the bustling cities of Port Elizabeth and East London, along the scenic Wild Coast or even inland, where many interesting game reserves and hiking trails are situated.

---

*Bright green caulerpa, a common shallow water algae on this coast, contrasts with the vivid pink sponge (**above**).*
*The Hole in the Wall (**left**), a natural sea arch near Coffee Bay, is a well known Wild Coast landmark.*

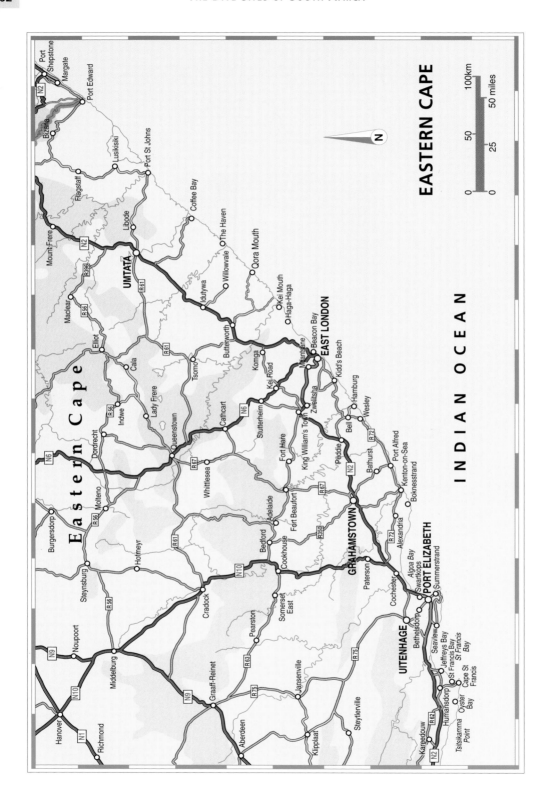

EASTERN CAPE

INDIAN OCEAN

Eastern Cape

The Wild Coast

The Wild Coast is renowned for its rugged scenery, good spearfishing and delicious seafood. While this is still true for many of the more inaccessible areas, pollution and indiscriminate harvesting of marine life have taken their toll of what used to be unspoilt wilderness.

Although there are many exciting reefs that remain to be discovered and explored, scuba diving is not particularly popular in this area. The coastline lies squarely in the path of the huge swells rolling in from the deep seas to the east, so there are few shore entries and those that do exist are quite tricky to negotiate. Because of the long distances between towns, the poor condition of the roads, the lack of facilities and the reasonably strenuous diving, this region is suitable only for completely self-sufficient parties of experienced divers with a bit of a pioneering spirit. It is a very popular destination for extended spearfishing trips.

The Wild Coast lies in a summer-rainfall region and, as many rivers flow into the ocean here, winter is the best time to dive. The conditions are very unpredictable and this should be borne in mind when planning a trip. The climate is most favourable during the months of May and June. Because of the river inflow and heavy swells, visibility is generally rather poor, usually in the region of 3m (10ft) with a maximum of 12 or 15m (40 or 50ft) in ideal conditions, a rather rare occurrence. Sea temperatures usually exceed 17°C (63°F) and can go as high as 23°C (73°F) when the warm Agulhas Current flows close to shore. The water is cleaned by the offshore south-westerly winds, which also flatten it to a degree, while the north-easter brings cold, dirty and choppy waters.

The dirt roads are generally in poor condition and road signs are unreliable. As many of the beaches are very remote, be sure to lock vehicles; you might even find it worth employing someone to guard your goods or vehicle. There have been incidences of muggings of small groups in isolated areas so, unless you are travelling in a group of at least five or six people, stick to the more populated spots.

As already stated, many virgin reefs wait to be discovered by divers with the necessary means, competence and adventurous spirit. In this section, however, the more accessible and regularly dived sites are described, but there are many other good spots available.

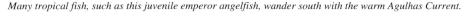

Many tropical fish, such as this juvenile emperor angelfish, wander south with the warm Agulhas Current.

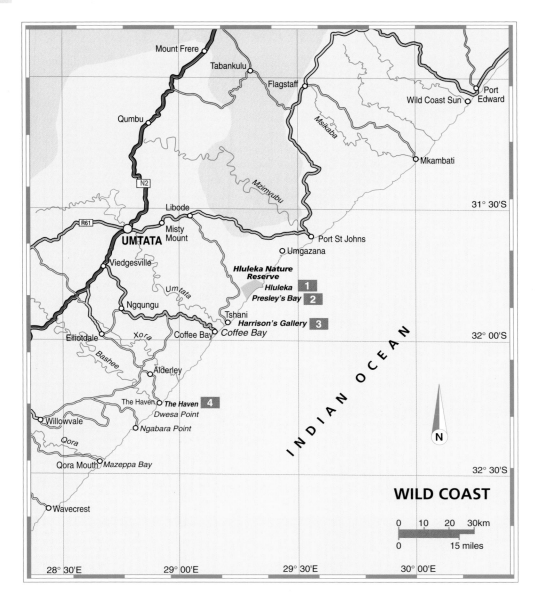

WILD COAST

0 10 20 30km

0 15 miles

---

1 HLULEKA

★★★★★★

Location: 31°49,00'S; 29°19,40'E, about 150-200m (500-650ft) out to sea, directly in front of the log cabins of the Hluleka Nature Reserve. See map this page.

Access: By boat from Mdumbi River, Tshani or Lwandile. About 12 minutes by boat from Presley's Bay (no. 2).

Conditions: Best dived during the winter months and there is always a possibility of a strong surge.

Average depth: 8m (25ft)

Maximum depth: 10m (33ft)

The reef falls within the Nature Conservation Area and consequently no crayfishing is allowed. However, it is one of the most rewarding spearfishing reefs along this coast, although spearfishing from the shore is not permitted and therefore can only be done from a boat. Its accessibility and facilities make it one of the most popular dive destinations along the Wild Coast. Caves add interest to the reef and the teeming fish life includes musselcracker, kabbeljou, bank steenbras, barbel, rockcod and rubberlips.

2 PRESLEY'S BAY

★★★★★

Location: 31°53,00'S; 29°16,30'E, to the north of the Mdumbi River mouth in front of Presley's Bay, some 800-1000m (2640-3300ft) out to sea. See map p. 64.
Access: By boat from Mdumbi River, Tshani or Lwandile.
Conditions: Best dived in winter.
Average depth: 15m (50ft)
Maximum depth: 22m (70ft)
This dive site consists of patches of rocky reef with pinnacles and extensive, but deep, reefs further out. It is a good fishing and spearfishing area.

3 HARRISON'S GULLEY

★★★★★

Location: 31°57,00'S; 29°13,50'E, to the left of the Mdumbi River mouth, north of the Umtata River mouth. See map p. 64.
Access: It is best to drive to the Umtata River mouth first and to take distances from there. Take the N2 south from Umtata and turn left onto the tarred Coffee Bay road, 20km (12.5 miles) out of Umtata. Carry on for 68km (42 miles) and turn left 6km (4 miles) before Coffee Bay onto the dirt road marked 'Umtata River mouth'. From here it is another 18km (11 miles) to the river mouth. Backtrack for 3km (2 miles) from the Anchorage Hotel and turn right where a sign says 'Thsane' (do not count on the sign still being there). After another 3.5km (2¼ miles) turn left where the road forks and go down the steep slope to the slipway at the bottom. Do not attempt this when the roads are wet.

There is a good launch site and the surf can generally be negotiated quite easily. This also serves as a launch for the other reefs further north. Harrison's Gulley is situated around the corner, to the south of the launch site. About 5.7km (3.5 miles) from the Umtata River mouth is another steep road which leads down to the river banks where, if desired, scuba diving is possible.

RIVER DIVING

The water in the Mdumbi River can be quite clean and the visibility is often better than in the sea. Both banks can be dived. and, although the river is only about 3m (10ft) deep, it can be very interesting and rewarding. Small tropical fish, as well as bigger fish, are often seen here.

CRAYFISH AND MORAY EELS

The crayfish in this part of the world have developed a protective commensal relationship with moray eels. These animals live in the same hole and when a predator, such as an octopus (or a diver), gets too close for comfort, the moray takes a quick, sharp nip. For this reason, when crayfishing, look very carefully before you stick your hand into any likely looking cranny.

Conditions: Heavy surge and big swells are common. It is best dived in winter, but the hydroelectric pump station in Umtata pumps water from the dam into the Umtata River during the months of May to September. This has been known to cause brown water and zero visibility around the mouth.
Average depth: 13m (43ft)
Maximum depth: 15m (5oft)
Rocky gullies run from shore for approximately 500m (⅓ mile), with the best diving approximately 300m (1000ft) offshore. It is a good fishing and spearfishing reef so local anglers can be consulted regarding the exact position of the reef. The reef life consists of colourful sponges, sea-fans and other common encrusting growth. A great variety of fish, including some small tropical fish right on the edge of their range, can be expected here. You may even spot some sharks, so be very wary if you are spearfishing.

4 THE HAVEN

★★★★★

Location: 32°15,00'S; 28°56,00'E, off the point to the north of the Haven Hotel, in front of the beach cottages. See map p. 64.
Access: Take the dirt road to Elliotdale (38km (24 miles) before Umtata on the East London side) and turn right to the Haven, 3km (2 miles) before Elliotdale. The hotel is another 78km (49 miles) from the turn-off. It is a total distance of 113km (70 miles) from Umtata and the journey takes about 2 hours. The reefs are reached by boat launched from the Mbashe (Bashee) River mouth. A reef finder is advisable if you are not diving with a local.
Conditions: It is best dived in winter when the water is cleanest. The Agulhas Current bounces off this part of the coast and swells can be huge with a strong surge. The Mbashe River muddies the water during the rainy season in the summer months.
Average depth: 12m (40ft)
Maximum depth: 15m (50ft)

The dive site consists of patches of rocky reef and sand with pinnacles rising to just below the ocean's surface. Fish of all kinds, ranging from game fish to small tropicals, may be seen and sharks, mainly hammerheads, are often encountered. These are also a good spearfishing reefs but, as the Haven falls within the Cwebe Nature Reserve, no crayfish, prawns, mussels or oysters may be taken. The mysterious wreck of the *Waratah* is rumoured to rest directly out to sea from the mouth, but numerous expeditions have produced no hard evidence.

> ## MARINE RESERVE
>
> The area between Nahoon Point and Gonubie Point has been declared a reserve, for three nautical miles out to sea. Shore angling, collecting of redbait and spearfishing are the only exploitations allowed. The areas between Christmas Rock and Gxulu River mouth, and Nyara River mouth and Great Kei River mouth, are also reserves for three nautical miles from the low-water mark.

East London

East London, the only river harbour and the fourth largest harbour city in the country, retains a distinctly sleepy, small-town atmosphere and offers a friendly reception to the visitor. Scuba diving is very popular but there are still numerous unexplored reefs, as well as a number of interesting wrecks, and local dive operators are opening up new dive sites regularly.

North-west and westerly winds clean the seas, southwesters cause swells to pick up, while the south-easterlies flatten the water. The easterly winds dirty the water and reduce visibility. The drought of the last few years has been disastrous for the farmers but has allowed for good diving conditions. The best time to dive is between December and March, as long as the rains have not been too heavy. June to August is usually fairly good, too, but autumn and spring (April to May and August to November) are very windy and the diving conditions are

Double-sash butterflyfish may be seen in the Cape.

not ideal. Water temperatures are usually 17-21°C (63 - 70°F) and visibility ranges from about 3-10m (10-33ft) with occasional days of very clear water. Because it is neatly sandwiched between warm and cold conditions, this area enjoys a wide species diversity and new, and sometimes unique, species are being found on a regular basis. Reef life is abundant and colourful with soft corals, bryozoans and sponges being numerous and varied. Fish are more of the edible type than the pretty tropical variety, with many red- and silverfish abounding, such as Roman, musselcracker and red and white stumpnose.

Non-diving companions can easily amuse themselves in East London by playing golf, tennis or other sports, or by visiting the nearby Mpanga Game Park. The East London Museum, which is famous as the institution responsible for the preservation of the first coelacanth specimen, is also definitely worth a visit. There are lovely beaches, beautiful walks, and excellent surfing and fishing when the conditions are right. There are sufficient shops, restaurants and other urban delights to prevent the city slicker from feeling too isolated.

5 GONUBIE POINT
★★★★

Location: 32°56,66′S; 28°02,18′E. See map p. 68.
Access: Take the N2 north and take the 'Eastern Beaches' turn-off. Follow the road signs to Gonubie and go along Main Road to the Gonubie Hotel. Turn right at the end of this road. The entry and exit points are at the old slipway, about 100m (330ft) further on, on the left. The reefs start from the shore and curve to the right for a considerable distance out to sea.
Conditions: Best dived on a high tide.
Average depth: 5m (16ft)
Maximum depth: 10m (33ft)
This is a good dive for the novice diver because of the easy entry and exit points and shallow depth. The reef is colourful with many sponges, gorgonians, sea-fans and small invertebrates occurring here.

The Agulhas Current a large, powerful, fast-flowing 'river' running southwards along the east coast of South Africa, is, in places, up to 160km (100 miles) wide and flows at speeds of up to 5 knots (9.25kph or 5.75mph). An extension of the South Equatorial and the Mozambique Currents, it carries warm water into the otherwise cool southern Indian Ocean, and is responsible for the southward extension of the range of many tropical fish species.

The current is influenced by the submarine topography, usually following the edge of the continental shelf. The continental shelf is relatively narrow off the coast of KwaZulu-Natal and becomes wider off the Eastern Cape, so the current swings away from the coast in this region, allowing the cooler water to remain inshore. Sometimes, for various reasons, the current flows closer inshore, bringing warm water and tropical fish species into the Eastern Cape, and, on rare occasions, as far as the Western Cape. When the current swings back, leaving these fish in colder water, they hide out in small nooks and crannies and, if the warm water doesn't return soon, die.

A number of currents flow in the opposite direction and have an enormous influence on the distribution of species along the coast. Close inshore, a cool counter-current flows northwards, sometimes petering out off the coast of KwaZulu-Natal, and is probably responsible for the annual arrival of huge schools of sardines and attendant predators in this region. It is likely that the ragged-tooth sharks utilize this current to migrate up to the KwaZulu-Natal South Coast, and that, on occasion, juveniles of this species follow this cold water from the Cape to the South Coast and may then be seen out of their usual range.

There are also a number of warm counter-currents which form circulation systems, ranging from inshore eddies, which complete a circulation in a few days or weeks, to huge oceanic circulations which take almost a year to complete a cycle. Many migratory animals utilize these cycles to mate under ideal conditions and to stay away from their adult habitat until they are old enough to avoid predators. This explains why you are unlikely to see, for example, baby loggerhead turtles on the coral reefs of Sodwana, even though they hatch on the nearby beaches. Those that survive the trek from their nest to the sea and the subsequent swim, enter the Agulhas Current and stay in the main circulation system for a few years, subsisting on the many floating organisms. The turtles only return to the coral reefs off Maputaland at the age of about three or four, when they are old enough to protect themselves and to begin breeding.

Divers, too, make use of this current. Off the southern Cape coast, spearfishers often travel way out to the Agulhas banks to shoot yellowtail and other pelagic fish, and, off the coast of KwaZulu-Natal, the presence of 'Mozambique water' close inshore is greeted with great enthusiasm. Divers revel in the wonderful warm, crystal-clear water off Sodwana, Aliwal Shoal and even sometimes as far down as the Cape.

Divers welcome the crystal-clear Agulhas water.

6 THREE SISTERS

★★★★★★★

Location: 32°58,34'S; 27°59,14'E, 1km (⅔ mile) off Bonza Bay (charted as Danger Point). See map this page
Access: Can be reached by boat from either Nahoon or Gonubie river mouth. The reef breaks at low tide and can be seen from the shore.
Conditions: It is best dived in winter (May to August). The water here is usually cleaner than for most shore dives in the area, as it lies further out to sea.

Average depth: 8m (25ft)
Maximum depth: 15m (50ft)
A beautiful and colourful reef, this is one of the more popular boat dives in the area and is regarded as one of the best in the East London region. Water temperatures range from a moderate 17-21°C (63-70°F).

The spectacular pinnacles, ledges and crevices are abundant in colourful invertebrates, such as sponges, gorgonians, and if you look carefully, camouflaged nudibranchs. Big reef fish abound on the pinnacles and it is consequently a popular spearfishing area. Spearfishing, however, is only permitted from shore. Ragged-tooth sharks have often been spotted on this reef.

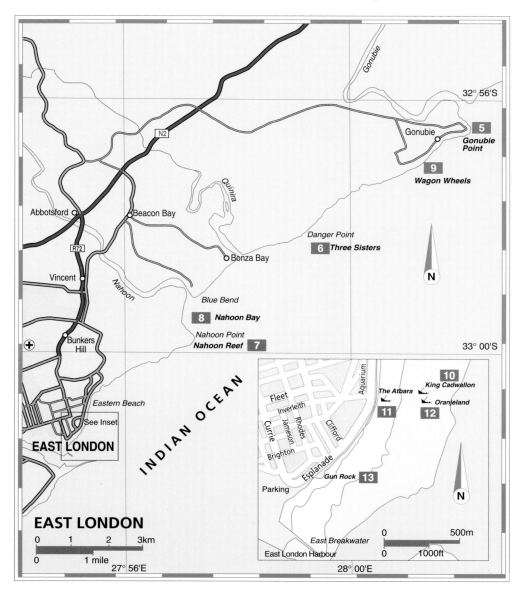

7 NAHOON REEF

★★★★★★

Location: 33°00,00'S; 27°57,30'E, to the west of the Nahoon River mouth. See map p. 68.
Access: Best dived from a boat launched through the Nahoon or Gonubie river mouth. The reef starts at the shore, extending a considerable distance out to sea, and can be dived from shore with an entry at Mermaid's Pool. This is also a popular night diving spot.
Conditions: There is a possibility of a strong long-shore current on an incoming tide.
Average depth: 10m (33ft)
Maximum depth: 12m (40ft)
The reef is full of holes and caves that are inhabited by many big fish, such as black steenbras and parrotfish, and there are many colourful corals and nudibranchs. Juvenile raggies are often spotted here. Just offshore are protected rock pools which offer good snorkelling.

8 NAHOON BAY

★★★★

Location: East of Nahoon Reef. See map p. 68.
Access: By boat launched from either Gonubie or Nahoon river mouths.
Conditions: Best dived on west to north-west winds, but is diveable all year.
Average depth: 10m (33ft)
Maximum depth: 18m (60ft)
This area offers three different dive sites with pinnacles protruding from a sandy seabed. Nahoon Bay is characterized by spectacular ledges and caves with a high concentration of soft corals and a wide range of reef fish. Juvenile tropical fish have accidentally wandered in along with the current occasionally. This is a great spot for those keen on macrophotography.

9 WAGON WHEELS OR REEF 200

★★★

Location: About 1.8km (just over a mile) out to sea, directly in line with 3rd Street, Gonubie, on the Nahoon side of Gonubie Point. See map p. 68.
Access: By boat from Nahoon or Gonubie river mouth.
Conditions: Strong currents are often encountered – excellent for drift diving.
Average depth: Anywhere between 10 and 30m (33 and 100ft)
Maximum depth: 30m (100ft)

This is a big reef with a large, flattish section and many pinnacles with small caves and crevices. Invertebrate life is colourful with sponges, basket stars and a wide range of soft corals. Big red- and silver reef fish also abound.

10 THE SS KING CADWALLON (1929)

★★★★

Location: 33°01,10'S; 27°55,50'E. See map p. 68.
Access: Park at the Aquarium on the beach front, a little to the east of the Kennaway Protea Hotel. Pace 40m (130ft) to the left (east) of the Aquarium, and look back towards the German memorial. Line up the wooden lamppost in front of a double-storey house with a tall metal lamppost in front and this line will lead directly to the wreck site, approximately 250m (825ft) out. Easy entry, but tricky exit.
Conditions: Surge can be heavy with strong currents.
Maximum depth: 8m (25ft)
The *King Cadwallon* burnt out and sank on 11 September 1929, after drifting with a fire in its bunkers for 41 days. It caught fire some 11km (7 miles) out of Durban on a voyage to Adelaide. Its bell can still be seen in the East London Museum. It was a British screw steamer, and its boilers still remain intact. It is a colourful dive with abundant fish life, including some tropical species.

11 THE ATBARA

★★★★

Location: 33°01,80'S; 27°54,85'E, in front of the Kennaway Protea Hotel, west of the Aquarium. See map p. 68.
Access: In front of the hotel, between beacons 'F' and 'G', there is a gulley approximately 150m (500ft) out to sea, leading to the wreck site. Choose alternative exits.
Conditions: Best dived on high tide.
Average depth: 6m (20ft)
Maximum depth: 7m (23ft)
There is not much left to be seen on this wreck as the area has been blasted, but its cargo of cement barrels have formed an interesting artificial reef which is rich in both invertebrate and fish life.

12 THE SA ORANJELAND (1974)

★★★

Location: 33°01,25'S; 27°55,50'E. See map p. 68.
Access: Between the 'L' and 'M' beacons on the sea-front, there are short concrete pillars, the remains of

diamond-shaped beacons. The wreck lies on a centre line between these beacons, about 300m (1000ft) out to sea. At low tide, bubbles and turbulence can be seen on the water above the wreck site. It is a rather long swim and is easier accessed by boat from the harbour.

Conditions: There can be surge on this reef.

Maximum depth: 9m (30ft)

The SS *Oranjeland* sank when it was caught in a north-east gale on 13 August 1974, after leaving the harbour on the way to Europe with a general cargo of 7500 tons, consisting mainly of granite. Nothing may be removed from the wreck. This is not a particularly interesting scuba dive but there are some fun swim-throughs. Wear gloves and beware of being swept onto sharp objects by the surge. This is more popular as a spearfishing spot.

13 GUN ROCK

★★★★

Location: 33°01,28'S; 27°55,26'E. See map p. 68.

Access: The entry is to the left of a prominent point, approximately 150m (500ft) to the right (facing the sea) of the Wimpy (a fast-food restaurant) on Aquarium Road.

Do not enter off the point and choose at least two alternative exits on either side of the point.

Conditions: This site can be tricky, so watch the sea for a while before committing yourself. Best dived at high tide. There can be surge when swells are running.

Average depth: 6m (20ft)

Maximum depth: 10m (33ft)

Gun Rock Reef is a long, flattish, rocky reef starting from shore, curving out to the left and running parallel to shore for a distance of 200m (650ft) out to sea. It is a colourful reef with blotches of red, orange and yellow sponges and other invertebrates such as sea-fans, gorgonians, sea stars, nudibranchs and soft coral. There is a variety of small fish, such as bigeyes, butterflyfish, blacktails and small sharks.

Port Alfred

Port Alfred is a picturesque little town at the mouth of the Kowie River, midway between Port Elizabeth and East London. A new marina has been built at the old harbour which was frequented by trading ships for more than 20 years during the nineteenth century.

Although days, or sometimes even weeks, of poor diving conditions may persist, particularly during the summer rainy season, this relatively unexplored part of the

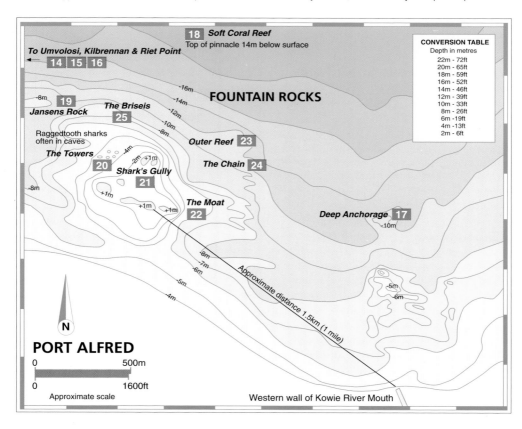

coast offers superb diving when conditions are good. The westerly winds clean the water, as does a light easterly wind, while a strong easterly dirties it. Warm *Berg* winds flatten the water but bring in cold water because of upwelling, and fog often presents problems. The western ocean currents clean the water and the opposite holds true for the eastern currents.

The best season for diving here is during the winter months (late March to late August), with the two best months being June and July. The average visibility (in diveable conditions) is around 6-10m (20-33ft), but it can be up to 20m (66ft) on exceptional days.

The water temperature ranges from 12-18°C (54-65°F) but can reach 25°C (77°F) occasionally in January, in which case it is usually very clean as well.

Fountain Rocks is an extensive reef to the south-east of the Kowie River mouth. Most launches are through the Kowie River mouth, which can be very dangerous in big seas, so it is sometimes not possible to dive because you cannot launch a boat. It is possible to launch an inflatable off Kleinmond Beach, though, about an hour's drive up the coast. Fish life is varied and big fish are particularly plentiful with many spotted ragged-tooth sharks and rays occurring in certain areas.

Non-diving companions can do an interesting two-day canoe trail on the Kowie River, explore the long, deserted beach or visit the nearby village of Bathurst with its lovely old buildings and craft centres, and its pleasant historic pub, the 'Pig and Whistle'. The Fish River Sun Casino in the Ciskei is only 28km (17 miles) from Port Alfred.

Striped grunters in large shoals often surround divers.

Conditions: Usually calm because of the depth.
Average depth: Fairly flat, all at 20m (65ft)
Maximum depth: 20m (65ft)
This British steel screw steamer had a short working life. It was built in 1903 and wrecked in 1907 when it struck a rock off Riet Point. It is relatively intact but is almost completely buried in the sand. It is well worth a dive with its interesting invertebrate life and variety of fish.

UMVOLOSI

★★

Location: About 300m (1000ft) offshore, 1km (⅝ mile) east of the Kleinmond River mouth. See map p. 70.
Access: Can be done as a shore dive but this is quite strenuous. Best dived from an inflatable launched off the beach or by boat from Port Alfred.
Conditions: Can only be dived in perfect conditions as it is very shallow.
Average depth: 7m (23ft)
Maximum depth: 12m (40ft)
There is not much fish or invertebrate life, but very keen wreck divers may find it interesting.

RIET POINT

★★★★

Location: About 12km (7.5 miles) east of the Kowie River mouth, about 3km (2 miles) offshore. See map p. 70.
Access: By boat from Port Alfred. It is best to take two tanks and perhaps combine a shallow dive here with a deeper one on the *Kilbrennan* (no. 15).
Conditions: Because the pinnacle comes up to about 6m (20ft), care must be taken when anchoring as the sea can pick up and tip a shallowly anchored boat.
Average depth: 10m (33ft)
Maximum depth: 22m (70ft)
This is an exceptionally colourful and prolific reef. Soft corals in many colours are abundant and, at greater depths, huge sponges dominate the reef. Because of the tricky anchoring, local fishermen avoid this spot and consequently, big reef fish abound.

15 KILBRENNAN

★★

Location: About 2km east of Riet Point. See map p. 70.
Access: By boat from Port Alfred (because of the long boat ride, it is best to bring two tanks and do two dives).

17 DEEP ANCHORAGE
★★

Location: On Fountain Rocks, slightly to the west of the Kowie River mouth. See map p. 70.
Average depth: 15m (50ft)
Maximum depth: 18m (60ft)
Ships used to anchor here during Port Alfred's active years as a port and an old anchor remains at the site. There are many bits and pieces of wrecks lying around.

18 SOFT CORAL REEF
★★

Location: On Fountain Rocks. See map p. 70.
Average depth: 15m (50ft)
Maximum depth: 25m (80ft)
There are beds of soft coral which dot the reef with brilliant colour, and drop-offs from 12m-25m (40-80ft). The top of the pinnacle rises to 14m (45ft) below the surface and the depth varies from 21m (68ft) on the shore side to 25m (80ft) maximum on the seaward side. It is unfortunately overfished, so the fish life is neither particularly abundant nor varied.

A cuttlefish swims by contracting its muscular mantle.

19 JANSSENS ROCK
★★★★

Location: North-east of Fountain Rocks. See map p. 70.
Average depth: 8m (25ft)
Maximum depth: 18m (60ft)
This site consists of a broken reef with four distinct pinnacles rising to a few metres below the surface, gulleys and a flat reef. The potholes are colourful with abundant sponges and soft coral growth. There is a tunnel approximately 8m (25ft) long running through the rock at a depth of about 9m (30ft) and raggies are often found in here. The tunnel is wide enough for four divers to swim through side by side with ease, a practice which is not recommended when the raggies are in residence.

20 TOWERS
★★★

Location: On Fountain Rocks. See map p. 70.
Average depth: 10m (33ft)
Maximum depth: 12m (40ft)
This is a majestic dive with sculpted pinnacles rising from coarse white sand. This spot hosts a small family of stingrays that appear to be very tame, allowing divers to approach them. Don't ever forget that stingrays, although usually quite passive, can inflict a very nasty wound if they feel threatened, trapped or annoyed.

21 SHARK'S GULLEY
★★★

Location: On Fountain Rocks. See map p. 70.
Average depth: 10m (33ft)
Maximum depth: 15m (50ft)
Ragged-tooth sharks are very often encountered here and as many as 30 have been counted on one dive. They do not harass divers, as long as they are not provoked or interfered with. There are also beautiful reef formations.

22 THE MOAT
★★

Location: On Fountain Rocks. See map p. 70.
Conditions: Only diveable when conditions are good.
Maximum depth: 12m (40ft)
This shallow dive offers some pretty tunnels.

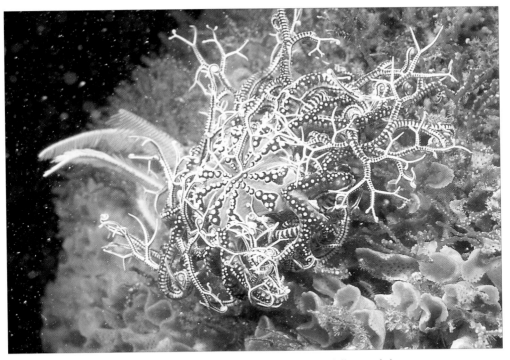

This basket star, resting on an orange bryozoan, has its feeding polyps partially extended.

23 OUTER REEF

★★

Location: On Fountain Rocks. See map p. 70.
Average depth: 10m(33ft)
Maximum depth: 18m (60ft)
This is an extensive reef with sandy patches where sand sharks and rays are often seen.

24 THE CHAIN

★★★

Location: On Fountain Rocks. See map p. 70.
Maximum depth: 18m (60ft)
This is the most colourful spot on the reef with gullies, overhangs and pinnacles, one of which rises to within a few metres of the surface. To the side is a flat area dotted with large potholes, some of which are so big that a pair of buddies can explore them together.

Reef fish such as stone bream, zebra fish and parrotfish are abundant. There are lengths of old anchor chain draped around the rocks and two old anchors, one of which is reputed to be more than 200 years old.

25 THE BRISEIS (1860)

★★★

Location: On Fountain Rocks. See map p. 70.
Conditions: Best dived during the period late May to mid-August, with some very good water during a short period in the months of January / February. Surge can be rough when seas are big.
The exact location of the 130-year-old wreck of the *Briseis* was established in July 1990 by Dennis Croukamp of the Kowie Dive School in Port Alfred. As is often the case, it is quite a distance from where it was originally thought to have come to rest.

The exact position will remain a bit of a secret until it has been properly researched and recorded, although Dennis will take sufficiently interested and qualified divers to this interesting site. Some promising and exciting discoveries have subsequently been made.

The Briseis was wrecked in a gale-force westerly wind during the night of 16 March 1859 when it struck Fountain Rocks and landed on top of the rocks, after which it broke up rapidly. It was en route from Bombay to London with a valuable cargo of ivory (some 250 tusks were trans-shipped with the crew at the time of wrecking), as well as carrying tin, cotton, sperm whale oil, carved teak furniture, guns and coir.

Although small, nudibranchs are some of the most spectacular marine animals, and are brightly coloured and often quite ornate in shape. The name nudibranch means 'naked gills' and these beautiful molluscs are totally without shells or other mechanical protection. The whole body is sometimes covered in long, fleshy appendages, the most common example of which is the gas flame nudibranch. Its appendages are coloured rather like a gas flame, in blue, yellow and white. These appendages increase the nudibranch's surface area and so facilitate oxygen exchange within the ocean, thereby acting like gills. Other species, of which the beautiful Spanish dancer is a notable example, have several bunches of gills encircling the anus. Two rhinophores, which may be feathery and quite decorative, are situated quite far forward on the animal, and serve as chemo-receptors, aiding it in its search for food.

Most nudibranchs are cryptically coloured, thus advertizing their inedible nature to potential predators.

*The cerata covering the bodies of the nudibranchs (**top and bottom right**) act as extra gills. Nudibranchs are hermaphroditic (**centre left**), usually brightly coloured (**bottom left**), but some are well camouflaged (**centre right**).*

Despite the nudibranch's lack of mechanical protection, it is not defenceless and displays various ingenious strategies to avoid becoming some other creature's lunch. It is slow moving, and usually depends on making itself unpalatable, often by 'borrowing' defence mechanisms from its prey. Some, such as the four-colour nudibranch, eat hydroids or anemones, extract the stinging cells and utilize them in their own defence. Some just taste awful but others are poisonous. *Phyllidia* sp., for example, are so noxious that fish kept in the same tank will die.

They are hermaphroditic and sexual union is always a two-way action with each individual both fertilizing the other and being fertilized. The eggs are laid in mucous sheaths, forming long ribbons or spirals.

This diver admires the spectacular invertebrate life which thrives in the strong current off Thunderbolt Reef.

26 THE KOWIE RIVER

★★★★

Location: Anywhere in the river. See map p. 70.
Access: Just hop in off the bank, but beware of boat traffic and tow a SMB (surface marker buoy) with flag alpha.
Conditions: When the sea is undiveable, the river is usually calm enough to dive. It is warmer than the sea and usually quite murky.
Maximum depth: 5m (16ft)
This is quite a fun dive as there are many rocks piled up on the outer edges of the river and many small tropical fish, such as butterflyfish, lionfish, and even juvenile angelfish, flit in and out of the nooks and crannies.

Port Elizabeth

Scuba diving is booming in Port Elizabeth, and the numbers of qualified divers are swelling at a tremendous rate. If you contact one of the dive schools or the Dolphin Underwater Club, you should not have to search long for a dive buddy or boat dive.

The south-westerly winds prevail in winter when they flatten and clean the water inside the bay, but roughen it up on the outside (west of Cape Recife point). The opposite holds true for the summer's south-easterlies. The best time to dive in this area is during the winter months of May through to September, but December and January

are also diveable. Average visibility in summer is around 5m (16ft) and in winter 8-15m (25-50ft). A variety of fish are found here and the reefs are densely populated. Shark species found here are ragged-tooth, hammerheads and the occasional Zambezi. The area around Bird Island to the east is well known for its population of great white sharks feeding on the seals, and is not recommended for recreational diving.

The Port Elizabeth area is a paradise for wreck divers with the remains of numerous wrecks, some of which are very old and historically significant, scattered on the reefs in the bay and on the seaward side of Cape Recife. Many are in shallow water and are not easily dived. Non-diving companions can lounge on the wide, open beaches, go to the very interesting Seafront Museum Complex, which includes an aquarium, or even visit the nearby Addo Elephant Park. Those with urban tastes will find shopping malls, cinemas, theatres and restaurants aplenty.

27 THE DODDINGTON (1755)

★★★

Location: 33°50,06'S; 26°17,40'E. See map p. 78.
Access: A long boat ride of approximately 60km (40 miles) from the harbour.
Conditions: Can be hazardous because of the large shark population, and usually clear because of the influence of the Agulhas Current.

Average depth: 4m (13ft)
Maximum depth: 6m (20ft)
Bird Island is inhabited by seals and there are, therefore, many great white sharks in the area. This fact, coupled with the strong currents and rough waters encountered here, make it unsuitable for novices. Landing on Bird Island is prohibited.

The *Doddington*, a 499 ton English East Indiaman, was wrecked on the reefs in the south-eastern corner of the island just after midnight on 17 July 1755, during a south-westerly gale. Only 23 of her crew of 270 survived and they had to endure seven months on the uninhabited island, living off edible shrubs and birds' meat and eggs. They built a 30ft (9m) sloop from the timbers of the wreck, setting sail to Delagoa Bay on 17 February 1756, arriving there after much hardship on 20 April 1756.

28 THE ST CROIX ISLAND SCUBA TRAILS

★★★★

Location: St Croix Islands: 33°47,80'S; 25°46,20'E. See map p. 78.
Access: A boat ride of 21km (13 miles) from the harbour.
Conditions: Can be surgy in the shallows.
Average depth: Slopes from 2-30m (6-100ft)
Maximum depth: 30m (100ft)
Divers can visit the reserve only when in possession of a permit issued by the Cape Nature and Environmental Conservation Department at tel. (041) 390-2147. The islands are heavily populated by jackass penguins, cormorants, gulls, terns and many other species of sea birds,

Yellow-bellied rockcod are seen on the edges of reefs.

THE NORTHEND WRECK SITES

The Great Gale of 1902 struck on 2 September, when Port Elizabeth harbour was hit by a gale force south-easter. Eighteen vessels riding at anchor were destroyed, causing the single largest ship loss in South African maritime history. The count of 18 does not include the many small craft that were also lost. The dead numbered more than 60, among them six brave rescuers.

The Northend area of the bay is consequently a graveyard of sunken vessels and it is almost impossible to try to identify the wrecks as their remains are scattered all over the ocean floor

---

and divers may not land on the St Croix Islands. The enforced closure of the reserve to fishing and spearfishing has paid off handsomely and the marine life is flourishing. Nothing may be taken from the water for a distance of 300m (1000ft) seawards from the islands.

The sea is rich in marine life and some of the fish species found here include yellowbelly, elf, grunter, piggy, Fransmadam, Roman, blacktail, steenbras, hottentot, bream, Scotsman, stumpnose, musselcracker, zebra, kob, geelbek, leervis and yellowtail.

Small tropical species, such as butterflyfish, may also be spotted in warm water conditions. Ragged-tooth, tiger and hammerhead sharks are often seen, together with the other smaller varieties such as dogfish and leopard sharks. The invertebrate life includes dense growths of giant sea-fans, sponges, brittle stars, starfish, anemones, soft and hard coral, sea urchins and nudibranchs.

The islands offer spectacular diving with interesting caves, drop-offs, walls and gullies, all covered in brilliantly coloured invertebrate life as mentioned above.

29 RIY BANK REEFS

★★★

Location: 34°00,00'S; 25°51,60'E. See map p. 78.
Access: 20km (12 miles) by boat from Port Elizabeth harbour or from Hobie Beach.
Conditions: Breaks heavily in big seas.
Average depth: Surface to 30m (100ft)
Maximum depth: 30m (100ft)
Terrific rock pinnacles rising from about 30m (100ft) to the surface are covered with invertebrate life and teem with fish. Game fish are often found here and it is also frequented by sharks. Boat trips are not run there on a regular basis, but can be organized through the local dive shops. This is a spectacular and interesting boat dive.

30 THE INCHCAPE ROCK

★★★★

Location: 33°56,00'S; 25°37,10'E. See map this page.
Access: The remains of the wreck can be seen sticking out approximately 300m (1000ft) off North End Beach. It can be reached by swimming out with full scuba gear or by boat from the harbour.

When doing a shore dive, care should be taken to avoid being washed against the *dolosse* (concrete harbour blocks). It involves a long swim out to the dive site and a boat dive is advisable. Shore diving here is not recommended for the novice.
Conditions: Best dived in May and June.
Average depth: 7m (23ft)
Maximum depth: 10m (33ft)
According to Malcolm Turner, author of *Shipwrecks and Salvage in South Africa, 1505 to the Present* (Struik 1988), this is almost certainly the wreck of the *Inchcape Rock*, which sank on 2 September during the Great Gale of 1902 when its cables parted. It was carrying a cargo of wheat from Portland in the United States.

31 PHILIP'S REEF

★★

Location: In the bay off Hobie Beach. See map this page.
Access: By boat from the harbour or Hobie Beach. It lies in a direct line with the FM radio mast and the harbour wall. Carry on along this line until the large water tank at the museum lines up with the centre of the Holiday Inn Garden Court.
Conditions: Best dived in winter.
Average depth: 14m (45ft)
Maximum depth: 18m (60ft)
This used to be known as Night Reef as the first night dives in the Eastern Cape area were done here when they were still a novelty. It was later renamed after Philip Coetzee, a marine biologist who did extensive research on the reef. Fish life is plentiful and varied and invertebrate life includes nudibranchs and shells. This reef should be studied at leisure and is ideal for macrophotography. It is flatter than Roman Rock (no. 32), and does not have quite such a prolific growth of invertebrate life, but is often dived because of its sheltered position in the bay.

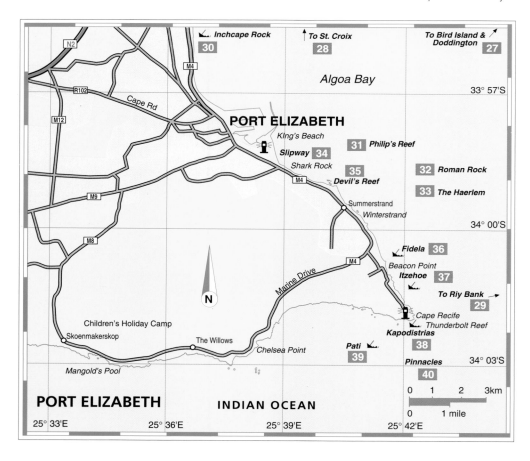

32 ROMAN ROCK

★★★

Location: 33°58,65'S; 25°40,10'E. See map p. 78.
Access: Ten minutes by boat from the harbour or five minutes from Hobie Beach.
Conditions: Best dived in winter.
Average depth: 15m (50ft)
Maximum depth: 18m (60ft).
This extensive reef is dominated by spectacular drop-offs and a single pinnacle rising to just below the surface. Great pods of redbait grow on this pinnacle and fish life abounds. The fish are very tame and often playfully follow divers around.

Many invertebrates are also found here; great gorgonians and sea-whips sway in the current, while a multitude of sponges, starfish, nudibranchs, anemones, feather stars and soft corals create a brilliant underwater garden. There is a good chance of sighting spotted ragged-tooth sharks here in April.

33 THE HAERLEM (1987)

★★★

Location: 34°58,86'S; 25°41,80'E. See map p. 78.
Access: Ten to 15 minutes by boat from the harbour or Hobie Beach. Get a local skipper to indicate the shore line-ups or use an echo-sounder to locate the wreck.
Conditions: Usually calm as it lies in the middle of the bay. Best dived in winter.
Average depth: 18m (60ft)
Maximum depth: 21m (69ft)
The *Haerlem*, an SA Navy frigate, was scuttled in November 1987, to form an artificial reef. It was in excellent condition at time of writing, with steel doors eerily screeching open and closed. Clouds of small fish hover around its upper deck and create marvellous photo opportunities. Sponges and fans have started growing on its rusting hull. A popular wreck dive, it is easy to reach and offers a variety of fish life. Because of its smallish size, it lends a very good perspective of an intact wreck, something not often encountered.

34 SLIPWAY

★★★★

Location: Off Humewood Beach, opposite Happy Valley. See map p. 78.
Access: Swim directly out from the six concrete pylons (all that remains of the old slipway) on the beach.

Conditions: This is usually a little cleaner than the other shore dives and is quite sheltered.
Average depth: 4m (13ft)
Maximum depth: 7m (23ft)
This very safe spot is a favourite for training dives and offers quite a bit to see. It is also good for night dives because of the safe conditions. Redbait, sponges and sea-fans abound and many small fish flit about the steel girders which remain on the site. Observant divers may spot an octopus hiding in its hole.

35 DEVIL'S REEF

★★★★★

Location: 33°59,00'S; 25°40,20'E. See map p. 78.
Access: Take Marine Drive towards Cape Recife and turn left into Bird Rock driveway just after Fourth Avenue and before the Marine Protea Hotel on the right. To the left of the parking lot is a stormwater pipe pointing straight out to sea and directly towards the reef. Line up with the pipe and swim straight out for approximately 150m (500ft). At low tide the reef is visible just below the surface.
Conditions: Sand can be churned up, which reduces visibility. An easy entry and exit at low tide, which is the best time to dive.
Average depth: 4m (13ft)
Maximum depth: 7m (23ft)
This lovely, very colourful, little reef is well worth the swim. Two rock pinnacles reaching to just below the surface play host to a variety of small to medium-sized fish such as blacktail and strepies. The invertebrate life consists of gorgonians, sponges and soft corals.

This is an easy and enjoyable dive for the novice, as well as the more experienced diver who doesn't have access to a boat. It can also be enjoyed on snorkel.

BELL BUOY AND ROMAN ROCK

The Bell Buoy used to be anchored on Roman Rock, but was moved approximately 400m (¼ mile) further out.

It is, however, still worth going round to the Bell Buoy as it offers shelter to a large number of seals who utilize it, fighting a continuous battle for space on the small superstructure, to the accompaniment of the loudly pealing bells.

The seals offer lovely underwater photographic opportunities, but the larger bulls should be treated with a great deal of respect as they are very protective and may react aggressively. Care must be taken not to startle or threaten them.

36 THE SS FIDELA (1873)

★★★★

Location: 34°00,60'S; 25°42,00'E. See map p. 78.
Access: Can be accessed from shore in the Cape Recife Reserve or by boat from Port Elizabeth or Sardinia Bay. To the left of the parking lot, 200m (650ft) inside the gate, there is a low concrete wall jutting straight out to the engine block that is clearly visible 400m (1320ft) offshore. A boat dive is much less strenuous.
Conditions: Often surgy due to the shallow depth.
Average depth: 4m (13ft)
Maximum depth: 6m (20ft)
The *Fidela* struck the reef on a voyage from Cape Town to Mauritius on 7 April 1873. It was a new steel screw steamer destined to serve as a mailship between Melbourne, Australia and New Zealand. Practise concrete 'bombs' were dropped on it during World War II and may still be visible on the site.

Marine life is typical of the area. Perlemoen (abalone) can be found from the shore out to the wreck site.

37 THE SS ITEHOE (1911)

★★★

Location: 34°01,30'S; 25°42,20'E. See map p. 78.
Access: The wreck site can be found some 700m (¾ mile) offshore, opposite the beacon to the left of the Cape Recife Lighthouse.
Conditions: A possibility of surge.
Average depth: 6m (20ft)
Maximum depth: 7m (23ft)

HISTORICAL WRECKS OF PORT ELIZABETH

There are many historically interesting wrecks off Cape Recife and Chelsea Point, some of which have been included as individual sites. The remains of most of these are scattered and many lie within the surf zone, so they will not be worth exploring except for divers particularly interested in wrecks.

The *Western Knight*, the *Ourimbah*, the *Strathblane* and the *Queenmoor*, off Chelsea Point, the *Sabina* off Cape Recife and the *Santissimo Sacramento* off Sardinia Bay, have not been included as individual dive sites. They are, however, interesting to dive or snorkel on the rare occasion that conditions allow.

MARINE RESERVE

The area from beacon PECR1, near, Schoenmakerskop, to beacon PECR2, near Bushy Park, for one nautical mile seawards from the high-water mark, is a marine reserve and nothing may be removed or disturbed.

The *Itzehoe* was a twin-funnelled screw steamer of German-Australian Lines carrying pianos and soft goods. Parts of the hull are still visible on the ocean bed. The marine life is typical of the area.

38 THE MV KAPODISTRIAS (1985)

★

Location: 34°02,40'S; 25°42,10'E, on Thunderbolt Reef. See map p. 78.
Access: About 20 minutes by boat from the harbour. The wreck is completely submerged.
Conditions: Very hazardous when even the smallest swell is running. The surge can be tremendous because of the shallow depth. There is a lot of jagged metal about and large gaping holes. This dive is only recommended for true wreck fanatics who are fit and experienced.
Average depth: 7m (23ft)
Maximum depth: 8m (25ft)
This 30000 ton Greek bulk carrier struck Thunderbolt Reef in calm weather on a voyage to Montreal on 29 July 1985, with a full cargo of manganese ore, zirconium sand, rutile and sugar. No lives were lost.

39 THE MV PATI (1899)

★★★

Location: 34°02,45'S; 25°41,40'E, on Thunderbolt Reef. See map p. 78.
Access: About 20 minutes from Hobie Beach, the *Pati* lies about 500m (⅓ mile) south of the *Kapodistrias* (no. 38).
Conditions: Surge can be extremely heavy, so should be dived only in very calm conditions.
Average depth: 7m (23ft)
Maximum depth: 8m (25ft)
The *Pati*, a Cypriot cargo vessel, lies in fairly shallow water. It struck the reef in fog on 17 May 1899 on a voyage from the Ivory Coast to the Persian Gulf with a cargo of cement. Many small fish and colourful invertebrates common to the reef are found on it.

The false plum anemone is very territorial and keeps other organisms at bay with its potent venom.

40 THE PINNACLES

★★★★

Location: 34°02,40′S; 25°42,10′E, seaward of Thunderbolt Reef. See map p. 78.

Access: By boat 25 minutes from the harbour, or 20 minutes from Hobie Beach.

Conditions: A very strong surge and current is frequently experienced because of the unprotected position in the path of oncoming swells, which can be huge. This dive should not be attempted in even when there is moderate surge conditions as anchoring can be very tricky.

Average depth: 20m (65ft)

Maximum depth: 30m (100ft)

This spectacular reef forms the western (outer) edge of the bay. Rock walls form brightly painted surfaces with sponges and other invertebrate life, and the sheer drop-offs and pinnacles lend a dramatic dimension to the underwater scenery when the visibility is good.

Fish life abounds and the occasional ragged-tooth shark or bronze whaler may be spotted. Invertebrate life is prolific and large gorgonians with basket stars clinging to them are a common sight. Hard coral of the semi-precious variety in colours of orange and lilac is found here, and was, in the past, harvested for jewellery-making. Fortunately this practice was stopped and heavy fines are now imposed on those who remove any coral. Multi-coloured sponges, big sea-fans, anemones and soft coral are common. Over the years many vessels have come to grief on this reef, which is named after HMS *Thunderbolt*, a wooden paddle-wheeled sloop which struck the reef on 3 February 1847, and sank in Algoa Bay.

Jeffreys Bay

J'Bay, as it is known to locals, has long been a mecca for local and international travellers in search of 'peace and the perfect wave'. The nearby St Francis Bay (see p. 86) also has some pretty spectacular surfing when the conditions are favourable, but it is not as dependable. During the summer holiday season, this area bursts at the seams with holiday-makers. It is also the centre of South Africa's *tjokka*, or calamari industry, so black-stained fishing boats speeding to and from the harbour are a regular sight.

Good surfing and diving conditions are not synonymous, and this area has never been a popular diving destination, but perlemoen abound and diving for them is a popular pastime in season. Succulent wild oysters are also found on most of the rocks and can be collected during low tide in season whilst alikreukels (giant periwinkles) can be harvested throughout the year. The area is virtually unexplored by scuba divers, though, and holds the promise of many new reefs to be discovered.

Sea urchins and starfish, probably among the most familiar sea creatures, are easily identifiable and common in tidal pools. Divers, however, get to see some of these echinoderms' more unusual relations on almost every dive as members of this family may be seen all along the coast from the intertidal zone to deep water.

Although there are exceptions, such as the pansy shells and heart urchins, echinoderms are mostly five-sided and radially symmetrical with two openings, one at the top (usually the anus) and one at the bottom (usually the mouth). Their spiny outer layer, from which the name 'echinoderm' arose, may be either brittle or extremely flexible, but will always carry spines, even if only vestigially.

A few minutes spent observing these animals closely can be very rewarding. For example, they walk in the most peculiar way. Lift a starfish gently and look at the underside of its 'arms'. You will see many tiny tube feet. The starfish walks by extending or contracting its tube feet by regulating the amount of fluid in each foot. When the foot is extended, the starfish moves it in the desired direction and then clings with its terminal sucker to the substratum. This is not exactly speedy, but it works.

Sea urchins, on the other hand 'walk' on their spines which are joined to their tough calcareous shell by ball and socket joints and can therefore be moved in any direction for locomotion or defence. The tube feet of the starfish also play an important role in

The beautiful diadema sea urchin has toxic spines and should be treated with great caution.

*These pale orange urchins and dull grey sea cucumbers (**top**) are offset by the vivid purple soft coral. A brittle star on a Sinuous sea-fan (**above left**), and crinoids, or feather stars, on an orange wall sponge (**above right**).*

feeding. A hungry starfish will envelop its prey, for example a mussel, and slowly pull the shell apart with its tube feet. There is no need for it to open the shell very wide because it doesn't remove the mussel from the shell – it exudes its own stomach into the shell and digests the mussel *in situ*!

The sea cucumber eviscerates its entire gut when threatened or annoyed, and can regenerate a new one in a short time.

The beautiful and delicate feather stars feed in a more usual fashion. Their slender, feathery 'arms' have central grooves into which the fine cilia push food particles. These are then transported to the mouth which is on the dorsal surface.

The brittle stars, on the other hand, are filter feeders and can often be seen half-buried in the sand, waving their 'arms' around in the current. In some places, it is common to see whole 'forests' of these little arms apparently growing out of the sand. They also use these long appendages for walking, possessing only vestigial tube feet, and are the fastest of the echinoderms.

Most spectacular of the brittle stars, though, is the somewhat more sedentary gorgons head, or basket star, which has continually branching 'arms' and, when feeding, this echinoderm spreads them out to form a huge 'basket', giving rise to one of its common names.

The Krom and Gamtoos rivers flow into the sea and cause muddy conditions after the rains. Strong winds blow during most of the year and the easterly winds that prevail in summer blow onshore and reduce visibility, while the offshore westerlies clean the sea during winter. Ground-swells occur and tend to pick up sand in shallow water. Visibility is usually about 2-6m (6-20ft) but can be as much as 15m (50ft), and water temperature ranges from 14-18°C (57-65°F). The best time to dive this area is during the month of November and from February through to September. Non-diving companions can go surfing, or enjoy the many beaches, shops and restaurants. This picturesque area is also well worth exploring.

41 VAN STADENS RIVER MOUTH

★★★

Location: 33°59,20'S; 25°13,20'E, in front of the Van Stadens River mouth, about 1.5km (1 mile) offshore.
Access: Approximately 30km (20 miles) west of Jeffreys Bay and 30-40 minutes by boat.
Average depth: 25m (80ft)
Maximum depth: 30m (100ft)
This reef is colourful and densely covered in marine growth, comparable to those of Philip's Reef (no. 31) in Port Elizabeth. Fish that are commonly sighted at Van Stadens River mouth include musselcracker, stumpnose, Roman and yellowtail.

42 GAMTOOS RIVER MOUTH

★★★

Location: 33°58,90'S; 25°03,56'E
Access: The Gamtoos River mouth is approximately 15km (9.5 miles) east of Jeffreys Bay and the boat ride there from Jeffreys Bay harbour takes 15-20 minutes.
Average Depth: 20m (65ft)
Maximum Depth: 25m (80ft)
This lies approximately 1.5km (1 mile) offshore and is actually a series of broken reefs rather than one continuous reef. The reef has similar invertebrate life to the Van Stadens River mouth dive (no. 41).

St Francis Bay

This is a popular perlemoen diving area with a few good scuba diving spots. When conditions are favourable, the surf in this area is absolutely superb, with Bruce's Beauties acknowledged to be one of the world's classic surf spots. St Francis Bay is approximately 16km (10 miles) from Humansdorp.

43 THE WATER TOWER REEF

★★★★★

Location: 34°01,30'S; 25°53,90'E, in front of the water tower on Paradise Beach.
Access: Turn off to Aston Bay from the Humansdorp-Jeffreys Bay road and follow Dolphin Road until it comes to a three-way stop. Turn right here into Johan Muller Road, carry on for about 1km (about half a mile) and turn left to the water tower, which is visible from quite a distance. By boat from St Francis Bay or Jeffreys Bay, or from shore to the shallower parts of the reef. The reef starts almost at the shore, but the shallower parts are not as spectacular as those deeper out.
Conditions: Can be surge on the shallower section and visibility may drop due to sand being picked up.
Average depth: 3m (10ft)
Maximum depth: 40m (130ft)
It appears to be one long reef running in a south-easterly direction for approximately 6km (4 miles), but is actually made up of interrupted sections. The best and most interesting dives are done from depths below 15m (50ft) where large sponges and soft corals are found.

44 BELLBUOY REEF

★★★★★

Location: Straight out from the Marina Martinique harbour which is situated just south of Jeffreys Bay. The reef is marked with a big buoy approximately 2km (1.2 miles) offshore.

A horsefish is often still – a photographer's delight.

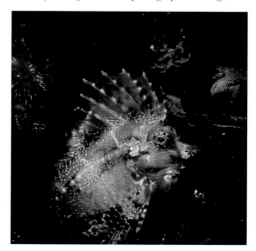

Access: A 10 minute boat ride from Jeffreys Bay or a 5 minute one from the Marina.
Conditions: Swells may be big on the shallower reefs. The water is normally clear after moderate south-westerly or westerly winds.
Average depth: 14-20m (45-65ft)
Maximum depth: 30m (100ft)
This very big reef caters for all levels of divers, including spearfishers and perlemoen divers. A popular site is at the buoy where it reaches a maximum depth of 20m (65ft). An abundance of small reef fish can be expected, as well as Red Romans, dageraad, Miss Lucy, parrotfish and an occasional big ray which normally hangs out in the vicinity of the buoy. Approximately 1.5km (1 mile) further offshore, a high-profile reef rises with deep gullies and drops of 4-7m (15-24ft). Raggedtooth sharks that swim lazily through the gullies are frequently sighted here, making this a first-class dive.

45 LIGHTHOUSE REEF

★★★★

Location: 34°12,80'S; 24°50,30'E
Access: A shore dive is possible from below the lighthouse, but the rip current can present problems, making this option advisable only for strong swimmers with good sea sense. To get to the lighthouse, carry on past the St Francis Bay turnoff. It is also accessible by boat launched in the Krom River, the slipway in St Francis or from Jeffreys Bay.
Conditions: A strong rip current makes a shore dive dangerous unless the sea is very calm, but this is safe for all levels of diver if done from a boat.
Average depth: 5m (16ft)
Maximum depth: 15m (50ft)
The reef starts about 100m (330ft) offshore and runs straight out from the Cape St Francis lighthouse in a south-easterly direction for approximately 3km (2 miles). It is colourful and well populated with marine growth typical to these waters. Fish abound and it is consequently a very popular spearfishing spot.

46 THE CAPE RECIFE (1929)

★★

Location: 34°12,70'S; 24°50,10'E, a little to the west of Cape St Francis lighthouse.
Access: Can be reached by boat from the launch as described for Lighthouse Reef (no. 45), or as a shore dive involving a swim of approximately 200m (650ft) from the lighthouse point.
Conditions: Strong rip currents are often present.

Average depth: 10m (33ft)
Maximum depth: 12m (40ft)
The *Cape Recife*, a British steam vessel, was on a voyage from Cape Town when it was wrecked in thick fog on 20 February 1929, a little to the west of Cape St Francis lighthouse. No lives where lost.
The wreckage lies scattered over an area about 100m (330ft) wide, 200m (650ft) off the point. The bronze propeller was salvaged in the 1970s. Two rusted cast-iron cannon can be seen in front of a house at the lighthouse, and many gardens in the area display pieces of wreckage. Various fish have made this wreck their home.

47 THE HMS OSPREY (1867)

★★

Location: 34°12,05'S; 24°48,20'E, 3km (2 miles) west of the Cape St Francis lighthouse.
Access: By boat launched as described for Lighthouse Reef (no. 45).
Conditions: A strong rip current is present, except in very calm conditions. The wreck lies on the outside or 'wild side' of the bay where huge swells can build up.
Average depth: 10m (33ft)
Maximum depth: 12m (40ft)
A British wooden steam screw gunboat, the *Osprey*, foundered during a westerly storm on 30 May 1867. The wreck site is in a shallow gulley and the remains that can be seen on the site include some bronze fittings, which may not be removed. Many species of fish common to the area can be seen on the wreck.

48 THE QUEEN OF THE WEST (1850)

★★

Location: 34°10,20'S; 24°32,20'E, approximately 30km (20 miles) west of Cape St Francis.
Access: A long trip by boat from St Francis Bay but a very interesting dive. The wreck is difficult to find and it is essential to take along a reef finder, or someone with knowledge of the area.
Conditions: Swells can become very big so it is only diveable in calm conditions.
Average depth: 18m (60ft)
Maximum depth: 20m (65ft)
The *Queen of the West*, a wooden British ship of 1160 tons, was wrecked on the Tsitsikamma coast on 16 June 1850 on a voyage from Bombay to London. It carried a cargo of cotton, wool and rope. All lives were lost and 30 bodies were washed up afterwards. There are still a plenty of brass and copper fittings on board, but none of these may be removed.

HOW TO GET THERE

WILD COAST

By road: The N2 runs through the middle of the Transkei and many smaller roads run off to the coast. To get from one coastal settlement to another, you usually have to go back to the N2 as there are many large rivers and most only have bridges on the N2. The roads are not good and should only be travelled in daylight as many cattle and other domestic animals stray onto them.

By air: You can fly as far as Umtata but from there you will have to rely on road transport. The buses are typically African; rather crowded, slow to leave every stop, but fast once they get going.

EAST LONDON

By road: East london is on the N2 and is easy to reach by road. Intercape buses run between East London and all the major centres.

By air: SAA flies to East London from the major centres.

PORT ALFRED

By road: To reach here by road, you will need to leave the N2 and take the coast road between East London and Port Elizabeth. Alternatively, you can leave the N2 at Grahamstown and drive straight down to the coast.

By air: There is a small airfield just outside the town but no scheduled flights.

PORT ELIZABETH

By road: Port Elizabeth is on the N2 and Intercape and Translux buses run to and from Port Elizabeth and Cape Town and East London.

By air: SAA flies to Port Elizabeth from the major centres.

JEFFREYS BAY AND ST FRANCIS BAY

By road: You will need to leave the N2 on the Cape Town side of Port Elizabeth to reach either of these towns. The roads are well-signposted.

WHERE TO STAY

WILD COAST

The **Wild Coast Sun** is a popular, upmarket tropical island hotel and casino, tel. (011) 780 7800. The **Hole in the Wall** hotel and holiday village, tel.

(0431) 31 2715, is near Coffee Bay. Basic supplies can be bought at Coffee Bay. The **Haven Hotel**, tel. (0471) 24 9410, offers accommodation in thatched rondavel-type chalets in the Cwebe Nature Reserve. Close to the beach and set in tropical gardens is the **Dwesa Nature Reserve**, which has self-catering wooden chalets on stilts with views of the sea. Bookings should be made through the Department of Agriculture and Forestry, Private Bag Umtata, tel. (0471) 24 322 or 24 9309. The **Mazeppa Bay Hotel**, tel. (0471) 2 5344/5/6, provide rooms, rondavels and the possibility of some good fishing.

EAST LONDON

The **Kennaway Protea Hotel**, tel. (0431) 2 5531, is a comfortable three-star establishment on the beachfront. For those on a tight budget, **East London Backpackers' Hostel**, 128 Moore St, tel. (0431) 2 3423, offers basic, but clean, cheap and pleasant accommodation. The **Gonubie Caravan Park**, tel. (0431) 40 2021, has beach and river frontage, or try **Roeberts Holiday Resort**, P O Box 5100, Greenfields, East London 5208, tel. (0431) 36 6381, which has self-catering cottages on the riverbank.

PORT ALFRED

The Halyards Hotel, Royal Alfred Marina, tel. (0464) 4 2410, is a very comfortable, reasonably priced three-star hotel with lovely views of the marina. **Rugged Rocks Beach Cottages** in Saltvlei Road, tel. (0464) 4 3112, has self-catering fishermen's cottages and wooden chalets right on the beach, 4km (2.5 miles) from the centre of Port Alfred. There are two campsites: **Riverside**, tel. (0464) 4 2230, is a few kilometres from the beach, and **Medolino**, tel. (0464) 4 1651, is close to the beach and about 2km (1.5 miles) from the business centre.

PORT ELIZABETH

The **City Lodge** in Summerstrand, tel. (041) 56 3322, fax (041) 56 3374, **Holiday Inn Garden Court** overlooking Kings Beach, tel. (041) 52 3720, fax (041) 55 5754, and the **Beach Hotel**, opposite Hobie Beach, tel. (041) 53 216, are all limited service hotels and offer

good value. **Marina View Holiday Accommodation**, tel. (041) 24 4180, offers self-catering units. The **Pine Lodge Resort**, P O Box 13033, Humewood 6013, tel. (041) 53 4004, has caravan sites and self-contained chalets on the beach at the edge of Cape Recife. Those on a very tight budget can expect typical backpacker's accommodation at **Port Elizabeth Backpackers Hostel**, 7 Prospect Hill, tel. (041) 56 0697. Alternatively, try the **Sea Acres Holiday Resort**, P O Box 13040, Humewood 6013, tel. (041) 53 3095, which offers caravan and tent sites, and self-catering cottages, rondavels and chalets close to Hobie Beach.

JEFFREYS BAY AND ST FRANCIS BAY

The **Savoy Protea**, tel. (0423) 93 1106, is a three-star hotel in Da Gama Street, close to the beach. The Intercape buses depart and arrive here. The **Beach Cabanas** in Da Gama Road, tel. (0423) 93 2323, have self-contained cabanas in a garden setting, and offer discounts for large groups in low season. **Jeffrey's Bay Holiday Resort**, tel. (0423) 93 1330, offers comfortable self-catering accommodation near the beach. **Jeffreys Bay Backpackers**, 12 Jeffrey St, tel. (0423) 93 1379, is a typical, friendly backpackers' hostel and you will find surfers from all over the world staying there. There is also a **municipal caravan park** here, tel. (0423) 93 1111. **The Bay Cove**, cnr Poplar and Da Gama roads, Wavecrest, is a highly recommended, friendly and affordable b&b, tel. (0423) 96 2622. **Island Vibes Backpackers**, 10 Dageraad Street, Pellsrus, has budget self-catering accommodation right on the beach, tel. (0423) 93 1625.

WHERE TO EAT

WILD COAST

All the hotels in this area have their own restaurant facilities.

EAST LONDON

Guido's, a chain of Italian-style restaurants, offers good food at reasonable prices. They have branches at Beacon Bay, tel. (0431) 47 3995, Devereux, tel. (0431) 5 6808, and Gonubie, tel. (0431) 40 1686. They are open for dinner on Mondays and Saturdays and lunch and dinner every other day. **Mövenpick**, in Orient Beach Esplanade, specializes in Swiss cuisine, tel. (0431) 21 840.

PORT ALFRED
Butlers, tel. (0464) 41398, is in Van der Riet Street and has a lovely river view. They serve steaks, seafood and curries. **Cockles and Mussels** also has a river view and specializes in seafood in the evenings and does light teas in the day. They are open from 10:00 till late, tel. (0464) 24 4873.

PORT ELIZABETH
La Vigie, at 22 Mount Road, is a very upmarket venue with a varied classic menu. Booking is essential, tel. (041) 54 4066. The **Bell Restaurant** at the Beach Hotel, Marine Drive, specializes in seafood, tel. (041) 53 2161 to book. **Cadillac Jack's** is a trendy rock 'n roll diner on the Boardwalk, Marine Drive, Summerstrand, tel. (041) 53 4408.

JEFFREYS BAY
There are several choices but **Chokkers Fast Food**, in Main Road, tel. (0423) 93 2673, offers very good quality fast food. The **Dock of the Bay Seafood Braai Restaurant** at the Marina Martinique Beachfront prepares excellent seafood on the braai, tel. (0423) 96 1565.

DIVE FACILITIES

WILD COAST
There was a dive operation at the Wild Coast Sun at Port Edward but it closed down, re-opened and closed down again. It is worth enquiring at the Wild Coast Sun reception or at Sun Diving at Park Rynie (see KwaZulu-Natal regional directory, p. 58) as they may take out charters on an *ad hoc* basis.

EAST LONDON
The following run courses, take charters, rent, sell equipment and offer air fills:
Pollocks Sports, tel. (0431) 2 4921.
Gonubie Dive School, tel. (0431) 38 1023.
Aqua Action, tel. (0431) 43 1128.
Dive Africa Tours, P O Box 2444, Beacon Bay 5205, tel. (082) 892 1492, organize country-wide diving trips and will take bookings for dive operators in most other centres.

PORT ALFRED
Kowie Dive School, in the Halyards Hotel, tel. (0464) 24 4432, run courses, do air fills and take charters out when conditions allow.

PORT ELIZABETH
Mike's Dive Shop, 63 Western Road, Walmer, tel. (041) 55 3367 and **Ocean Divers International**, Kine Park, Rink Street, Walmer, tel. (041) 51 5121 sell and service equipment, offer courses and air fills. **Scubaventures**, 21 5th Avenue, Walmer, tel. (041) 51 5328, offer specialised training, equipment rental and dive charters.

JEFFREYS BAY AND ST FRANCIS BAY
There are no dedicated dive facilities but Bob Meikle from **Meikle's Hardware**, tel (0423) 94 0324, offers air fills, rents equipment and runs charters. **Bay Diving**, 6 Mimosa Street, offers equipment rental, air fills, training and dive charters, tel. (0423) 96 2171.

REGIONAL HIGHLIGHTS

WILD COAST
This region is characterized by great surf and long, deserted beaches which are well suited for walking and hiking (unfortunately only advisable in reasonably large groups). Fishing and spearfishing is very rewarding.

EAST LONDON
The **East London Museum** in Oxford Street, tel. (0431) 22 623, is well worth a visit and there are many lovely beaches on the outskirts of town. **Hogsback**, not too far away, offers lovely day walks in a beautiful mountain forest. Tolkien fans will appreciate the Middle Earth quality of this place as it was here that he found his inspiration for *The Hobbit*. Contact Hogsback Inn, tel. (045642) and ask for 6.

PORT ELIZABETH
The **Oceanarium and Museum Complex** in Beach Road, Humewood, tel. (041) 56 1051, has an oceanarium, an aquarium and a snake park, and is well worth a visit. The nearby **Addo Elephant Park**, tel. (0425) 40 056, fax (0425) 40 0196, offers reasonably priced camping and self-contained chalets, and

is home to many elephants. The somewhat more upmarket **Shamwari Game Reserve**, tel. (042) 851 1196, fax (042) 31 1391, offers escorted game drives and a number of charming accommodation choices.

JEFFREYS BAY AND ST FRANCIS BAY
This area is a magnet for surfers from all over the world. Non-surfers, too, are drawn here, often simply to collect the many and varied shells which are washed up on the beach. Collecting of shells is permitted, only from the beach.

INFORMATION AND BOOKING

National Parks Board, P O Box 787 Pretoria 0001, tel. (012) 343 1991 or P O Box 7400 Roggebaai 8012, tel. (021) 22 2810.
National Hiking Way Board, Private Bag X447, Pretoria 0001, tel. (012) 310 3839 (for booking hiking trails).
Eastern Cape Nature Conservation, tel. (0431) 41 2212, fax (0431) 41 3266.
Cape Nature and Environmental Conservation Department, tel. (041) 390 2147.
Port Alfred Publicity Association, tel. (0464) 4 1235 / 24 4139.
Port Elizabeth Publicity Association, tel. (041) 52 1315.
Jeffreys Bay Publicity, tel. (0423) 93 2588.
Transkei Tourism Board, tel. (0471) 2 6685.

EMERGENCY NUMBERS

There are large **hospitals** in Port Elizabeth, Umtata and East London:
Port Elizabeth tel. (041) 33 7811
Umtata tel. (0471) 3 1116
East London (0431) 2 7350
Recompression facilities are available at the SAS Port Rex in East London, tel. (0431) 2 2494 or 2 2415. The SAS Donkin, in Port Elizabeth, tel. (041) 502 2006, at the time of writing has two portable mono-place chambers which can be used in an absolute emergency. A larger chamber will be acquired in the future.
DivEvac Emergency Number: (011) 403 7080 or toll-free 0800 02 01 11
General Emergency Number :10 111
Ambulance: 10 177

THE GARDEN ROUTE

This long and beautiful stretch of coastline, extending from Mossel Bay to the Tsitsikamma National Park, is known as the Garden Route and includes the attractive resort towns of Plettenberg Bay and Knysna. This area is regularly visited by divers and holidaymakers from all over the country and abroad. The beaches are magnificent, the water reasonably warm and the surrounding scenery, with its sheer cliffs and tangled forests, create the perfect holiday environment. The prevailing wind directions are south-east in summer and south-west in winter and the rain-bearing cold fronts that pass over the Western Cape can influence the weather in this region, particularly to the west.

There is often much suspended planktonic matter in the water which provides nutrients for a spectacular growth of invertebrate life. Many people who dive here for the first time are initially disappointed by the lack of colourful tropical fish but, by changing their focus and perspective, are soon overwhelmed by the wealth of colourful reef life. Because the water temperature lies between that of the warmer KwaZulu-Natal coast and the colder southern Cape, much of the underwater fauna here is found nowhere else in the world.

The most reliable time to dive this area is during the winter months of May to September, while December and January can also offer excellent diving conditions. Visibility ranges, on average, between 5 and 15m (16–50ft) but can increase to over 20m (65ft) on occasion. During summer, the water temperature can rise as high as 25°C (77°F) and drop to 10°C (50°F) after a strong south-easter, when upwelling takes place. In winter the fluctuations are not nearly as great and the average temperatures range between 16 and 18°C (61–65°F).

There are active diving schools and clubs in Mossel Bay, Knysna and Plettenberg Bay, where instruction courses, gear rental, air-filling facilities and boat charters are available. The roads in the area are excellent, there are numerous lovely resorts and camping sites to choose from, and plenty of non-diving activities for those who prefer to stay out of the water.

---

*Nudibranchs (**above**) are some of the more colourful and fascinating reef inhabitants in this area.*
*The most popular dive in the Knysna Lagoon (**left**) is the Paquita, situated in the mouth known as The Heads.*

Tsitsikamma

The Tsitsikamma National Park covers some of the most exquisite and inaccessible stretches of coastline in the country. Situated halfway between Knysna and Humansdorp, 90km (55 miles) from either, the park is administered and protected by the National Parks Board.

No boats are allowed in the area that stretches from the Groot River at Nature's Valley in the west to the other Groot River near Oubos in the east. The western section of the Park reaches out to sea for a distance of 800m (½ mile) and the eastern section for 5.5km (3.5 miles). This effectively rules out most of the diving in the area as shore entries are difficult because of the steep and inaccessible coastline. No spearfishing is allowed and no shells (even dead ones) or other marine organisms may be removed or disturbed.

There are two areas in this National Park where sport diving and snorkelling are allowed (see map on page 93); these are the official scuba and snorkelling trails which are clearly demarcated.

This is not really a diving destination as it is visited more for the lovely scenery, beautiful forest walks and the prolific bird life, with diving is regarded as a bonus if the conditions are favourable.

1 THE SCUBA TRAIL
★★

Location: 34°01,40'S; 23°53,98'E. See map p. 91.
Access: Drive or walk to the restaurant at the eastern end of the camp and enter in the sandy cove.
Conditions: Rough most of the time. Visibility is rarely more than 10m (33ft) and usually about 5m (16ft).
Average depth: 6m (20ft)
Maximum depth: 10m (33ft)

The rocks are covered with typical invertebrate life, sponges, starfish and small molluscs, and fish such as galjoen or dogfish, may be seen.

2 THE SNORKEL TRAILS
★★★

Location: The two snorkel trails in the area are located in fairly sheltered places. The deeper snorkel trail is to be found below the restaurant in the scuba area and the

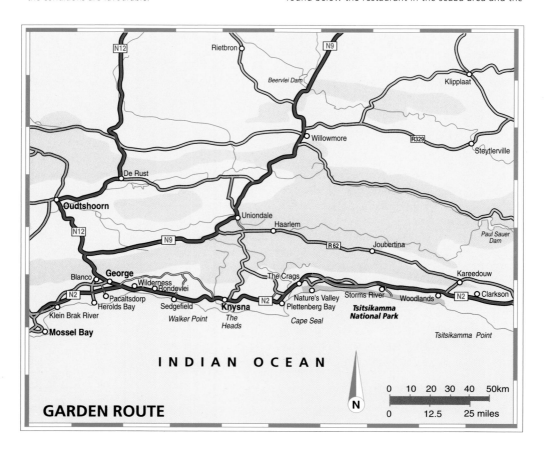

GARDEN ROUTE

PARK RULES FOR DIVERS

In an effort to prevent accidents, the Parks Board has laid down regulations which are strictly enforced:
• All scuba divers have to report to reception or the park headquarters to register before diving.
• All scuba divers must produce proof of their scuba qualifications.
• NAUI Open Water One, SAUU One-star divers and those of equivalent qualification must be accompanied by a diver of higher qualification.
• Nothing may be removed.
• No spearfishing or angling is allowed.
• No aquatic crafts are allowed.

shallower one on the western side of the oceanettes (chalets) at the start of the Otter Trail. See map this page.
Conditions: Pretty rough most of the time. When it's diveable, visibility is rarely more than 10m (33ft), and is more usually about 5m (16ft).
Average depth: 6m (20ft)
Maximum depth: 10m (33ft)

Although the two snorkel trails here are in fairly protected areas, diving is only recommended when the sea is calm. In summer months guided 'tours' are organized by park officials. The shallower pool is generally diveable more often than the deeper area. A wide variety of fish and invertebrates can be found in the pools.

Plettenberg Bay

Plett – as this holiday and residential resort is popularly known – was given the name of *Bahia Formosa*, meaning Beautiful Bay, by the Portuguese seafarers of old. It was aptly named as it is one of the loveliest bays to be found along the southern African coastline.

During the summer holiday season this quiet seaside town is transformed into a little metropolis by holiday-makers from all over the country, and is visited by many anglers and divers throughout the year. In spring, whales regularly swim into the protection of the bay to mate and calve, and dolphins often frolic in the waves close to shore. The water temperature is moderate with an average of around 18°C (65°F), and visibility is usually between 5 and 10m (16-33ft). The best months to dive the area are September through to October, but fair conditions

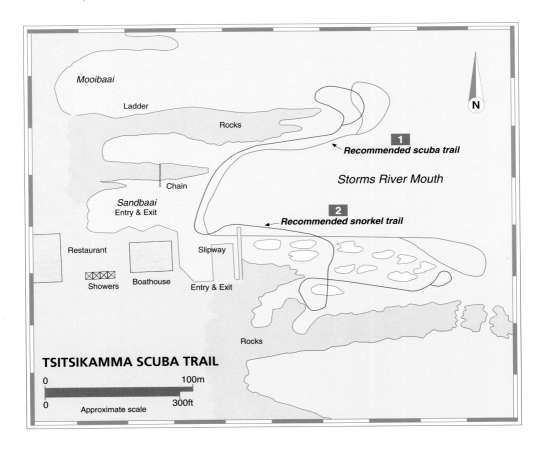

Mooibaai

Ladder

Rocks

N

1 Recommended scuba trail

Storms River Mouth

Chain

Sandbaai
Entry & Exit

2 Recommended snorkel trail

Restaurant

Slipway

Showers   Boathouse   Entry & Exit

Rocks

TSITSIKAMMA SCUBA TRAIL

0   100m

0   300ft
Approximate scale

WHEN THE DIVING GETS TOUGH ...

The 'Scubaquarium' at the Beacon Isle Hotel is a large tank through which sea water is circulated. It is stocked during the holiday season with fish, chunks of living reef, and other marine life. Novice divers wanting to experience the undersea environment in complete safety can do so here. It is also a great attraction for children, who can watch the divers swimming among the sea creatures.

prevail all year round. The onshore south-easterly winds tend to churn the sea up in summer, while the westerlies clear the water in winter. Horse trails, bicycle trails, golf, tennis, sailing, canoeing on the lagoon and lovely walks are available for energetic non-divers. The more relaxed visitor can visit one of the many excellent restaurants, or just lounge around the pool at one of the hotels.

3 PLAYGROUND

★★★

Location: Between Groot Bank (no. 5) and Nature's Valley. See map p. 94.
Access: By boat from Plettenberg Bay.
Conditions: The water is usually colder and cleaner here than around Plettenberg Bay.

Average depth: 15m (50ft)
Maximum depth: 24m (80ft)
There are big terraces going down from 10-24m (33-80ft). The marine life is not quite as abundant as at Virgin Reef (no. 4), but the pretty relief makes this an interesting dive when visibility is good. Big mako sharks have been spotted here on occasion.

4 VIRGIN REEF

★★★★

Location: About 1km (²/₈ mile) east of Groot Bank (no. 5). See map p. 94.
Access: By boat from Plettenberg Bay.
Conditions: Usually cleaner and colder than around Plett as it is further out to sea.
Average depth: 18m (60ft)
Maximum depth: 34m (112ft)
This is a big reef, similar to Groot Bank (no. 5). Virgin Reef is not often dived and consequently has profuse and colourful invertebrate life.

5 GROOT BANK

★★★★

Location: 34°00,40'S; 23°29,38'E, to the east of Plett, between Keurbooms River and Nature's Valley, about 12km (7.5 miles) north-east of Plett. See map p. 94.

Starfish, sea-fans and sponges are typical of the marine life along the Garden Route.

This giant fan-worm has its feeding organs extended. If it is approached too closely, it will retract them.

Access: By boat launched from Hobie Beach to the east of the Beacon Isle Hotel or by inflatable from the hotel.

Average depth: 20m (65ft)

Maximum depth: 25m (80ft)

Described by locals as the 'Sodwana' of the east coast, this reef starts 30-40m (100-130ft) offshore, but is, strictly speaking, a boat dive because the shore entry entails an extremely long walk.

There are fantastic pinnacles dropping from approximately 9-25m (30-80ft), and the rock formations form large amphitheatres and caves. You can also swim through and explore the huge tunnels here when the conditions are favourable.

Big gamefish such as steenbras, musselcracker, Romans, parrotfish and ragged-tooth sharks frequent this reef. The dense marine growth that covers the rock is vividly coloured and of great variety.

6 REDBAIT REEF

★★

Location: 34°03,60'S; 23°22,92'E, off the small beach in front of the Beacon Isle Hotel. See map p. 94.

Access: A short swim of 30m (100ft) to the reef. An easy entry and exit from the little beach in front of the hotel.

Conditions: Best on high tide when surge is lowest.

Average depth: 4m (13ft)

Maximum depth: 8m (25ft)

This reef is not as colourful as the others in the area because the marine life has been quite depleted by divers spearfishing and collecting oysters. Some big fish visit the reef but sharks are hardly ever spotted.

Beyond the reef is the site of an old shipwreck, which is identified by many bricks. The reef seems to be in a sorry state, and diving here is not highly recommended. It is an easy shore dive for the novice and the visibility here is sometimes a lot better than on the deeper reefs.

7 DEEP BLINDERS

★★★★★

Location: 34°03,56'S; 23°33,10'E, seaward of the three blinders in front of the Beacon Isle Hotel. See map p. 94.

Access: By boat launched from Hobie Beach to the east of the Beacon Isle Hotel or by inflatable from the hotel. Approximately 300m (1000ft) offshore, this dive can be done from shore by strong swimmers. To the right of the blinders is a rip current that can be used to take you out and around. It is a short trip by boat from any of the other launching points.

Conditions: Although this site can be dived on any tide, high tide is the best as the water is cleaner and calmer.

Average depth: 8m (25ft)
Maximum depth: 18m (60ft)
A great reef to dive on as there are drop-offs to a depth of 15m (50ft), and, seaward of the rocks, up to 18m (60ft). Behind the reefs is a sandy area where one is almost certain to see stingrays and bull rays. The shallower part of the reef is densely covered with redbait pods.

8 SHALLOW BLINDERS

★★★★

Location: 34°03,56'S; 23°22,95'E, 70m (230ft) shorewards of the three blinders off the Beacon Isle Hotel. See map this page.
Access: A shore or boat dive, it is only 150m (500ft) from the little beach in front of the hotel.
Conditions: Diveable on both high and low tides, but best done on high tide if dived close to the blinders.

Average depth: 8m (25ft)
Maximum depth: 9m (30ft)
Richly coloured and densely covered in marine growth, it is a big, flat reef, sloping up to about 5m (16ft) at the shallowest point. Close to the pinnacles are a number of gullies and the occasional ragged-tooth shark can be spotted here. They have never bothered scuba divers, but should not be harassed.

9 DOLPHIN COLUMN

★★★

Location: About 100m (330ft) behind the Blinders (nos. 7 and 8). See map this page.
Average depth: 12m (40ft)
Maximum depth: 18m (60ft)
The reef consists of a pinnacle and a number of gullies. The invertebrate life is very similar to that found on the

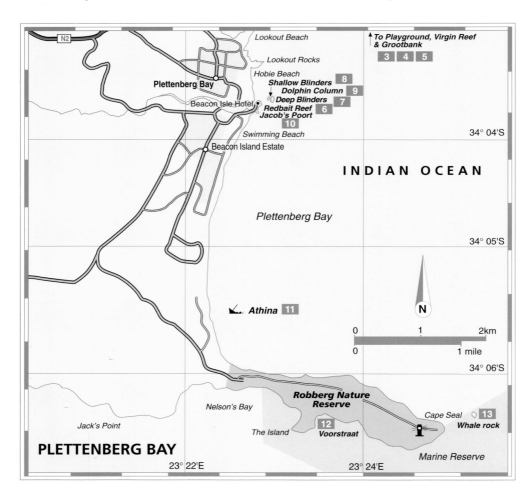

MARINE RESERVE

Other than shore angling, no marine animal may be disturbed or removed from the area one nautical mile seawards from the high-water mark in the Robberg Nature Reserve. This area includes the wreck of the *Athina*, and the dive sites Voorstraat and Whale Rock (dive nos. 11, 12 and 13).

Blinders (nos. 7 and 8) but the chance of spotting a school of dolphins swimming past makes this dive that little bit more exciting. Raggies have also been seen here.

10 JACOB'S POORT

★★★★★

Location: 34°03,70'S; 23°23,00'E. See map p. 94.
Access: Very close to the Beacon Isle Hotel by boat, and a swim of approximately 300m (1000ft) from the shore.
Conditions: The reef lies in the protection of the bay and is generally diveable.
Average depth: 12m (40ft)
Maximum depth: 16m (52ft)
The reef is covered in luxuriant and colourful invertebrates with sea-fan forests, white and red coral, sponges, sea-whips, soft coral, anemones, urchins, and masses of redbait pods which attract numerous fish. The smaller fish are tame and make good photographic subjects. Of the bigger fish that might be spotted are black parrotfish,

red steenbras, as well as small pyjama, dog and cat sharks. Divers often encounter dolphins in the vicinity of the reef, whilst whales sometimes come in close.

The very rare sunfish has been spotted lying on the bottom here, and big rays are also frequently seen. Worth looking out for is the family of yellow-bellied rockcod that live on the edge of the drop-off towards the east. Feathery black and white stinging hydroids are common on the reef and divers should beware of touching these as an itchy, burning rash results.

11 THE MFV ATHINA (1967)

★★★★

Location: 34°05,60'S; 23°22,90'E, a little east of Robberg Nature Reserve, in front of the Robberg Holiday Resort and Caravan Park; 150m (500ft) west of the caravan park and 50-75m (165-230ft) offshore. See map p. 94.
Access: By boat, it is approximately 4km (2.5 miles) from Plett. From shore, there are steps leading down to the beach from the caravan park and the wreck can clearly be seen at low tide.
Conditions: Best dived on high tide because of the shallow depth and strong surge when swells are big.
Average depth: 7m (23ft)
Maximum depth: 9m (30ft)
The MFV *Athina*, a Greek trawler of 814 tons, carried a full cargo of fish when it hit Whale Rock and sank on the eastern side of the Robberg on 1 August 1967. On days when the water is clear, the outline of the wreck can be seen from the lookout point in the Robberg Nature Reserve. The stern section protrudes above the

---

Soft corals, anemones and sea-fans contribute to this colourful display on Jacob's Poort.

waves with the bow pointing towards the shore. This can be a penetration dive, but should not be attempted except under the calmest conditions as surge and suction can be hazardous.

Robberg Nature Reserve is a lovely place for a day's outing and, with its breathtaking views and interesting walks, should not be missed when in the area.

12 VOORSTRAAT OR THE ISLAND

★★★★★★

Location: On the eastern side of the island on the southern side of Robberg Peninsula. See map p. 94.
Access: It can be snorkelled from the shore but, as it involves a long walk, should be accessed by boat launched from Plettenberg Bay if done as a scuba dive.
Conditions: Because of its position on the sea side of Robberg, it can be dived in a moderate easterly, but is totally undiveable if the wind is west to north-west.
Average depth: 6m (20ft)
Maximum depth: 18m (60ft)
The site consists of large round boulders with big caves worth exploring, and colourful invertebrate life.

13 WHALE ROCK

★★

Location: 34°06,60'S; 23°25,32'E, off Robberg Point, south of Plettenberg Bay. See map p. 94.
Access: By boat from Plettenberg Bay, approximately 7km (4.5 miles).
Conditions: Diving should only be attempted when the sea is very calm and conditions are ideal, as a strong current rips through here, and there are often big stand-up swells off the Point.
Average depth: 24m (80ft)
Maximum depth: 30m (100ft)
Whale Rock is a large pinnacle that can be seen breaking some 900m (just over half a mile) off the point of the magnificent Robberg Peninsula. It is a sharky area, with many raggies, and some big fish may be seen. The rocks are covered in sea-fans, soft corals and colourful sponges, typical of south-eastern Cape waters.

This site is not often dived as conditions are rarely good enough. It is definitely not a novice dive and best attempted with someone who knows the area. There is a breathtakingly scenic walk along the nature reserve to the point, from where Whale Rock can be seen.

The bright green caulerpa contrasts sharply with the pastel sea anemone and the red algae on this shallow reef.

Knysna

This lovely town is a favourite holiday destination, best known for its beautiful lagoon which empties into the sea through a spectacular mouth known as The Heads. The nearby forests have many lovely hiking trails and are home to a few elusive forest elephants.

The water is clear and warm for most of the year, with the winter months offering the best visibility, although good visibility of 15m (50ft) and more can be expected under ideal conditions in December and January. Up-welling occurs after a strong south-easter, which makes the water much colder; sea temperatures of as low as 9°C (48°F) have been recorded. There are no major rivers flowing into the sea, except for the algae-rich water of the Knysna Lagoon. This does not greatly influence the visibility but does bring nutrient-rich water to the nearby reefs, encouraging prolific growth of invertebrate life.

The inviting aquamarine to emerald green waters of the lagoon offer protected diving even when the sea is rough, so the visiting diver does not have to leave without the chance of getting wet. The visibility changes quickly with the tides and winds. The best time to dive is on high tide when the ocean water pushes in as far as the bottom bridge over the lagoon.

The lagoon area is under the protection of the National Parks Board, whose offices can be found at the end of Thesen's Jetty. They insist that divers tow or display the flag Alpha when diving in the lagoon as boat traffic can be heavy and hazardous to the unwary. Exciting drift dives can be done on an incoming tide and a great distance can be covered in a relatively short time. Local divers have covered the 3.5km (2.25 miles) from the Heads to Thesen's Jetty in a time of one hour and 20 minutes.

Non-diving companions can go for long and scenic walks in the nearby forest, do a bicycle or horse trail, paddle a canoe across the lagoon, explore the Featherbeds Nature Reserve, visit a museum or even pan for gold in one of the streams in the forest. If this all sounds too energetic, there are a number of good coffee shops, restaurants, pubs and craft shops to visit.

14 DAGLEISH BANK

★★★

Location: 34°11,60'S; 22°57,40'E, south of Buffels Bay, 16km (10 miles) from Knysna Heads. See map p. 99.
Access: By boat launched through The Heads or from Buffels Bay.
Average depth: 30m (100ft)
Maximum depth: Beyond sport diving depths.
A large pinnacle rising to 27m (90ft) below the surface, this fabulous reef is covered in colourful hard and soft coral and hosts a multitude of big gamefish, rockcod and

The dainty seahorse is often seen off Thesen's Jetty.

other species. Dagleish Bank is a dive site that is not regularly visited due to the rather long distance from the launch sites, and is therefore still relatively unspoilt.

15 EAST CAPE REEF

★★★

Location: 34°05,33'S; 23°05,76'E, off East Cape point, approximately 150-200m (500-650ft) offshore to the east of the Heads. See map p. 99.
Access: By boat launched through The Heads.
Conditions: Diving is possible even when there are fairly big swells running.
Average depth: 20m (65ft)
Maximum depth: 24m (80ft)
There are overhangs, drop-offs and caverns covered in soft corals. Game fish, rays and sharks, such as ragged-tooths are often seen. This reef is so extensive that its can only be fully explored by doing a number of dives.

16 BRUCE SE BANK ('BRUCE'S BANK')

★★★★

Location: 34°05,68'S; 23°04,78'E. See map p. 99.
Access: Approximately 15 minutes by boat from the Heads, and 2.5km (1.5 miles) to the east. An echo-sounder is needed to locate the pinnacles, or dive with a local skipper who knows the shore markers.
Average depth: 25m (80ft)
Maximum depth: 31m (100ft)

The distinctive white 'cauliflower' soft coral is typical of this area and dominates the invertebrate life on the pinnacles. The effect of the delicate soft corals is simply marvellous. Interspersed with the whites are pastel pinks and oranges and bright mauves. Some hard corals can be seen here too. Basket stars cling delicately to the sea-fans and numerous soft corals and brightly coloured sponges in red, yellow or orange are evident.

Not many colourful fish are found on the reef, but Chaetodons (butterflyfish) are sometimes seen as they dart gracefully around, pecking at the growths with pointed mouths. Sizeable pyjama sharks are often seen sleeping in crevices.

The reef is extensive and rises to two peaks well below the surface. Because of the depth and the delicate nature of the invertebrate life, this site is definitely not for the inexperienced diver. It is, however, one of the most beautiful reefs along the entire coastline.

KNYSNA HEADS

The entrance to the Knysna Lagoon is guarded by the spectacularly rugged Heads which can be explored on foot on the eastern shore. Boat trips can also be arranged to the very beautiful and deserted western side. Divers, anglers and others who exit the lagoon through The Heads have the best view of these scenic cliffs with their many caves and magnificent sea-arches.

appearance of the reef below this level is reminiscent of Bruce se Bank (no. 16), with masses of colourful growths such as basket stars and spectacular starburst soft corals.

17 THE PINNACLE

★★★

Location: 34°05,25'S; 23°03,36'E, about 750m (½ mile) out, slightly to the west of The Heads behind a blinder. See map p. 99.
Access: By boat launched through The Heads.
Average depth: 12m (40ft)
Maximum depth: 20m (65ft)

The pinnacle, after which this site is named, is about the size of a double garage. It is covered with dense redbait pods down to about 12m (40ft) below the surface. The

---

Soft corals and anemones on a redbait pod.

18 THE FAIRHOLME (1888)

★★

Location: 34°05,00'S; 23°02,60'E. See map p. 99.
Access: By boat launched through The Heads, approximately 10 minutes or 1.5km (1 mile) from The Heads in a westerly direction.
Conditions: The sea has to be very calm with little swell to allow diving here as the wreck lies in shallow water, close to the rugged and steep coastline.
Average depth: 10m (33ft)
Maximum depth: 13m (43ft)

The *Fairholme* caught fire off Cape Agulhas on the way from Calcutta to New York with a cargo of jute. This British iron ship of almost 2000 tons drifted a considerable distance until it came to rest in its present position on 1 April 1888. Its ribbed remains can still be seen clearly on the site about 100m (330ft) offshore. It lies in a north-south direction, with the bows pointing roughly to the south. Small fish swim around the rusty remains and many sea-fans, basket stars and tubeworms grow on it.

19 THE PAQUITA (1903)

★★★★★

Location: 34°04,60'S; 23°03,60'E, in The Heads, on the eastern side. See map p. 99.
Access: Safe entry and exit points can be reached from the parking area at The Heads. The wreck lies below the white beacon on the eastern shore of The Heads.
Conditions: It is essential that you dive The Heads only 30 minutes before the turn of the tide, preferably at high tide when water is generally cleaner. Best dived during

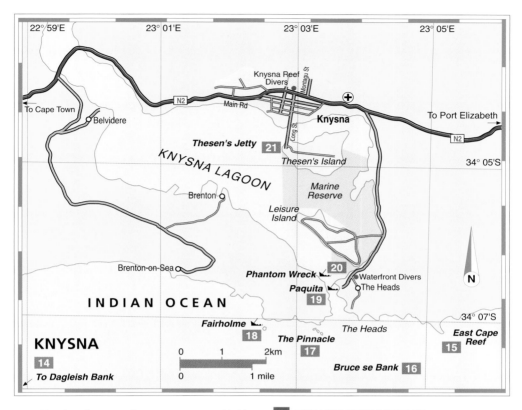

neap tide when the current is not as strong. At mid-tide the current travels through The Heads at nine knots (nearly 5m or 16ft per second)!
Average depth: Bow in 4m (13ft)
Maximum depth: 20m (65ft)
The *Paquita* was a majestic German iron barque of some 484 tons that sank at The Heads on 19 October 1903 under sand ballast, after offloading creosote in the lagoon. As there are no waves breaking on it, it is remarkably well preserved for a wreck of this vintage, and the shape and size can still be determined. There are two big anchors and many interesting nooks and crannies in the rusted remains. The bow lies in a sandy patch and is sparsely covered with marine growth, while the stern section on the reef has more colour.

The rocky reefs are covered with colourful invertebrate life such as starburst coral in pinks and white, with many red, yellow and orange sponges. Basket stars are plentiful and sea-whips and fans are common.Small reef fish hover around but seem quite wary of divers. The marine growth on the sides of the drop-off is luxuriant and vivid. There is, unfortunately, also a great deal of fishing line and other junk on the wreck, which is periodically cleared by local divers. Strictly speaking fishing is not allowed on the site, but this rule is often disregarded by many. There are showers and toilets in the National Parks Board small wooden ablution block next to the entry and exit point.

20 THE PHANTOM WRECK
★★

Location: 34°04,18'S; 23°03,45'E. See map this page.
Access: A shore dive can be done from the entry points of the *Paquita* (no. 19), but the dive is more easily done off a boat launched from the slipway in front of the Angling and Dive Club.
Conditions: It is best dived on a slack tide (approximately 30 minutes before the turn of tide), with high tide usually the best time.

BLENNIES

These comical fish of the family *Blenniidae* are tiny, usually less than 7cm (3in), and hide in small holes in the shallow part of the reef. They have big eyes, expressive mouths and antler-like growths where mammals would have eyebrows, and are well worth looking out for. They are also sometimes spotted 'jumping' over rocks in tidal pools.

The reefs off most of South Africa's coastline are not rich in the colourful tropical fish that many divers have come to expect on every dive. They are, however, very rich in colourful invertebrate life and do support a large variety of monochromatic fish in shades of red or silver. These are, however, often more prized for their flesh rather than for their appearance.

The seabreams (family *Sparidae*) are probably the most significant. Of the 100 species known worldwide, 41 occur off the South African coast, and of those, 25 are endemic. The rocky reefs from the Eastern Cape to the South-western Cape are home to many of these.

The red stumpnose *(Chrysoblephus gibbiceps)* is easy to identify and is aptly named; it is mostly red, with a few blackish spots, and has a short, concave snout. It feeds on molluscs and crustaceans, the shells of which it can easily crush with its powerful jaws. Not alike in appearance is the white stumpnose *(Rhabdosargus globiceps)*, which is very common in the colder Cape waters, particularly in False Bay. It has a convex snout and is characterized by five or more faint, sooty, vertical bars. It frequents the edges of rocky reefs where it feeds on shellfish, mostly at night.

Also common in the Cape, is the very distinctive Roman, or red Roman, *(Chrysoblephus laticeps)* which is closely related to the red stumpnose. It is an orangey-red fish with two very distinctive white 'saddles', and is usually found hiding under overhangs in the rocky reefs. Like the red stumpnose, this fish undergoes a sex change. All young fish are female and become male when they are older and bigger. As there are always more smaller fish than bigger ones, this strategy is very successful in maintaining an optimum sex ratio. The Roman is greatly prized as an angling and spearfishing species and, with its richly flavoured flesh, is a very popular table fish.

Big-eyes are one of the main attractions of coral reefs and also extend their range along the Cape coast.

Hottentots, common in the Cape, surround this diver.

Bronze bream are a popular spearfishing target.

Some of the more insignificant little fish which are often ignored by scuba divers are also seabreams. The hottentot *(Pachymetopon blochii)* is a common and very small silvery fish often found on Cape reefs. They can be something of a nuisance to underwater photographers, as they seem to be attracted to the whine of a charging flash and will swarm so closely around your camera that it is impossible to photograph them or anything else.

The strepie *(Sarpa salpa)* is characterized by delicate horizontal yellow stripes against its silver body and swims in big schools along the whole Cape coast, often totally encircling a diver.

The zebra *(Diplodus cervinus)* has, not surprisingly, evenly spaced vertical black stripes on its silver-coloured body. It is also called the *wildeperd,* which means wild horse in Afrikaans.

Also very common on rocky reefs is the *Diplodus sargus,* otherwise known as a blacktail or dassie. Its common names refer to the black spot at the base of its tail and its habit of hanging around just above the rocks rather reminiscent of the locally common land mammal, the hyrax, colloquially known as a dassie, or a rock rabbit.

Most of the popular game fish are also not particularly brightly coloured, such as the magnificent Cape yellowtail *(Seriola lalandi)*, the garick or *leervis (Lichia amia)*, shad *(Pomatomaus saltatrix)*, and the kobs (family *Sciaenidae*), which include the daga salmon *(Argyrosomus hololepidotus)* and the geelbek *(Attractoscion aequidens)*.

Endemic to South African waters are two species of the beautiful galjoen, which is much prized as an angling fish and is also a popular spearfishing target. The galjoen *(Coracinus capensis)* is a small, robust deep-bodied fish whose colour ranges from almost black to silvery-bronze. It is common in the surf zone and in rocky gulleys or kelp beds. It feeds on algae, small molluscs and ascidians (redbait).

Closely related is the banded galjoen *(Coracinus multifasciatus)* which is found along the Eastern Cape and KwaZulu-Natal coast and also around Madagascar. It frequents turbulent gullies between rocky reefs and subsists mostly on ascidians, Bryozoa and molluscs.

The galjoen is South Africa's national fish and is, unfortunately, endangered because of the delicious flavour and delicate texture of its distinctively marbled flesh.

Average depth: 5m (16ft)
Maximum depth: 6m (20ft)

The rather mysterious name of *The Phantom Wreck* was given to this wreck by local divers who had great difficulty in finding it after passing it on a speedy drift dive in the lagoon. It is reputed to be the wreck of the *Piesang*, but its origins and date of demise are unknown. The wood and iron remains are found in shallow water scattered over an area of approximately 100m² (1000 sq feet) and are covered with marine growth and algae. Ask a local diver to take you there or you may miss it.

21 THESEN'S JETTY

★★★★

Location: 34°02,90'S; 23°02,76'E. See map p. 99.
Access: Turn into Long Street off the main road on the Port Elizabeth side of town and carry on over the railway line to the restaurant and pub on the jetty.
Conditions: Best dived approximately three hours after the turn of tide to high, when clear sea water pushes in. Visibility is usually about 2-8m (6-25ft).
Average depth: 6m (20ft)
Maximum depth: 10m (33ft)

This is a junkyard of tyres, glass, bottles and items of dubious origin, but do not despair! Under the jetty, in the grasslike algae, dwell the extremely dainty, hard-to-find

and fascinating little seahorses with their tiny tails curled round the waving stems. These delicate creatures are protected and may not be removed or disturbed in any way; those who do so will incur a heavy fine.

Small and brightly coloured tropical fish flit inbetween the jetty supports when warm water enters the lagoon. Some seahares and many fragile nudibranchs are also found though they may need a gentle dust-off to see them properly!

This is a different dive experience that can be very interesting if you disregard the garbage. A regular clean-up of the area, coupled with anti-pollution measures, could turn this into a popular and safe dive, and no-one need die of dehydration afterwards!

SHARK ATTACK

Diving in the proximity of Seal Island off Mossel Bay without a cage (as is the case with all seal-inhabited islands off the coast) is not recommended and should be regarded as hazardous.

The world's first recorded fatal shark attack on a kitted-out scuba diver took place here in June 1990 when the 21-year-old Monique Price was attacked by a great white while on the surface and died as a result of her injuries.

The delicate structure of the feeding fans of this tubeworm, or fan worm, is clear in this macro photograph.

Mossel Bay

Mossel Bay's claim to historical fame is as the site where Bartholomeu Dias and his crew first set foot on the shores of South Africa in 1488, after unknowingly rounding the Cape. This fairly large seaside town which marks the beginning of the Garden Route has experienced a tremendous growth lately due to the presence of the Mossgas offshore gas project, and many people have since moved into the area.

The bay is one of the most sheltered on the South African coastline as it is protected from the open ocean by Cape St Blaize. The water inside the bay is free from dangerous currents and generally very calm and clear, ensuring good diving conditions for most of the year.

The best time to dive is late summer and early autumn, from December to early May, when the westerly winds clean and flatten the sea. South-easterly winds blow from September to early December and churn up the sea. After a strong south-easter has blown, upwelling takes place, and this can reduce sea temperatures to as low as 9°C (48°F). Average visibility is around 4-6m (13-20ft), increasing to 10m (33ft), maybe more, in summer.

The invertebrate and vertebrate life encountered in these waters is typical of the Eastern Cape and is both varied and colourful. In the summer months, small tropical fish sometimes appear when the water temperature is high enough, and even Moorish idols, which are usually found only in much warmer seas, have been spotted here. Pansy shells (similar to sand dollars) are often found by divers, but only dead ones should be removed. Between September and November (spring), whales come into the bay to calve in its protected waters. There is a colony of seals on Seal Island, and they form an important part of the diet of great white sharks which are, consequently, found in abundance in the area around the island. Large schools of small hammerhead sharks are also often seen in the area.

Intrepid companions or divers seeking a dive with a difference can take a short drive to the Gouritz River Bridge where they can do a bungee jump or a bridge swing – an experience guaranteed to get the adrenalin of even the most experienced scuba diver pumping. This is usually only in operation over weekends and sometimes during the week in season. Less adventurous divers and non-diving companions can choose between visiting the museum, exploring the beaches, going fishing or spending a few hours shopping.

Soft coral with its feeding polyps extended.

situated approximately 400m (¼ mile) offshore, slightly towards the Hartenbos side of the mouth. The echo-sounder will indicate a depth of 15m (50ft), getting shallower. Continue in this direction until a reading of 8m (25ft) is reached and anchor. It is a boat trip of about 8km (5 miles) from Mossel Bay.

Conditions: Not to be dived in low visibility as there are many sharks in the area and they feed in murky water.
Average depth: 8m (25ft)
Maximum depth: 15m (50ft)

It is a large reef dominated by a pinnacle approximately 15m (50ft) in diameter at the top. The main attraction of this reef is the enthralling caves which have stunning rock formations and a number of pinnacles. The reef is well populated with a variety of big fish and covered in invertebrate life typical of the area.

23 STINGRAY REEF

★★★★

Location: 34°10,00'S; 22°07,40'E, about 100m (330ft) offshore from Die Bakke Caravan Park. See map p. 104.
Access: Drive along George Road, turn into the caravan park at the 'Die Bakke' sign, and turn left towards the thatched chalets. Enter from the beach in front of the furthest chalet, which is no. 1. The reef lies at an angle of approximately 30° to the shore.

22 KLEIN BRAK (LITTLE BRAK)

★★★

Location: 34°05,70'S; 22°09,00'E, off the mouth of the Klein Brak River. See map p. 104.
Access: By boat launched from the slipways. The reef is

A sea spider walks carefully over encrusting sponge.

green eyes, just sticking up out of the sand, or maybe you will be treated to the sight of three or four stingrays gliding past, especially in December or January.

This reef is sometimes called *Ou Skoen*, meaning old shoe, but the reason for this name has long since walked off in search of a partner. Stingray Reef is one of the more easily accessible dives in the area, and is therefore very popular with locals.

24 MITCH'S REEF

★★★★

Location: 34°10,20'S; 22°07,90'E. See map this page.
Access: Drive along George Road, turn into the caravan park at the Die Bakke sign and park in front of the ablution block closest to the main (thatched) entrance to the park. Ask at the caravan park office for a key to the gate, walk down the steps and enter across the rocks. Swim for about 150m (500ft) at a 90° angle from shore until you cross the reef, and follow it in the direction of the harbour. By boat it involves a short trip from the harbour.
Conditions: Generally calm and fairly clear.
Average depth: 6m (20ft)
Maximum depth: 9m (30ft)
This large reef is well covered with big sea-fans, soft corals, feather stars and large sponges. The outer edge is

Conditions: Can be surge due to the shallow depth.
Average depth: 6m (20ft)
Maximum depth: 8m (25ft)
It is a smallish reef interspersed with sand gullies with marine life that resembles Mitch's Reef (no. 24) but without the big fish. If you look carefully, you will see pairs of

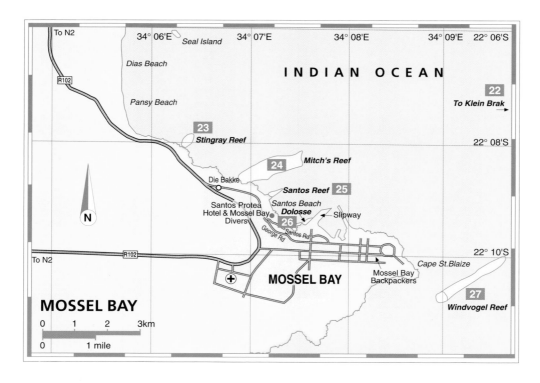

visited by a good variety of big fish including Romans and rockcod. Most of the fish are very tame and can be observed at close quarters. Many pyjama sharks can be found lying about in the crevices between the redbait and octopuses often hide in rocky holes where the reef meets the sand. Spearfishing is discouraged on this reef because of the tameness of the resident fish.

25 SANTOS REEF

★★★★

Location: 34°10,30'S; 22°08,00'E, on the northern border of Santos Beach. See map p. 104.
Access: Drive along Santos Road down to the main beach and park next to the Pavilion Restaurant. Kit up in the carpark and walk down the path to the beach. The reef can be seen breaking about 150m (500ft) to the left.
Conditions: Protected and generally calm.
Average depth: 6m (20ft)
Maximum depth: 8m (25ft)
Santos Reef starts at the shore and tapers to a point out to sea. An outstanding feature is the delicate hue presented by the great number of lovely tubewormsthat live on the reef. There are large redbait pods, sponges and sea stars everywhere as well as many small fish. Dead pansy shells are often found on the sand.

Don't search too hard but the remains of the wreck of the *Galera* (1892) can be found on the deepest part of the reef, furthest from the shore. It sank in a southeast gale on 25 August 1892 with a cargo of copra on a voyage from the Friendly Isles to Marseilles. Unfortunately most of the wreck is covered in sand and therefore not much of it can be seen.

26 DOLOSSE

★★★★

Location: 34°10,70'S; 22°08,48'E, on the western side of Mossel Bay harbour wall. See map p. 104.
Access: Take Church Road into the harbour and drive to the yacht club. The dive site is accessible from the *dolosse* (concrete breakwater blocks) on the western side of the harbour wall, which can be easily reached by a short walk. It is easier to enter and exit at the slipway but it involves a slightly longer swim.
Conditions: Calm and protected.
Average depth: 4m (13ft)
Maximum depth: 6m (20ft)
This is an artificial reef formed by the *dolosse* stacked against the outside (western side) of the harbour wall. The crevices formed by these concrete structures are filled with marine life, and when the water is warm, small

When disturbed, sun-burst coral withdraws its polyps.

tropical fish flit in and out of the holes. Take a torch along to enable you to explore the exciting labyrinth of nooks and crannies properly.

27 WINDVOGEL REEF (SHALLOW AND DEEP BLINDERS)

★★★★

Location: 34°11,38'S; 22°10,00'E, 800m (½ mile) to the east of Cape St Blaize. See map p. 104.
Access: A 25 km (1.25 miles) boat ride from the slipway in the harbour.
Conditions: This reef falls outside the protection of the bay and can only be dived when the sea is calm with no white water breaking on the blinders. There are strong currents in the area.
Average depth: 12m (40ft) on Shallow Blinders
Maximum depth: 27m (90ft) on Deep Blinders
The reef is topped by two pinnacles that rise to within 3m (10ft) of the surface and the rock formations form impressive drop-offs, with some caves and swim-throughs. Deep Blinders is fairly flat with huge boulders, covered with large sea-fans, a tremendous variety of pink and mauve soft coral, and large red and orange sponges. This makes for a colourful and thrilling dive, not to be hurried.

How to Get There

By road: The N2 runs through the entire Garden Route and all the towns are well-signposted.

By bus and train: Intercape buses run between East London and Cape Town, passing through all the Garden Route towns, as does the railway.

By air: The only major airport in this area is at George, about halfway between Mossel Bay and Knysna.

Where to Stay

TSITSIKAMMA

The **Tsitsikamma Coastal National Park,** has chalets for hire and camp sites. Bookings are made through the National Parks Board at Storms River Mouth (see p. 107). Situated in indigenous forest 10km (6 miles) from the Storms River mouth is the **Tsitsikamma Forest Inn,** which has an à la carte restaurant and a bar, P O Box Storms River 6308, tel. (042) 541 1711. The **Tsitsikamma Lodge,** P O Box 10, Storms River 6308, is also situated in a forest setting. It is 20km (12.5 miles) from the Tsitsikamma National Park and 8km (5 miles) east of the Storms River bridge. It has a buffet restaurant and a ladies' bar. Tel. (04230) 802 to book. **Hiker's Home,** 411 St Patricks Road, Nature's Valley, tel. (04457) 6805, is a superb B&B establishment with comfortable dorm accommodation for hikers and budget travellers.

PLETTENBERG BAY

The **Beacon Isle,** tel. (04457) 3 1120, is a comfortable RCI-affiliated (Resort Condominium International) time-share resort and hotel. It is right on the beach, has a convenient launching spot just in front of the lawn, and a dive operation on the premises. The **Formosa Country Inn Hotel,** P O Box 121, Plettenberg Bay 6600, tel. (04457) 3 2060, is 2km (1.25 miles) from Plettenberg beach. It offers in the hotel gardens, à la carte and carvery restaurant, a cocktail bar and lounge. Also in a garden setting is the **Stromboli Inn,** P O Box 116, Plettenberg Bay 6600, tel. (04457) 7760, which has 17 cottages, a table d'hôte restaurant and a ladies' bar. Divers on a tighter budget will find friendly backpackers' accommodation at

The Albergo, 8 Church St, tel. (04457) 3 4434. Another budget option is the **Robberg Holiday Resort,** P O Box 81, Plettenberg Bay, tel. (04457) 3 2571, which offers caravan sites, camping and self-catering accommodation. Some 8km (5 miles) from Plettenberg Bay is **Dune Park Holiday Resort,** P O Box 658, Plettenberg Bay 6600, tel. (04457) 9606, which offers self-catering accommodation in luxury and budget units, as well as caravan and tent sites.

KNYSNA

Close to the *Paquita* wreck and the launch site near The Heads is **Ai Due Camini,** tel. (0445) 82 5339, a comfortable, upmarket bed and breakfast establishment, and **Under Milkwood,** tel. (0445) 2 2385, which offers self-catering chalets. **Belvedere House,** tel. (0445) 87 1055, a well-run upmarket guest house, is situated in a magnificent historic homestead right on the Lagoon. The three-star **Knysna Protea Hotel,** tel. (0445) 2 2127, is an historic hotel which offers comfortable standard hotel service. Those on a tight budget will find private, train-compartment style accommodation at **The Caboose,** corner of Grey and Trotter Streets, tel. (0445) 82 5850, at only slightly more than backpacker rates. **Knysna Backpacker's Hostel,** 42 Queen Street, tel. (0445) 2 2554, is a typical backpackers' hostel with the youthful atmosphere. A rather fun option is to rent a houseboat from **Lightley's Holiday Cruisers,** tel. (0445) 87 1026, and cruise the lagoon. **Lake Brenton Holiday Resort,** P O Box 235, Knysna 6570, tel. (0445) 81 0060, offers self-catering accommodation and camping. It is situated on the western shore of Knysna Lagoon. **Monk's Holiday Accommodation** on Knysna Lagoon, P O Box 379, Knysna 6570, tel. (0445) 22 609, offers self-catering accommodation, and both caravan and tent sites with full ablutions.

MOSSEL BAY

The **Santos Protea Hotel,** tel. (0444) 7103, is a three-star hotel overlooking Santos Beach. **Huis de Marquette,** 1 Marsh Street, tel. (0444) 91 3182, is a pleasant guest house. **Mossel Bay Backpackers** is in an adjoining, but totally separate, building. **Die**

Bakke/Santos Holiday Resort, P O Box 25, Mossel Bay 6500, tel. (0444) 91 2915, is on the seashore and has self-catering accommodation, caravan and tent sites with full ablutions. Chalets, caravan and tent sites on the seafront are also available at **Diaz Beach Chalets and Caravan Park,** Private Bag X29, Mossel Bay 6500, tel. (0444) 95 1740.

Where to Eat

TSITSIKAMMA

The National Park has a restaurant, a take-away kiosk and a shop selling basic supplies. It is a good idea, however, to bring your own provisions.

PLETTENBERG BAY

There is no shortage of restaurants in this tourist town but, as a treat, try **Stromboli's Inn,** tel. (04457) 7760, 8km (6 miles) on the Knysna side of town. They do a superb table d' hôte dinner and an à la carte lunch in a lovely country setting. **The Islander** on the National Road towards Knysna, serves a seafood buffet. It is advisable to book, tel. (04457) 7776. For a seafood barbecue, **The Look Out Restaurant** at Look Out Beach, is the place to go, tel. (04457) 31 379. The **Pelican Restaurant** in the centre of town (Woodmill Lane Shopping Centre) serves Cajun food and seafood steaks, tel. (0445) 82 5711. Pizza fans should visit **Cranzgots Pizzeria** in the Main Street, tel. (04457) 31 660.

KNYSNA

Knysna has a host of restaurants and coffee shops and **Cranzgots,** right on The Heads, has it all. There is a coffee shop by day and a pizzeria and pub by night. The food is good and the view wonderful. Tel. (0445) 23629. **Featherbeds Tavern,** tel. (0445) 81 0590, in the Featherbeds Nature Reserve on the western Head, does great seafood in a beautiful setting. For a pub lunch on the lagoon, try **Crabs Creek Waterfront Tavern,** Belvedere, tel. (0445) 87 1043, or **Jetty Tapas,** Thesen's Jetty, Long Street, tel. (0445) 21 927.

MOSSEL BAY

The **Post Tree Restaurant,** Powrie St, tel. (0444) 4402, is reputed to be the best in town and serves seafood and pasta. **Tidals Waterfront Seafood Tavern & Pub** at the Point, tel. (0444) 91 3777, is great for seafood and pub lunches. If you are staying at Die Bakke Caravan Park, try **De Bakke Restaurant** in George Street, tel. (0444) 91 2321.

DIVE FACILITIES

TSITSIKAMMA
There are no dive facilities available in the Tsitsikamma area , so bring all your own gear along. The nearest air station is in Plettenberg Bay.

PLETTENBERG BAY
Plett Dive Centre, Shop 6, Milkwood Centre, Hopwood Street, tel. (04457) 3 0303, fax (04457) 3 2046. **Indian Ocean Divers**, Beacon Island Hotel, tel. (04457) 3 1158, run charters and certification courses, rent and sell equipment, and offer air fills.

KNYSNA
Waterfront Divers, Bottom Car Park, Knysna Heads, tel. (0445) 2 2938, are very conveniently situated for shore dives on the *Paquita* and are also close to the launch site near the Heads. They run charters, offer PADI courses, and air fills, as well as the renting and selling of equipment.

MOSSEL BAY
Mossel Bay Divers, Santos Protea Hotel, Santos Road, tel. (0444) 91 1441, offer the full range ofl facilities.

REGIONAL HIGHLIGHTS

TSITSIKAMMA
There are beautiful walks around Storms River Mouth and the five-day **Otter Trail**, one of the most popular hiking routes in South Africa, starts here. If you are quiet and look very carefully, you may be rewarded by the sight of a Knysna lourie flitting through the forest canopy. Just off the N2, the **Big Tree**, a giant yellowwood estimated to be over 800 years old, is worth a short detour.

PLETTENBERG BAY
The **Robberg Nature Reserve** offers lovely walks, superb scenery and good bird-watching. **Equitrailing**, P O Box 1373, Plettenberg Bay 6600, tel. (04457) 9718, offers full- and half-day horse trails as well as champagne breakfasts and catered moonlight rides.

KNYSNA
This lovely town has become an artists' retreat so there are many interesting craft shops in town and shopaholics will thrive here. The **Angling Museum**, in the old gaol, is unique. **Millwood House Museum** is a reconstructed miner's house and has exhibits dating back to the Knysna Gold Rush. If the museum interests you, contact Sam's Tours, tel. (0445) 2 3522, and enquire about their escorted gold-panning expeditions. There are magnificent walks in the Knysna Forest and you may be fortunate enough to see one of the few elusive elephants that live there. For mountain- bike trails in the forest, contact **Cycles in the Forest**, tel. (0445) 3 3272. A trip to **Featherbed Nature Reserve**, on the western Head, is highly recommended. Access to the reserve is by boat. Steam train enthusiasts will be enthralled by a ride between Knysna and George in the **Outeniqua Choo-tjoe**, tel. (0441) 738202 to book, and even those who do not find trains particularly fascinating will be impressed by the scenery. Food fans can sample fresh oysters at the **Knysna Oyster Co.**, tel. (0445) 2 2168.

MOSSEL BAY
The **Bartholomeu Dias Museum** houses exhibits relating to the history of Mossel Bay, particularly its links with Portuguese seafarers, and is home to the original Post Office Tree. Boat trips to **Seal Island** to view the seals are fun for divers and non-divers alike. These and other cruises start from the harbour.

CLOSE BY
Noetzie, east of Knysna, is a tiny haven on the coast, famous for its unusual castles (these are private residences). The Noetzie ('black') River runs into a lagoon here. **Wilderness**, west of Knysna, is a small seaside resort and is the start of the Cape's Lake District. This area is popular among water-sport enthusiasts, as well as anglers, bird-watchers and hikers. The interesting inland town of **Oudtshoorn**, home of the country's ostrich industry, is not too distant. A day trip here could include a visit to the spectacular **Cango Caves** or to an **ostrich farm** where you can view these fascinating birds and, if adventurous, even ride one.

There are numerous beautiful drives in the vicinity. The most spectacular is probably the **Swartberg Pass**, between Oudtshoorn and Prince Albert, with its hairpin bends and stark scenery. The **Seweweekspoort** (Seven Weeks Pass) through the same mountains, also offers superb scenery, lovely waterfalls, and pools in which to cool off. The **Bloukrans Pass** in the Tsitsikamma area, unlike most passes, goes down and then up, passing through some absolutely spectacular forest scenery.

INFORMATION AND BOOKING

National Parks Board, P O Box 787, Pretoria 0001, tel. (012) 44 1191 or (012) 343 1991.
National Parks Board, P O Box 787, Pretoria 0001, tel. (012) 343 1991, or P O Box 7400, Roggebaai 8012, tel. (021) 22 2810.
National Parks Board, Storms River Mouth, tel. (042) 541 1607.
National Hiking Way Board, Private Bag X447, Pretoria 0001, tel. (012) 310 3839 (for booking hiking trails).
Plettenberg Bay Publicity Association, Victoria Cottage, 12 Kloor Street, Plettenberg Bay, tel. (04457) 3 4065.
Garden Route Tourism Office, 124 York Street, George, tel. (0441) 73 6314 or (0441) 73 6355.
Knysna Publicity Association, 40 Main Road, Knysna, tel. (0445) 2 1610.
Mossel Bay Publicity Association, tel. (0444) 22 2221.

EMERGENCY NUMBERS

There are **hospitals** in Mossel Bay, Knysna and George:
Mossel Bay tel. (0444) 91 2011
Knysna tel. (0445) 23 123
George tel. (0441) 74 5122
The nearest **recompression facilities** are in Cape Town (see p. 155.)
Divevac Emergency Number: (011) 403 7080 or toll-free 0800 02 01 11
General Emergency Number: 10 111
Ambulance: 10 177

THE SOUTHERN CAPE COAST

This is a popular holiday area and many small settlements are scattered along the coast. Hermanus, with its busy fishing harbour, is the biggest and is a bustling residential and holiday village with a well-developed tourist infrastructure. Other popular dive areas along this shoreline are Waenhuiskrans (Arniston), Struisbaai, Gansbaai, Cape Hangklip and Cape Agulhas. Cape Agulhas is the southernmost point of Africa and it is the official meeting place of the Indian and Atlantic oceans. The water temperature is sometimes dominated by the warmer waters of the Agulhas Current, when temperatures rise to the region of 14–20°C (57–68°F) but, under the influence of the Benguela current, the sea becomes icy cold, and can drop to as low as 8°C (46°F).

Fishing is of major economic importance, and perlemoen and crayfish are plentiful in this region. The area is also popular with divers who enjoy spearfishing and scuba diving. The kelp beds are sparse (compared with the South-Western Cape), with Cape Agulhas being the eastern limit where South African kelp is found.

Most rain falls in winter, when cold fronts pass through from the west, and the prevailing winds are the westerlies in winter and south-easterlies during summer. As a rule, the winter westerlies clean and flatten the sea and offer diving with visibility ranging from 5–8m (16–25ft) while in summer the average visibility is only a few metres. Summer can offer excellent diving, though, when upwelling brings cold, clear water in under the murk and creates a sharp thermocline. When these conditions prevail, visibility can exceed 20m (65ft) and temperature is often as low as 10°C (50°F).

Even very experienced divers, if they have only dived in tropical locations, will find the conditions in this area a bit harsh. The cold water orientation courses offered in Hermanus are highly recommended, not only in order to dive safely, but also to learn something about the very different and colourful reef life encountered in these cold, nutrient-rich waters.

*The beautiful klipvis (**above**), seen here nestled in an orange sea-fan, is one of the most common of the Cape fishes. Hermanus (**left**), a popular resort on the Southern Cape coast, offers interesting dives with spectacular reef life.*

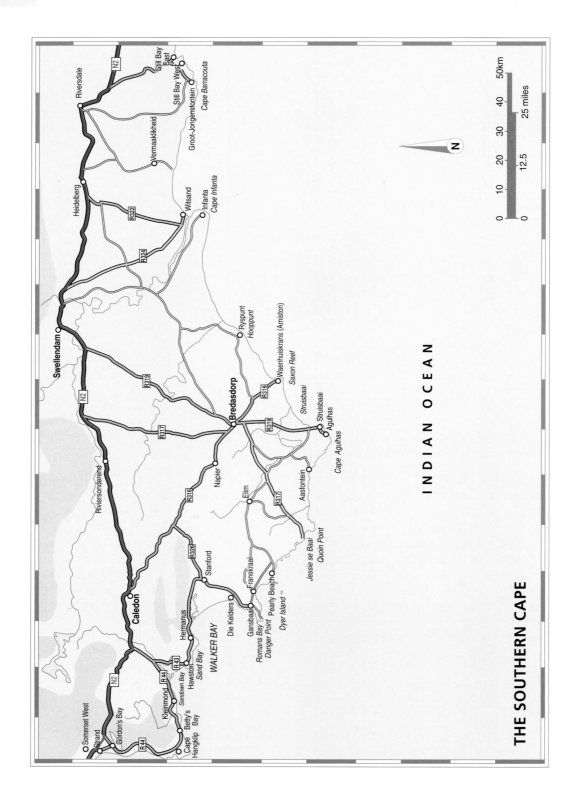

THE SOUTHERN CAPE

Waenhuiskrans
(Arniston)

This holiday and fishing village is a popular spearfishing destination, and many Cape Town divers go there for weekends. Scuba diving is not particularly popular, but the wreck of the *Arniston*, from which the town derives its unofficial name, is worth a dive. Visibility is usually about 2-6m (6-20ft), but can exceed 15m (50ft).

1 THE ARNISTON (1815)

★★

Location: 31°41,40'S; 20°14,60'E, 900m (just over half a mile) offshore, straight out to sea from the slipway. See map p. 114.
Access: By boat launched from Waenhuiskrans. Avoid the concrete block in line with the slipway, about 100m (330ft) out, as it is not easily seen, especially at high tide.
Conditions: There can be heavy surge and low visibility because of its shallow depth.
Average depth: 5m (16ft)
Maximum depth: 6m (20ft)
The *Arniston, a* British transport ship, ran aground near Waenhuiskrans on 30 May 1815, during a storm on a voyage from Ceylon (Sri Lanka) to England. On board were Viscount and Lady Molesworth and many wounded soldiers. Only six of the 378 people on board survived after getting to shore by clinging to pieces of wreckage. They were rescued after 24 days of living on shellfish and food washed ashore from the wreck. A monument in honour of the deceased was erected sometime later on the camp site can still be seen.

The ship was 270ft (82m) long and 40ft (12m) wide and was built in 1794. Archaeological work was done on this wreck by divers as a project for the University of Cape Town in 1982, when test excavations were made and some interesting artefacts were recovered and catalogued. Iron beams, anchors and iron cannon remain on the site, standing as a reminder of the tragedy. Absolutely nothing may be removed.

Struisbaai

This attractive fishing village, rather like Waenhuiskrans, is popular with visiting fishing and spearfishing enthusiasts as well as being an important commercial fishing centre. There are no diving facilities in the village, although it is possible to charter a local fishing boat. Blessed with picturesque thatched, whitewashed fisherfolk's cottages and often having clear blue skies, it offers superb photographic opportunities and is, like Waenhuiskrans, a very popular spot with painters.

Prepared for the cold water in full wetsuit and gloves, these divers admire the abundant Southern Cape reef life.

2 FIVE-MILE BANK

★★★★★★

Location: 34°50,20′S; 20°07,60′E, approximately 8km (5 miles) off the coast. See map p. 114.

Access: By boat launched from Struisbaai.

Conditions: The reef lies in the clear water of the Agulhas Current so visibility is usually between 10 and 20m (33-65ft). The current can be very strong, as much as 5 knots (2.6m or 8½ft per second).

Average depth: 25m (80ft)

Maximum depth: 30m (100ft)

This deep and extensive reef teems with marine life, particularly game fish, and is a favourite spearfishing spot, obviously not for beginners. It can also be a very interesting scuba dive.

3 THE MV ORIENTAL PIONEER

★★★★★

Location: 34°48,50′S; 20°05,30′E, about 1km (²/₈ mile) offshore, in line with the water tower at Struisbaai. See map p. 114.

Access: By boat launched from Struisbaai.

Conditions: Can be surge and is usually not too clear.

Average depth: 10m (33ft)

Maximum depth: 12m (40ft)

This Chinese bulk carrier sprung a leak and sank on 22 July 1974 with 50000 tons of iron ore on board. It has broken up completely and lies not far below the surface, creating hazardous shipping conditions. The wreck teems with fish and is a favourite spearfishing venue. It is an interesting scuba dive and the sounds the wreck makes when the current buffets its steel plates is eerie.

Gansbaai

This is a small, sleepy fishing village with a busy harbour used mainly by trawlers. Divers often visit the area for scuba diving on the wreck of the *Birkenhead* (1852) and perlemoen or crayfish diving. Charters to Dyer Island for shark cage diving among the large community of great white sharks are run on an *ad hoc* basis.

4 THE HMS BIRKENHEAD

★★★★

Location: 34°38,60′S; 19°70,30′E, the wreck lies on the western side of Birkenhead Rock, approximately 2.5km (1.5 miles) off Danger Point. See map p. 114.

Access: By boat from Gansbaai harbour or Kleinbaai. Kit up in the boat and descend as soon as you hit the water as it is not a good idea to hang around on the surface in these waters. When exiting, it is recommended that buddy pairs surface one at a time and enter the boat quickly so that no-one has to hang around waiting.

Conditions: A strong undercurrent and big swells, as well as the depth, make this a dive only for the experienced diver, preferably accompanied by someone with knowledge of the site. The top of the pinnacle is 3m (10ft) below the surface and breaks in all but the calmest conditions. Great white sharks are common, so take careful note of the advice above and don't hang around on the surface.

Maximum depth: 28m (92ft).

This wreck is of great historical significance because of the many brave lives that were lost and the still undiscovered fortune that it was thought to have carried. It was one of the first British iron paddle frigates to be built and was later converted to a troopship.

The wreck consists of three main sections: the bows, the engine room and the stern. This site is rarely dived by sport divers on account of the distance from Cape Town, the depth (allowing only limited bottom time), and the rough sea conditions. For divers willing to make the effort, though, a thrilling and fascinating experience is guaranteed. Absolutely nothing may be removed.

5 DYER ISLAND

★★★★★

Location: Approximately 8km (5 miles) south of Franskraal to the west of Gansbaai. See map p. 114.

Access: Can be reached by boat from Gansbaai harbour. Diving without a cage is not recommended at all. Contact the Two Oceans Aquarium in Cape Town for information on charter dives.

Conditions: The channel between the rocks and the island is usually reasonably calm but there can be a swell running. Visibility is usually only a few metres and the water temperature ranges from 10-15°C (50-60°F).

Average depth: 2m (6ft)

THE STRUIS STINGRAYS

There are a number of big stingrays which always seem to swim around the slipway between the moored boats. You could get a good look at them in the shallows by going out on snorkel, but remember that they can inflict a very nasty wound if they are frightened or annoyed.

'They shall not say in England,
that we fought
With shameful strength,
unhonour'd life to seek;
Into mean safety, mean deserters, brought
By trampling down the weak.'

The troopship HMS *Birkenhead*, carrying reinforcements for the Eighth Frontier War, struck a submerged rock off Danger Point in the early hours of the morning of 26 February 1852. As well as the soldiers, there were many women and children on board.

The captain tried to steam off the rock but this caused further damage as it increased the size of the hole in the hull, allowing the cold water to rush in and swamp the boilers. The ship was then helpless and started breaking up and sinking rapidly.

'And ever like base cowards,
who leave their ranks
In danger's hour, before the rush of steel,
Drifted away disorderly the planks
From underneath her keel.'

The men were ordered to line up on deck and bravely watched as the women and children were rowed to safety. Although the same discipline was displayed ten years earlier during the wrecking of the *Abercrombie Robinson*, the wrecking of the *Birkenhead* is credited with initiating the maritime tradition of 'women and children first'.

'Then amidst oath, and prayer,
and rush, and wreck,
Faint screams, faint questions
waiting no reply,
Our Colonel gave the word,
and on the deck
Form'd us in line to die.'

After the women and children were safely in the boats, the horses were cut loose and the men told to jump and try to save themselves. As the ship disappeared beneath the waves many of the soldiers, few of whom could swim, drowned. Others were taken by great white sharks which were attracted to the area by the commotion. To this day, Gansbaai locals call great whites 'Tommy sharks' in memory of all the Englishmen they ate. Of the total number of 638 passengers on board, 445 died but all the women and children were rescued.

Over the years many unsuccessful salvage attempts have been made, and large amounts of money spent to try and recover the legendary treasure of £300 000 in gold specie which was rumoured to have been carried to pay the army.

The most recent, best-equipped and most scientific attempt was launched in 1985 by a group of Johannesburg and Cape Town divers. They designed a small dive saturation unit but were unable to use it because of the strong bottom currents and big swells. Despite the fact that the salvage operation lasted for more than two years, the main body of treasure was not found. The few coins that were recovered most likely came from the private cache of one of the officers.

Although the salvors were disappointed at the elusiveness of the treasure, they did succeed in salvaging many historically valuable artefacts. They also accurately recorded their finds and the exact position of the wreck for posterity.

There was much controversy at the time of the salvage as the wreck is a war grave and so should not, according to some, be disturbed in any way.

' – What follows, why recall! –
The brave who died,
Died without flinching
in the bloody surf:
They sleep as well
beneath that purple tide,
As others under turf.'

The exerpts are from the poem *Loss of the Birkenhead* by Sir Francis Hastings Doyle. Further information on the wreck and the subsequent salvage attempts, can be found in *Salvage of the Birkenhead*, Allan Kayle (Southern Book Publishers, Johannesburg, 1990).

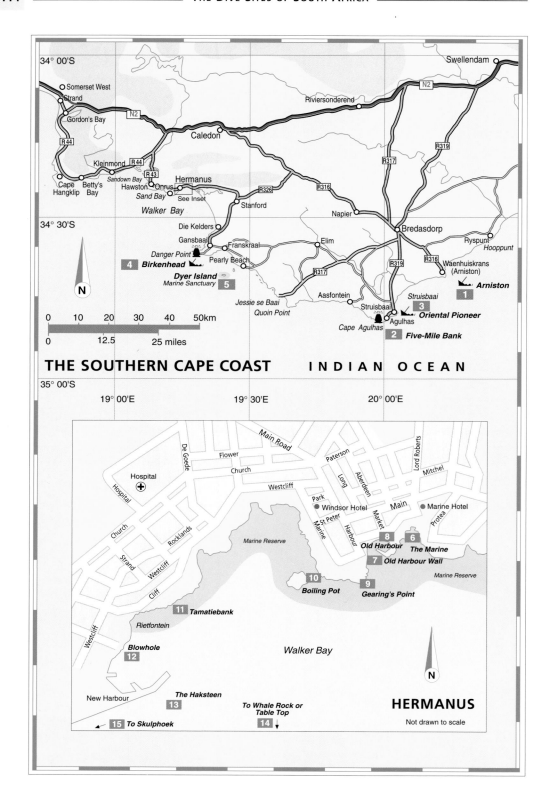

34° 00'S

Swellendam

Somerset West
Strand
Gordon's Bay
N2
R44
Caledon
Riviersonderend
N2
R319
R317
Kleinmond R44
R44
Sandown Bay
Betty's Hawston Onrus
Cape Bay Sand Bay
Hangklip See Inset
Hermanus
Stanford
R326
R316
Napier
Bredasdorp
Ryspunt
Hooppunt

Walker Bay

34° 30'S

Die Kelders
Gansbaai
Franskraal
Elim
Waenhuiskrans
(Arniston)
4 **Birkenhead**
Danger Point Pearly Beach
R319
R316
Dyer Island
Marine Sanctuary **5**
Aasfontein
Struisbaai
3
R317
⚓ **Arniston**
1

Jessie se Baai
Quoin Point
Struisbaai
Oriental Pioneer
Cape Agulhas Agulhas
2 **Five-Mile Bank**

N

0 10 20 30 40 50km

0 12.5 25 miles

THE SOUTHERN CAPE COAST   I N D I A N   O C E A N

35° 00'S

19° 00'E 19° 30'E 20° 00'E

Main Road
De Goede
Flower
Paterson
Lord Roberts
Hospital
Church
Mitchel
Westcliff
Long
Aberdeen
Park
Church
Windsor Hotel
Main
Marine Hotel
Hospital
St Peter
Market
Protea
Marine
Harbour
Rocklands
Church
Marine Reserve
8
6
Strand
Old Harbour **The Marine**
Westcliff
7 **Old Harbour Wall**
Cliff
Marine Reserve
10
9
Boiling Pot **Gearing's Point**
11 **Tamatiebank**
Rietfontein
Westcliff
Blowhole
12
Walker Bay
New Harbour
The Haksteen
13
To Whale Rock or
Table Top
15 **To Skulphoek**
14 ↓

HERMANUS

N

Not drawn to scale

This area is home to many sizeable great white sharks who subsist very well on the large seal colony on the island. Shark cage charters are run to this site from time to time, although there does not seem to be sufficient demand to support a full-time operation.

They usually work something like this: a fishing boat (often quite smelly) is chartered from Gansbaai. Once at the island, chum, consisting of blood, old bits of fish and whale oil (if available and obtained from dead stranded whales) is put into the water. After a while, the cage is lowered. The top of the cage is buoyed to remain on the surface and a large piece of bait (seal or whale meat if available; otherwise any meat) is attached to the cage. Divers are then lowered into the rocking cage, *sans* fins and wait around (usually two at a time) until a shark comes to investigate the bait. Sightings are not guaranteed and it is advisable to plan to go out two or three days in a row if you want to be sure of a sighting.

This dive is uncomfortable, involves long periods of hanging around on a rocking fishing boat and is not for the squeamish or nervous. It is, however, highly recommended for competent, confident divers.

Hermanus

This is the largest town in the area, with commercial fishing and tourism being the main industries. The water temperature ranges from about 10-22°C (50-72°F) and the visibility is usually about 4-6m (13-20ft). In summer, though, the south-easter often brings in cold, clear water and visibility can be 20m (65ft) or more under the thermocline (of course it's also cold). The reef life is spectacularly colourful and prolific. Although the conditions are most consistent in winter (June to September), most

MARINE RESERVE

The area around Dyer Island is a perlemoen (abalone) sanctuary. No perlemoen may be removed from an area of two nautical miles from the high-tide mark on Dyer Island (it's not a good place to snorkel, anyhow).

diving is done in summer when they are less predictable but can be much better. This is because migratory southern right whales spend the winter in Walker Bay to calve and mate and it is almost impossible for divers to avoid them. This may sound like a wonderful opportunity to dive with them, but failing to keep a distance of 300m (1000ft) from these animals in South African waters carries a large fine, a jail sentence of six months and, for foreign visitors, deportation. Winter is still a great time to visit, though, as the whales are easily visible from the shore and offer hours of entertainment as they cavort in the water, often breaching or doing a classic dive showing their distinctive tail flukes.

Snorkel diving for crayfish and perlemoen is rewarding and is a very popular pastime with the locals. Check with local divers before collecting any seafood as the limits of the reserves may change from time to time.

Non-diving companions can spend hours exploring this fascinating town with its many craft shops, characterful restaurants and interesting museum at the Old Harbour. The magnificent walk along the top of the cliff overlooking the bay can be stretched out to fill a whole day if you pack a picnic basket.

These spectacular orange 'wall' sponges are restricted to the Southern and South-Western Cape.

This pipefish peers out from its hiding place in the soft coral. Note the extended feeding polyps.

6 THE MARINE

★★

Location: 500m (⅓ mile) offshore in front of the Marine Hotel. See map p. 114.
Access: Usually done as a boat dive, but can be accessed from the tide pool in front of the hotel by very fit divers.
Average depth: 18m (60ft)
Maximum depth: 24m (80ft)
This is a flattish reef with soft corals and colourful invertebrate life. The tide pool at the entry point offers fun snorkelling for beginners, but be careful of sea urchins.

7 OLD HARBOUR WALL

★★★★

Location: Just on the outside of the harbour wall. See map p. 114.
Access: Easy shore entry through the harbour (it is no longer used so there is no boat traffic).
Conditions: Should not be dived in a big swell.
Average depth: 6m (20ft)
Maximum depth: 10m (33ft)
This lovely dive features beautiful hard and soft coral and occasional kelp and redbait.

8 OLD HARBOUR

★★★★★

Location: About 200m (660ft) directly out from the Old Harbour Wall reef (no. 7). See map p. 114.
Conditions: Can be surge in a big swell.
Average depth: 10m (33ft)
Maximum depth: 17m (55ft)
This is a very attractive reef with steep drop-offs, cold-water corals, sea-fans, gorgon's heads or basket stars (*Astrocladus* sp.) and many species of nudibranchs.

The old harbour itself is an interesting little museum with exhibits relating to the colourful fishing history of Hermanus and also has an interesting section on whaling and the many uses of whale products.

MARINE RESERVE

The area stretching from Kraal Rock in Walker Bay to Rietfontein, Hermanus, for a distance of 500m (⅓ mile) out to sea from the high-water mark, is a reserve. No marine animals may be collected or disturbed with the exception that rock and surf angling from the shore are both allowed.

MARINE RESERVES

Nothing may be removed from the following reserve areas but rock and surf angling are allowed:
• The area within Harder Bay, near Onrus;
• The Mudge Point Marine Conservation Area, from the eastern limit of the Frans Senekal Game Reserve to the western limit of the Hawston Harbour for 100m (330ft) seawards (commercial exploitation, subject to permits and quotas, is allowed here);
• The Betty's Bay Reserve, from beacon B1 at Stoney Point to beacon B4 to the east of Jock se Baai also known as Jock's Bay, for two nautical miles seaward of the high-water mark.

9 GEARING'S POINT

★★★★

Location: Just to the right as you swim out of the Old Harbour entrance. See map p. 114.
Access: Swim out through the Old Harbour mouth.
Conditions: The reef starts near the surface and there can be surge in the shallows.
Average depth: 10m (33ft)
Maximum depth: 18m (60ft)
This reef has prolific invertebrate growth but is marred by the incredible amount of junk, such as plastic bags, which all seem to collect here after blowing into the sea. Local divers and the resident sea-life would benefit if visiting divers would pick up and take out any garbage, especially plastic, they come across.

10 BOILING POT

★★★★★

Location: Off Gearing Point, about 100m (330ft) off-shore, in line with the Windsor Hotel. The reef runs from Gearing Point to Boiling Pot. See map p. 114.
Access: By boat from the New Harbour.
Conditions: Can be surgy in a big sea when bubbling is visible around the pinnacle, hence the name.
Average depth: 10m (33ft)
Maximum depth: 23m (75ft)
This is quite a narrow ledge with two distinctly different pinnacles. The southernmost one is covered entirely in redbait (*Pyura stolonifera*) which shelters many small octopuses and crayfish. The northernmost pinnacle, in contrast, hosts beautiful colonies of hard and soft corals, sponges and many waving sea-fans.

11 TAMATIEBANK

★★★★★★

Location: Near Rietfontein Bay. See map p. 114.
Access: Either by boat from the new harbour or as a shore dive. The entry involves a giant stride off a ledge of about 1m (3ft) and the exit has to be timed so that you can catch a swell back onto the ledge.
Average depth: 10m (33ft)
Maximum depth: 17m (55ft)
This is a broken reef with plenty of gulleys. The vertical sides are encrusted in soft corals and crinoids while the top is covered in redbait.

12 BLOWHOLE

★★★★

Location: Just to the left (facing the sea) of the new harbour entrance. See map p. 114.
Access: The walk down to the water's edge is very steep and slippery and great care should be taken. The entry itself is an easy giant stride and the exit is a simple plop onto a ledge where you can remove your fins and just step onto the shore.
Conditions: Usually reasonably sheltered as it is near the harbour entrance. Boat traffic must be considered a major hazard and a SMB (surface marker buoy) with flag alpha is essential.
Average depth: 3m (10ft)
Maximum depth: 9m (30ft)

A false plum anemone on the marine algae, codium.

There is a lot of kelp and redbait in the vicinity. The planking and keel of the *South West Pelican*, which sank here after breaking its moorings in 1993, can be seen. Ensure that you do not enter the harbour limits. Look out for the fence with the harbour light on it and ensure that you do not swim past that point.

13 THE HAKSTEEN

★★★

Location: A few hundred metres in front of the New Hermanus harbour. See map p. 114.
Access: A very short boat trip from the harbour, not recommended as a shore dive.
Conditions: Usually calm because of the depth. It is also deep enough and far enough from shore to benefit from thermoclines.
Average depth: 18m (60ft)
Maximum depth: 26m (85ft)
The Haksteen is a spectacular pinnacle which comes to within 4m (13ft) of the surface and has steep drop-offs with a number of diveable surfaces between 16 and 22m (52 and 72ft). The top of the reef is covered in redbait

---

PERLEMOEN IN KELP

First catch your perlemoen and leave it in fresh water until it dies. This prevents it getting tough. Find a nice fresh *Ecklonia* stipe (the hollow variety). Remove the perlemoen from the shell, wash it well, trim off the frilly bits and cut it into bite-sized cubes. Cut the fronds off your kelp stipe while keeping the float intact. Cut the stalk about 50cm (20in) from the top. Then cut two rings of about 5cm (2in) each. Cut these rings into little strips. Wash the stipe well and pack the perlemoen into it, adding garlic and fresh herbs if you like. Plug the open end of the stipe with the little strips of kelp and place directly on the coals for about 20 minutes and serve with a crisp Cape wine. Delicious!

---

and kelp while the sides host a multitude of beautiful hard and soft cold-water corals, brightly coloured sea-fans, and many crayfish. The reef is dissected by a large sand gulley which separates the shallow pinnacle from the deeper pinnacle and the drop-off.

At first glance, the klipvis seems quite drab but closer inspection reveals beautiful markings.

14 WHALE ROCK OR TABLE TOP

★★★★

Location: A few 100 metres in front of the New Harbour, further south than the Haksteen (no. 13). See map p. 114.
Access: A very short boat trip from the harbour, not recommended as a shore dive.
Conditions: Usually calm because of the depth and it is deep enough and far enough from shore to benefit from thermoclines.
Average depth: 12 or 22m (40 or 72ft)
Maximum depth: 40m (130ft)
This spot is known as Whale Rock to the fishing folk, but divers call it Table Top, because of the underwater topography. It consists of a large flat section at about 12m (40ft) with a moderate drop-off to 22m (72ft), and then a spectacular sheer drop-off to 40m (130ft).

As seems to be common in this area, the very top of the reef is covered in redbait while the sides and lower surfaces are graced by beautiful hard and soft corals, seafans, bryozoans and sponges.

A typical feature of this reef is the pink hard coral with yellow, brown and orange crinoids growing out of it. This is a popular crayfishing and fishing spot so divers should be very careful of fishing boats. Always use a SMB (surface marker buoy), and carry a knife as there may be bits of rope, crayfish nets or even fishing line entangled in the reef. These are, however, not usually a major hazard as they become encrusted very quickly.

15 SKULPHOEK (SHELL CORNER)

★★★

Location: 4-6km (2.5-4 miles) from the New Harbour, travelling south along the coast. See map p. 114.
Access: By boat from the harbour.
Conditions: Usually not much surge as it is quite deep.
Average depth: 20m (65ft)
Maximum depth: 36m (120ft)
This is an extensive reef, stretching for 2km (just over a mile) with big, flat, bare areas and a profusion of pink cold-water coral on the steep drop-offs.

Cape Hangklip

The sheer sides of Hangklip (literally, 'hanging rock') tower over the coastline and can be seen from as far away as Cape Point to the west and Danger Point to the east. This is a popular spot for gathering perlemoen and, to a lesser extent, crayfish, but the spearfishing is not wonderful. Other than the wreck of the *Meridian*, there is nothing worth diving on scuba as the sea is very shallow

Cape long-legged spider crab on a sinuous sea-fan.

for a few hundred metres from shore, and visibility, usually less than 5m (16ft). It is a convenient spot to dive out a few perlemoen, and also lovely for a beach braai (barbeque) of freshly caught seafood.

Non-diving companions can amuse themselves on the nearby sand-dunes, possibly even doing a beginner's paragliding course.

16 THE MERIDIAN (1828)

★★

Location: 34°22,50'S; 18°52,90'E, on the east side of Silver Sands Bay at Cape Hangklip.
Access: The site is to the west of a prominent slanting rock that protrudes above the surface in front of the steps leading down to the water.
Conditions: Usually flat as the bay is very sheltered.
Average depth: 4m (13ft)
Maximum depth: 5m (16ft)
No lives were lost when this British brig of 144 tons was wrecked on 19 May 1828 on a voyage from Singapore and Batavia to Table Bay. Two anchors and six cast-iron cannon mark the site of the wreck but it is not easy to find. This dive is only recommended for serious wreck enthusiasts as the sea life is not very exciting.

BASKET STARS OR GORGON'S HEADS

These beautiful echinoderms are modified brittle stars with repeatedly branching arms. They are usually found on sea-fans, the most common being *Lophogorgia flammea*. At night, or in a strong current with much suspended planktonic matter, they feed by spreading their arms into the current, creating a beautiful 'basket'.

How to Get There

WAENHUISKRANS
There is no public transport. The best way to get there is to turn off the N2 towards Bredasdorp and continue along that road to Waenhuiskrans (Arniston).

STRUISBAAI
There is no public transport. The best way to get there is to turn off the N2 at Caledon, go through Bredasdorp and then continue to Struisbaai.

GANSBAAI
From Cape Town, the route through Hermanus is the easiest. If you are travelling from the east, you may wish to drive through Caledon and enjoy some lovely rural scenery.

HERMANUS
The turn-off from the N2 is well marked. An alternative route (if you are coming from Cape Town) is to take the Gordon's Bay turn-off from the N2 and to follow the scenic coastal road past Cape Hangklip, through Betty's Bay follow the signs to Hermanus from there.

CAPE HANGKLIP
Take the Gordon's Bay turn-off from the N2 and then continue on this road for a few kilometres past Rooiels until you reach Cape Hangklip.

Where to Stay

WAENHUISKRANS
The three-star **Arniston Hotel**, tel. (02847) 5 9000, is a very comfortable, stylish establishment right on the beach. **Waenhuiskrans Camping Site** offers self-catering bungalows, and caravans and camping near the beach, tel. (02841) 5 9620, P O Box 51, Bredasdorp 7280. Self-catering accommodation with a picturesque sea view can be found at the thatched, white-washed **Arniston Seaside Cottages**, P O Box 403, Bredasdorp, 7280, tel. (02847) 59 772 for more information.

STRUISBAAI
The **Struisbaai Hotel**, tel. (02846) 5 6625, is a comfortable and unpretentious one-star establishment with en suite accommodation in rondavels. The

Struisbaai Caravan Park, tel. (02846) 5 6538, offers grassed and partially shaded camping and self-catering chalets right near the beach. **Mooi Nooientjie**, on the corner of Van der Stel and Vasco da Gama streets, is a pretty thatched, white-washed self-contained cottage with three double bedrooms. Tel. (0221) 63 1160 for bookings and further ßinformation.

GANSBAAI
De Kelders Hotel, tel. (02834) 4 0421, is situated on a cliff with lovely sea views. It offers reasonably priced accommodation, as does the **Sea View Hotel** at 12 Mark Street, tel. (02834) 4 0211, which has an à la carte restaurant, a bar and a slipway available. There is a **Municipal Campsite**, tel. (02834) 4 0872 and, 6km (4 miles) away, the **Uilenkraalsmond Camp Campsite**, tel. (02834) 8 0200, offers camping, caravan sites and chalets. It also has a small shop on site.

HERMANUS
The **Windsor Hotel**, tel. (0283) 2 3727, is conveniently placed for the launch site at the harbour and for a shore dive or snorkel on *Tamatiebank*. The three-star **Marine Hotel** overlooking Walker Bay, tel. (0283) 2 1112, is slightly more upmarket. **Hermanus Youth Hostel**, 15 Church St, tel. (0283) 2 1722, will provide adequate accommodation for those on a tighter budget. For self-catering accommodation, try **Zoete Inval**, 23 Main Road, Hermanus 7200, tel. (0283) 21 242, which is a double-storey guest house with eight bedrooms and a loft – it sleeps 17. **Paradise Park Holiday Camp** in Onrus, just 7km (4½ miles) from Hermanus, offers self-catering accommodation, caravan stands and camping. Dive clubs wishing to stay here will be offered a 10% discount. Tel. (0283) 76 3402 to book.

CAPE HANGKLIP
The Hangklip Lodge, tel. (02823) 28 277, is the only place where you will find accommodation here. The lodge offers bungalows, chalets, camping and caravan stands, plus they have two bars and a restaurant. Alternatively, try nearby Gordon's Bay for accommodation (see Regional Directory on p. 154).

Where to Eat

WAENHUISKRANS
If you feel like treating yourself, the **Arniston Hotel** will provide you with an excellent meal in an elegant restaurant with a lovely view of the sea. Tel. (02847) 5 9000 to book. If staying in self-catering accommodation, the few stores in the town will adequately provide you with basic supplies.

STRUISBAAI
The **Struisbaai Hotel** in Minnetokka Street serves modest but enjoyable fare in an à la carte restaurant, tel. (02846) 5 6625. Also in Minnetokka Street is the **Beachcomber Restaurant** which offers seafood and steaks, tel. (02846) 5 6000. Otherwise you'll have to rely on takeaways from the cafe or bring and prepare your own provisions.

GANSBAAI
Ciro's, 15 Franken Street, tel. (02834) 4 1106, is situated in a tastefully renovated fisherfolk's cottage and serves pasta, seafood and grills.

HERMANUS
This touristy but attractive town is characterized by fashionable restaurants and coffee shops so you will have no lack of variety. For something quite different, though, try **Bientang's Cave**, which really is a cave. It is characterful and serves an excellent seafood buffet. Tel. (0283) 2 3454 / 2 3651 to book. **The Burgundy** in Market Square, tel. (0283) 2 2800, is renowned for its Cape-style cuisine and was voted one of the top 10 restaurants in the Western Cape. Do a little wine-tasting while you're there at the Hamilton Russell shop next door to the Burgundy. **Something Special**, 16 Mitchell Street, behind Wolfswinkel, tel. (0283) 22 0033, serves delicious teas and light lunches. **Rossi's Italian Restaurant**, 10 High Street, offer excellent steaks, as well as delicious pasta and pizzas in a friendly atmosphere. Tel. (0283) 22 848 to book. Seafood lovers should visit **Greens Wine Bar and Bistro**, 310 10th Street, Voelklip, tel. (0283) 77 1048. **Charlie's Tapas**, a restaurant and pub in Harbour Way, serves tasty, light meals in a vibrant atmosphere. Tel. (0283) 70 0110.

DIVE FACILITIES

HERMANUS
Scuba Africa, tel. (0283) 6 2362, run regular charters and dive courses.
BS Divers, tel. (0283) 2 1376, also do charters and offer advanced mixed gas deep diving courses from time to time.

REGIONAL HIGHLIGHTS

WAENHUISKRANS
The name of this town means wagon house cliff, and refers to a spectacular sea cave which is literally big enough to house an oxwagon. A lovely walk along the coast leads to this cave. The entrance is only accessible at low tide, but as it does not flood completely, the worst that can happen if you get caught out is to have to wait a while or swim a few hundred metres.

The **Shipwreck Museum** in near Bredasdorp, tel. (02841) 4 1240, is a must for keen wreck divers. It is open from 09:00 to 16:45, Mondays to Fridays, 09:00 to 13:00 and 14:00 to 15:45 on Saturdays, and on Sundays from 11:00 to 12:30.

STRUISBAAI
Struisbaai is a small fishing town and is popular mainly with fishermen and swimmers. This is the closest town to **Cape Agulhas**, the most southerly point of Africa, a rather wild, bleak and dramatic spot. The **Cape Agulhas lighthouse** was completed in 1848 and is the second oldest in South Africa. It has been declared a national monument and lays claim to the only lighthouse museum in the country.

GANSBAAI
Gansbaai harbour shelters a fleet of fishing boats which operate in Walker Bay and on Agulhas Bank. The nearby **De Kelders**, which means the cellars, is another interesting sea cave but, unlike Waenhuiskrans, this one is connected to a large limestone network. To see the cave, collect a key from De Kelders Hotel. Don't be tempted to wander off into the tunnels as you may get lost. In spring and winter, southern right whales come very close inshore and can be observed from the rocks. It is illegal to approach within 300m (1000ft) of them.

HERMANUS
The southern right whales can be seen to even better advantage off Hermanus. In late winter/early spring the town goes 'whale crazy' and they hold a **whale festival**. During this time the whales come into the Walker Bay to calve and are heralded by the town's official 'whale crier'. The **Old Harbour Museum** is situated in the disused fishing harbour and has both indoor and outdoor exhibits. When the whales are in attendance, an underwater microphone transmits their songs to shore and you can listen to them 'conversing' with each other.

There is a good **golf course** here and **fishing trips** can be arranged from the harbour. The surrounding mountains, which encompass the spectacular **Fernkloof Nature Reserve**, offer lovely walks, especially in spring when the *fynbos* (heath-type vegetation) is at its best. The **Hermanus Lagoon** is a very popular dinghy sailing venue and is the home of the Hermanus Yacht Club. In summer, tourists flock here from all over the country and it can get very crowded. Walkers will delight in the 12kms (7.5 miles) of scenic **cliff path** which leads along the coastline.

CAPE HANGKLIP
Cape Hangklip was once a refuge for runaway slaves and cattle-rustlers. It is a lonely place with nothing much to see besides the new automatic **lighthouse**. The nearby **Harold Porter Botanical Gardens** at Betty's Bay is very picturesque, especially in spring. The Gardens is renowned for its wealth of wild flowers, especially ericas and the red disa. Also near Betty's Bay are high, white sand dunes which offer great sandskiing (you need a piece of masonite with a rope handle) and are also the accepted 'beginners slopes' for the Cape Town paragliding schools.

CLOSE BY
Inland **Caledon** is famous for its hot springs. The springs produce 900 000 litres of water daily. The beautiful botanical garden in Caledon is world renowned for its flowers and a flower show is held here every September.

The **Salmonsdam Nature Reserve** near Caledon is a sanctuary for animals and plant sanctuary of the area. The deep valley offers walks or a dramatic mountain drive for cars. Camping facilities are available. These are controlled by the Caledon Divisional Council.

Between Waenhuiskrans and Port Beaufort, 50km (30 miles) east of Bredasdorp, lies the 36 000 ha **De Hoop Nature Reserve**. There are cottages and campsites here, hiking, game-viewing, bird-watching, mountain-bike trails and good whale-viewing in season. Contact De Hoop Nature Reserve, Private Bag X16, Bredasdorp, 7280, to book, preferably a few months in advance.

Bontebok National Park, about 7km (4½ miles) from Swellendam, is a small sanctuary for the bontebok and various other antelope. Over 500 plant species are found here, some of which are rare. The Park has walking trails, fishing and swimming in the Breede River, views of the Langeberg Mountains, a shop and petrol. Accommodation is available at a restcamp. Information and bookings can be made through the National Parks Board (see below for details).

INFORMATION AND BOOKING

National Parks Board, P O Box 787, Pretoria 0001, tel. (012) 343 1991, or P O Box 7400, Roggebaai, 8012, tel. (021) 22 2810.
National Hiking Way Board, Private Bag X447, Pretoria 0001, tel. (012) 310 3839 (for booking hiking trails).
Captour, Adderley Street, Cape Town 8001, tel. (021) 418 5214
Hermanus Publicity Association, Information Centre, Main Road, Hermanus, tel. (0283) 2 2629.

EMERGENCY NUMBERS

The nearest **recompression facility** is in Cape Town, tel. (021) 787 3821.
There are **hospitals** in Bredasdorp, Caledon, Hermanus and Cape Town:
Bredasdorp tel. (02841) 4 1167
Caledon tel. (0281) 2 1070
Hermanus tel. (0283) 2 1166
Cape Town (Groote Schuur) tel. (021) 404 9111
DivEvac Emergency Number: (011) 403 7080 or toll-free 0800 02 01 11
General Emergency Number: 10 111
Ambulance: 10 177

THE SOUTH-WESTERN CAPE

Although the convergence of the Atlantic and Indian oceans is not at Cape Point but at Cape Agulhas, the South-Western Cape is affected by both the Agulhas and the Benguela currents. The difference in sea temperature is responsible for a marvellous diversity of underwater life and scenery, so the Cape diver literally enjoys the best of two worlds.

The region falls well within the winter rainfall area with north-westerly and westerly winds prevailing from early May to late August. These winds clean and flatten the eastern side of the Peninsula (the western side of False Bay) but blow onshore along the western side of the Peninsula, creating big swells and breakers with dirty water for most of the season. The best time to dive this side of the coast is in summer, from September to April, when strong south-easters blow offshore, causing upwelling of clear, cold water. This is also the best time to dive the eastern side of False Bay while the western side is rough and murky.

The climate is moderate with wet winters and dry summers. The temperature never falls below freezing with minimum winter temperatures around 5°C (41°F), rising to about 30°C (86°F) and higher in summer. The coast is a graveyard of shipwrecks, most of which met their fate during spectacular winter storms, and many interesting wreck dives can be done from a boat or from the shore.

Kelp beds are dense and plentiful and take some getting used to. The reef life is spectacular. Hard and soft cold-water corals in shades of pale pink, bright purple, red and orange are set off by a background of sulphur-yellow or bright orange sponges, and bright blue, violet or pale green anemones. It is not uncommon for observent divers to be rewarded by the sighting of between five and 15 different species of nudibranchs on one dive.

Non-divers will not be bored in Cape Town and will have difficulty deciding whether to visit Table Mountain, Cape Point or the Kirstenbosch National Botanical Gardens. Indoor pursuits, such as visiting museums, art galleries or antique shops, will also tempt them. Coffee shops, restaurants and theatres provide more than adequate *après*-dive entertainment.

Common in the Southern and South-Western Cape is the ornate topshell (**above**) *which is often found on sea-fans.*
This classic shot of Table Mountain (**left**) *was taken from Bloubergstrand, a popular area for surf and crayfish.*

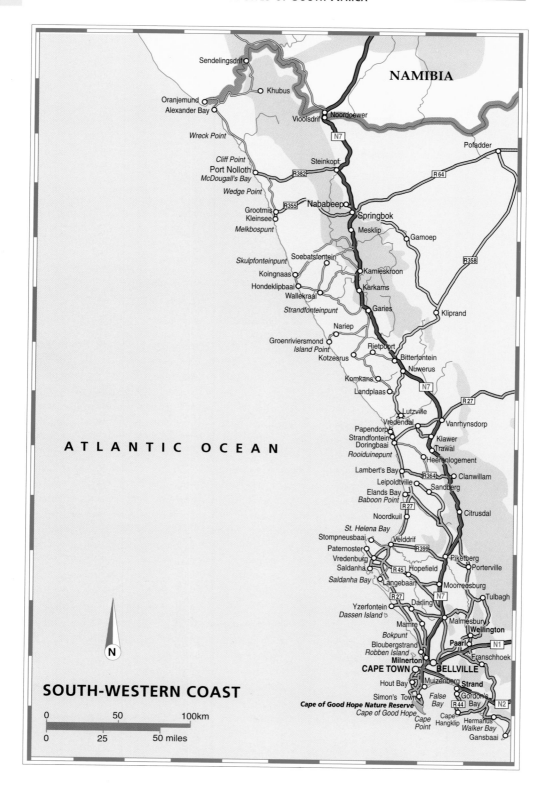

Sendelingsdrif

NAMIBIA

Khubus

Oranjemund
Alexander Bay

Viooolsdrif Noordoewer

N7

Wreck Point

Pofadder

Cliff Point
Port Nolloth
McDougall's Bay

Steinkopf

R382

R 64

Wedge Point

R355 Nababeep
Grootmis
Kleinsee

Springbok

Mesklip

Melkbospunt

Gamoep

Skulpfonteinpunt Soebatsfontein

R358

Koingnaas

Kamieskroon

Hondeklipbaai
Wallekraal

Karkams

Strandfonteinpunt

Garies

Kliprand

Nariep

Groenriviersmond
Island Point
Kotzesrus

Rietpoort

Bitterfontein
Nuwerus

Komkans

N7

Landplaas

R 27

Lutzville

ATLANTIC OCEAN

Vredendal
Papendorp
Strandfontein
Doringbaai
Rooiduinepunt

Vanrhynsdorp

Klawer
Trawal

Heerenlogement

Lambert's Bay

R364

Clanwilliam

Leipoldtville
Elands Bay
Baboon Point

Sandberg

R 27

Noordkuil

Citrusdal

St. Helena Bay
Stompneusbaai
Paternoster
Vredenburg
Saldanha

Velddrif

R399

Piketberg

Porterville

R 45 Hopefield

Saldanha Bay

Langebaan

Moorreesburg

R 27

N7

Tulbagh

Yzerfontein
Dassen Island

Darling

Mamre

Malmesbury

Bokpunt

Wellington

Blouberg strand
Robben Island

Paarl

N1

Milnerton

Franschhoek

CAPE TOWN

BELLVILLE

Hout Bay

Muizenberg Strand

Simon's Town

False
Bay

Gordon's
R 44 Bay

N2

Cape of Good Hope Nature Reserve
Cape of Good Hope

Cape
Point

Cape
Hangklip

Hermanus
Walker Bay

Gansbaai

N

SOUTH-WESTERN COAST

0	50	100km

0	25	50 miles

The Eastern Shore of False Bay

This stretch of scenic and rugged coastline on the slopes of the Hottentots Holland mountains between Gordon's Bay and Rooiels, is best dived in summer after a south-easterly wind. The water temperature usually ranges from 14–16°C (57–62°F) but can drop to 11 or 12°C (52 or 54°F). Visibility averages from 6–8m (20–25ft) but can be up to 20m (65ft) on a good day.

The entire area offers excellent scuba diving and snorkelling, best done from a boat as the mountainside is very steep, making shore entries tricky and quite strenuous. There are some good crayfishing and perlemoen spots, the best of which are found at the eastern extreme of the region near Cape Hangklip.

Non-diving companions can do a day tour of the nearby Stellenbosch Winelands, visiting beautiful Cape Dutch wine farms, or lunch in one of Stellenbosch's fine restaurants. There are also a number of good coffee shops, craft shops and antique shops in Stellenbosch, as well as in Somerset West, and the nearby seaside resorts of the Strand and Gordon's Bay.

Orange sea-fans, one of the more common sights in this area, can grow to over a metre in length.

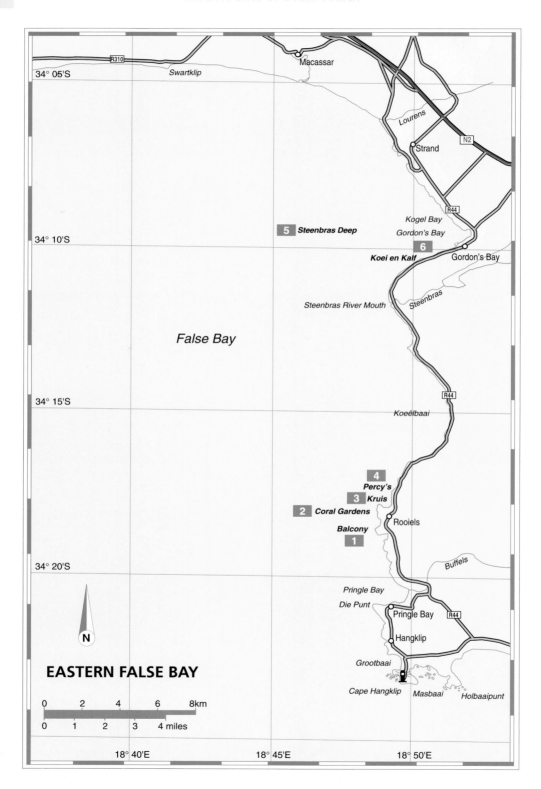

34° 05'S

R310

Swartklip

Macassar

Lourens

Strand

N2

Kogel Bay

R44

5 **Steenbras Deep**

Gordon's Bay

34° 10'S

6

Koei en Kalf

Gordon's Bay

Steenbras River Mouth

Steenbras

False Bay

34° 15'S

R44

Koeëlbaai

4

Percy's

3 **Kruis**

2 **Coral Gardens**

Rooiels

Balcony

1

34° 20'S

Buffels

Pringle Bay

Die Punt

Pringle Bay

R44

Hangklip

Grootbaai

N

EASTERN FALSE BAY

Cape Hangklip

Masbaai

Holbaaipunt

0   2   4   6   8km

0   1   2   3   4 miles

18° 40'E

18° 45'E

18° 50'E

1 BALCONY

★★★★

Location: 34°18,28'S; 18°48,96'E. See map p. 126.
Access: Turn down the road at the Rooiels Café, then turn left into a dirt road, turn right at the end and then second right into the parking area opposite a double-storey house. You have to walk over a pebble beach to an easy entry. Swim through the kelp to the dive site which is approximately 50m (165ft) out, directly opposite the white-tipped pinnacle rock on the shore.
Conditions: It is sheltered from the south-easter.
Average depth: 6m (20ft)
Maximum depth: 15m (50ft)
Pinnacles rise from the sandy ocean bed, their sides covered in feather stars, sponges, anemones and other colourful invertebrates. Crayfish and perlemoen are abundant and may be taken on snorkel, in season only by permit holders (see pages 25 and 26).

2 CORAL GARDENS

★★★★★

Location: 34°18,00'S; 18°51,00'E, north end of Rooiels. See map p. 126.
Access: Take the road from Gordon's Bay and turn right at the T-junction into Rooiels. Turn left and continue down to the shore. The entry involves clambering over rocks and a tricky swim through a gulley to the left. The reef goes off to the right of the gulley.
Conditions: This is not a very sheltered spot and the entry and exit can be rough.
Average depth: 12m (40ft)
Maximum depth: 15m (50ft)
It is a beautiful dive with plenty of invertebrates, crayfish, fish and perlemoen.

3 CROSSES (KRUIS)

★★★★★★

Location: 34°17,00'S; 18°49,44'E, 18km (11 miles) south of Gordon's Bay. See map p. 126.
Access: From Gordon's Bay, drive towards Rooiels and park at Buoy 20 (signposted on the road) on the grassy picnic spot. Follow the path to the left till you reach a long gulley. The easiest entry is to jump off the point at the mouth of the gulley, but you can clamber off the rocks into the gulley if you prefer. The dive site is just behind a submerged shelf of rock. To exit, swim into the gulley and then into the lee of the little rock almost at the

end, where it is sheltered and you can scramble onto the rocks. This can be done as a boat dive; it is a ride of about 16km (10 miles) from Gordon's Bay harbour.
Conditions: The shelf of rock running out to sea, behind which the main dive site is situated, can pick up rather dramatically on a low tide and high swell, so great care should be taken when swimming over it.
Average depth: 12m (40ft)
Maximum depth: 18m (60ft)
The rocky sea bed is colourful and there is an abundance of marine life. The best spot is the outer side of the submerged point which forms a small wall down to about 8m (25ft) and then slopes gently to 18m (60ft). The 'wall' is covered in redbait and many colourful invertebrates, and also shelter many crayfish in inaccessible holes.

This is a lovely site, named because of the crosses on the cliffside. Although novices can safely enjoy this dive from a boat, the shore entry is for moderately experienced divers only, and should not be attempted without either local expertise or a very thorough site survey.

4 PERCY'S

★★★★★★

Location: 34°16,50'S; 18°49,80'E, 18km (11 miles south of Gordon's Bay). See map p. 126.
Access: Park at Buoy 20 and follow a steep but well-worn path heading off towards the right. The entry is off the rocks into a small sheltered gulley. This can be done as a boat dive; it is a ride of about 16km (10 miles) from Gordon's Bay Harbour.
Conditions: This is best dived after a south-easterly wind. It is slightly sheltered from the south-west swells, if they are small.
Average depth: 12m (40ft)
Maximum depth: 21m (69ft)
This is a colourful dive with enormous sea-fans and 'forests' of feeding brittle stars half buried in the sand with just the tips of their arms showing. Nearby is a family of friendly seals, the younger members of which may possibly come to play. It is a good spot for night dives on perfectly calm, moonlit summer nights.

The knobbly anemone and the ladder ascidian are both common in South-Western Cape gullies and kelp forests.

5 STEENBRAS DEEP

★★★★

Location: 34°12,64'S; 18°45,50'E, approximately 6km (4 miles) off the mouth of the Steenbras River. See map p. 126.
Access: The best launching spot is Gordon's Bay Harbour. Travel on 265° for about 11.5km (7 miles) and then start searching with an echo-sounder.
Conditions: Because of its depth it can be dived in a moderate swell, but can be very surgy and choppy in a south-westerly wind.
Maximum depth: 30m (100ft)
The pinnacle starts at 17m (55ft) and is covered with sea-fans, big sponges and other invertebrate life, similar to Koei en Kalf (no. 6). There are plenty of fish to see. It is not recommended for novices.

6 KOEI EN KALF (COW AND CALF)

★★★★

Location: 34°10,20'S; 18°50,62'E. See map p. 126.
Access: The easiest way to access this site is by boat from Gordon's Bay Harbour. Follow the coastline until you see the two rocks opposite the five houses on the hillside. If you wish to do a shore dive, take the road from Gordon's

Bay south to Rooiels. Just before the Gordon's Bay municipal border signpost are five houses above the road and a clump of trees below it. Park there and look for the two rocks (Cow and Calf) lying approximately 100m (330ft) out. This entry involves a steep and tricky climb.
Conditions: This is best dived after a south-easter but, due to its sheltered position, is also diveable, but there can be surge during a south-westerly wind.
Average depth: 7m (23ft)
Maximum depth: 13m (43ft)
It is a very colourful reef with nudibranchs, anemones, urchins, starfish, sea-fans and sponges. Fish such as Roman, hottentot and other small varieties, are plentiful.

ROCK ENTRIES AND EXITS

These are not usually graceful. To enter, the slither-slide-flop method is most often employed, although a giant stride is sometimes possible. Never turn your back to the sea. Exiting is even less digni-fied, with the safest method as follows: wait for a nice big swell and fin your way as far as you can up the rocks and then hold on tight so you don't get sucked back into the sea. Wait for the next swell to push you a little further and then crawl out of the surf zone. Do not try to stand up in the surf zone or you may be knocked down on the rocks, possibly causing injury or loss of equipment.

The Western Shore of False Bay

This western side of False Bay forms the eastern coast of the Cape Peninsula. The Main Road (M4) runs along this coast, as does the southern suburbs railway line to Simon's Town. It is a well populated area with a series of suburbs nestled inbetween the mountain and the sea.

In winter, the prevailing north-westerly winds bring rain, and clean and flatten the sea as they blow offshore. This is consequently a great time to dive this lovely coast, if you can brave the inclement topside weather. The good road infrastructure makes it easy to reach most of the dive sites from land, and shore dives are the norm.

The water along this side of the bay is always a few degrees warmer than that of the western side of the Peninsula and can reach as high as 18°C (65°F), although it can drop as low as 12°C (54°F). The visibility is usually between 5 and 10m (16–33ft) but can reduce to almost zero when the south-easter has been blowing (usually in summer). It can, however, quite often be a spectacular 30m (100ft) in winter.

This area is a part of metropolitan Cape Town and so is close enough for non-diving companions to take full advantage of the city's many and varied attractions.

Tambja capensis, *a fairly common nudibranch of False Bay, nestles between a feather star and bryozoan.*

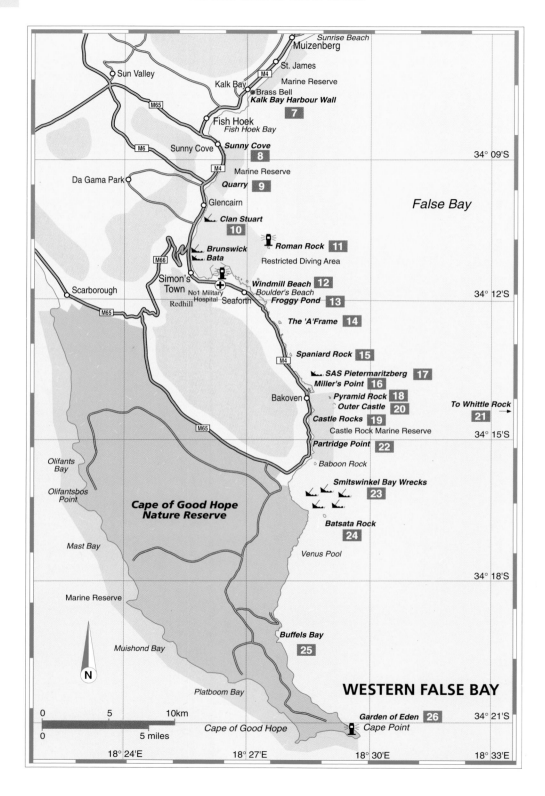

Sunrise Beach
Muizenberg
Sun Valley
St. James
M4
Marine Reserve
Kalk Bay
Brass Bell
Kalk Bay Harbour Wall
7
Fish Hoek
Fish Hoek Bay
Sunny Cove **Sunny Cove**
8
34° 09'S
Da Gama Park
M4 Marine Reserve
Quarry 9
Glencairn
False Bay
Clan Stuart
10
Brunswick
M66 **Bata**
Roman Rock 11
Restricted Diving Area
Simon's
Town No1 Military
Scarborough Hospital Seaforth
Redhill
Windmill Beach 12
Boulder's Beach
Froggy Pond 13
M65
34° 12'S
The 'A'Frame 14
Spaniard Rock 15
M4
SAS Pietermaritzberg 17
Miller's Point 16
Bakoven
Pyramid Rock 18
Outer Castle 20
To Whittle Rock
21
M65 **Castle Rocks** 19
Castle Rock Marine Reserve
34° 15'S
Partridge Point 22
Olifants
Bay
Baboon Rock
Olifantsbos
Point
Smitswinkel Bay Wrecks
23
**Cape of Good Hope
Nature Reserve**
Batsata Rock
24
Mast Bay
Venus Pool
34° 18'S
Marine Reserve
Muishond Bay
Buffels Bay
25
N
Platboom Bay
WESTERN FALSE BAY
0   5   10km
0   5 miles
Garden of Eden 26 34° 21'S
Cape of Good Hope **Cape Point**
18° 24'E   18° 27'E   18° 30'E   18° 33'E

Kalk Bay

Kalk Bay is a quaint suburb which has a fishing village atmosphere and a characterful working harbour. There are also lovely mountain walks here and some easy-to-explore caves. The village itself is charming and has a wealth of fascinating craft and antique shops, as well as a number of small, bohemian restaurants and coffee shops.

7 KALK BAY HARBOUR WALL

★★★★★

Location: 34°07,72′S; 18°27,06′E. See map p. 130.
Access: This dive is best reached by jumping off the harbour wall, some 2-4m (6-13ft) high, depending on the tide. The exit is by means of a steel ladder in the wall. It is not easy with full dive gear so is best done in two trips, with one buddy in the water while the other one ferries the gear up. An easier alternative is to enter or exit off the shelving rocks to the south of the harbour.
Conditions: This site can only be dived in very calm conditions, usually in mid-winter. It is absolutely essential to carry a knife as there is a lot of discarded fishing line in which you could become entangled.
Maximum depth: 6m (20ft)
Although the sea bed is littered with old tyres, fishing line and bits of net, it is an interesting dive. Most locals dive this site to salvage lead sinkers, which they melt down for diving weights, and *tjokka* jigs (the lures used for catching squid) which they sell back to the fishing boat crews. If you swim out 100m (330ft) or so, you will come across a family of seals who sometimes play with divers.

Fish Hoek

This comfortable seaside suburb has a beautiful beach with good sailing, windsurfing and swimming in temperate waters. The coastline is enhanced by a paved walkway, Jager's Walk, which extends the whole length of the southern end of the bay.

8 SUNNY COVE

★★★★

Location: 34°08,68′S; 18°26,30′E, on the south side of Fish Hoek bay. See map p. 130.
Access: Park next to the Sunny Cove railway station, 0.7km (just less than half a mile) south of Fish Hoek. Cross the railway line over the bridge, follow the paved walkway to the right of the beach and choose one of the many easy entry and exit points.

Conditions: This shallow dive site is sheltered in Fish Hoek bay and thus is often calm and clear when the rest of the area is not diveable.
Average depth: 7m (23ft)
Maximum depth: 10m (33ft)
Although the rocky reefs are covered in rich marine growth because there is plenty of sunlight, the invertebrate life is not as colourful as the spots further south. Small fish abound and a few elusive pipefish and hard-to-spot sea horses have been seen lurking in the waving green 'meadows' of Caulerpa (sea grass). This is a favourite place for night dives, during which half-buried soles and small dog sharks are often seen.

9 QUARRY

★★★★

Location: 34°09,20′S; 18°26,26′E, approximately 2km (1.5 miles) south of Fish Hoek. See map p. 130.
Access: Measure 2.2km (1.5 miles) from the Fish Hoek traffic circle and park in the parking area on the left. Kit up alongside the vehicle and cross the railway line to the

Herbivorous topshells seen grazing on kelp.

flat, rocky formations directly ahead. This is a fairly easy entry, but time your exits carefully. The reefs extend straight out from the shore.

Conditions: It is best dived during winter after a strong north-westerly wind. The surge can be strong as it is quite shallow and in the path of oncoming swells.

Average depth: 7m (23ft)

Maximum depth: 10m (33ft)

This site gets its name from the Glencairn quarry on the mountainside opposite. The reefs consist of rocky gullies running out to sea and there is an artificial reef created by numerous old car tyres that were dumped into the sea to attract sea life. It has been a success and a variety of reef fish are found there. There are many nudibranchs and big sea-fans. Playful seals are sometimes encountered.

Simon's Town

This fascinating town with its characterful Victorian buildings, pubs and coffee shops, is intimately tied up with the history of both the Royal and the South African Navies, which gives it a decidedly nautical atmosphere.

10 THE CLAN STUART (1914)

★★★★

Location: 34°10,20'S; 18°25,90'E, 4km (2.5 miles) from the Fish Hoek traffic circle on the road to Simon's Town. This wreck is close inshore and is situated in the restricted diving area. See map p. 130.

Access: Permission to dive on this wreck must be obtained from Naval headquarters at Simon's Town, tel. (021) 86-2300, or you may find yourself accosted by a patrol of navy divers or, even worse, surfacing in the midst of an artillery practice. They are quite relaxed about giving permission and will only refuse if they are planning

PROPOSED UNDERWATER HISTORICAL HERITAGE SITE

A proposal has been made, and accepted in principle, that the many wrecks in Simon's Bay be declared national monuments. It is hoped to place plaques on site or make underwater 'maps' of the wreck sites available to divers so that these historically significant wrecks can be fully appreciated. The first wrecks to be included will be the *Clan Stuart* (no. 10), the *Brunswick* and the *Bata*. Information on the latter two will become available as the trail is developed.

some sort of activity in the vicinity where you plan to dive. It is a short swim of about 50m (165ft) offshore with easy entry and exit points. The ship's engine block can be seen protruding from the sea.

Conditions: This bay is almost always sheltered except in a strong north-easter. Because of the shallow depths there can be surge when a swell is running.

Average depth: 6m (20ft)

Maximum depth: 8m (24ft)

The *Clan Stuart*, a 3500-ton British turret steamer carrying a cargo of coal, sank after dragging its anchors in a south-east gale on 21 November 1914. Its shallow depth allows plenty of sunlight to penetrate and the wreck is covered with dense marine growth, attracting a large number of fish. This wreck will be part of the proposed Simon's Bay wreck trail.

11 ROMAN ROCK

★★★★★★

Location: 34°10,51'S; 18°27,36'E, this spot is marked by an obvious light and can easily be seen from Simon's Town or Glencairn. It is in the restricted diving area. See map p. 130.

Access: It is essential to obtain permission from the Naval headquarters before diving this spot (see dive no. 10). It is a short boat ride from Simon's Town harbour.

Conditions: This is a sheltered winter dive.

Average depth: 15m (50ft)

Maximum depth: 25m (80ft)

This is a site which is not often dived in the past because of the inconvenience of obtaining permission from the navy, but it is much easier now. The marine life is abundant with colourful invertebrates and reef fish typical of False Bay. This is another of those spots where you may encounter playful seals.

12 WINDMILL BEACH

★★

Location: 34°12,06'S; 18°27,40'E, just south of Boulders Beach, below the golf course. See map p. 130.

Access: Drive out of Simon's Town to the south, turn left into Bellevue Road, and then first right into Links Road, just past the golf course. Park at the end of the road and walk about 100m (330ft) to the beach. The entry and exit are both very sheltered, gently sloping sand beaches.

Conditions: This site is almost always sheltered and the entry is probably the easiest on the entire South African coast. Wave action is usually no more than an inch or two and is rarely more than 30cm (1ft) high. There can be a little surge round the point if there is a big swell.

A typical False Bay rock reef, covered in a multitude of invertebrate life and stopping abruptly at the sand.

Average depth: 6m (20ft)
Maximum depth: 8m (25ft) off the point
There is a rocky point going out to sea for about 100m (330ft) from the middle of a gentle beach. It is a favourite training dive as you can enter from the beach on one side of the rocks, swim round the point and exit on the other side of the rocks, on the same beach. Plenty of kelp, red and green seaweed, nudibranchs, sea cucumbers, urchins, dogfish and pyjama sharks can be seen.

13 FROGGY POND

★★

Location: 34°12,26'S; 18°27,56'E, a little bay 5km (3 miles) from Simon's Town on the road to Cape Point (just before the 'A' Frame, no. 14). See map p. 130.
Access: Park on the opposite side of the road and kit up there or on the lawn in front of the beach. It is an extremely easy entry and exit from the little beach to the right of the rocky cluster jutting into the sea. Enter and swim to the left and around this cluster where you can descend and start exploring.
Conditions: A sheltered spot, usually flat and clear.
Average depth: 5m (16ft)
Maximum depth: 7m (23ft)
Being in shallow water, the rocks are densely covered in red, green and brown seaweed, but the invertebrate life is not particularly colourful. There are a number of small fish flitting about and cuttlefish and octopuses have been spotted there. This is a relaxed dive, ideal for the novice or out-of-practice diver.

14 THE 'A' FRAME

★★★★

Location: 34°12,48'S; 18°27,66'E, just past Froggy Pond (no. 13), approximately 5km (3 miles) from Simon's Town. See map p. 130.

Access: Follow directions as for Froggy Pond (no. 13) but continue for about 400m (about ¼ mile) until you see some cottages on a large green lawn on the sea side of the road. Park on the main road, kit up there and walk down to the mast on the rocks which has replaced the A-frame structure after which this site was named. You can enter from the flat rock below the mast or over the round boulders about 50m (165ft) to the south. The flat rock is usually easier at low tide and the boulders at high tide.

Conditions: There can sometimes be a bit of a surge on the outer side of the big rock, but it is usually calm inshore, especially in winter.

Average depth: 8m (25ft)

Maximum depth: About 15m (50ft) on the outer side of the big rock.

The best spot to descend is on the landward side of the big round rock, after a swim of about 60m (200ft). There are some deep holes and overhangs and the side of the rock abounds with colourful invertebrates of all descriptions. Fish are tame and include Roman, hottentot, dassie and stompneus (stumpnose) and occasionally the bright yellow juvenile parrotfish. Friendly, playful seals are sometimes encountered. Small, harmless sharks, such as dogfish and pyjama sharks, are often seen. Octopuses and cuttlefish are not uncommon.

The smaller rock to the left of the round one has a lovely cave with huge sponges and colourful invertebrates. It can, unfortunately, sometimes be silted up for a few weeks, especially at the beginning of winter.

BOULDERS BEACH AND THE PENGUINS

This is one of the prettiest and most sheltered beaches on the Peninsula and has a resident population of endangered jackass penguins. They can be observed from the paved walkway above the beach and also from the water. This is a lovely snorkelling spot for beginners and lucky divers may catch sight of a penguin 'flying' underwater.

15 SPANIARD ROCK

★★★★

Location: 34°13,00'S; 18°28,00'E, about 6km (4 miles) past Simon's Town, towards Cape Point. See map p. 130.

Access: It is a short, steep climb down to the entry and exit points and then a swim of about 75m (250ft) to the large rock which can be seen from the road.

Conditions: A strong surge can develop when a swell runs in the bay. The water is usually clear in winter.

Average depth: 8m (25ft)

Maximum depth: 12m (40ft)

This colony of endangered jackass penguins, sunning themselves at Boulders Beach, are protected by law.

The rock and the surrounding reefs are covered in brightly coloured sponges and marine growth, dominated by vivid yellows and reds, which give the site the name 'Spaniard Rock'. Reef fish typical of False Bay, such as Roman, hottentot, butterfish and Janbruin (John Brown), are plentiful.

16 MILLER'S POINT

★★★★★

Location: 34°13,90′S; 18°28,60′E, in front of the Cape Boat and Ski-Boat Club slipway and clubhouse on the road from Simon's Town to Cape Point (M4). See map p. 130.
Access: There are several easy entry and exit points close to the launch site or the tidal pool in sheltered waters.
Conditions: The water is usually calm and clear because of the protected location. It is essential to dive with a marker buoy and Alpha flag because of boat traffic.
Average depth: 7m (23ft)
Maximum depth: 18m (60ft) at the blinder
The reefs in this area consist mainly of low walls and gullies covered in marine growth and patches of kelp. There is a blinder further out to the east, approximately 200m (660ft) from shore. Marine life is not particularly colourful, except on the blinder.

17 SAS PIETERMARITZBURG (1994)

★★★

Location: About 2km (1.25 miles) north of the Miller's Point slipway. See map p. 130.
Access: A short boat ride from Millers Point slipway.
Conditions: Best dived in winter, it should be reasonably unaffected by surge as it is quite deep.
Average depth: 16m (52ft)
Maximum depth: 20m (65ft) on the sand
This ship has a very interesting history. It was formerly HMS *Pelorus* and led the D-day invasion of Normandy in the Second World War. It was bought by the South African Navy in 1947 for use as a training vessel and was later converted to a minesweeper.

The *Pietermaritzburg* was scuttled on 12 November 1994 to form an artificial reef and, unlike most of the artificial reefs in this area, has been placed in relatively shallow water. It lies straight up on the sand.

It is anticipated that the growth of marine life on this wreck should be much quicker than it was on the Smitswinkel Bay wrecks (no. 24; see the comparative photographs on p. 147) because of the shallower depth. The ship is, at present, in perfect condition, making an interesting and eerie dive.

Blue choirboys, a common sea-squirt, with crinoids.

18 PYRAMID ROCK

★★★★★★

Location: 34°14,24′S; 18°28,72′E, just to the north of Castle Rocks (no. 19). See map p. 130.
Access: This is a pyramid-shaped rock which sticks up about 1m (3ft) above the water, about 75m (250ft) from the northern edge of Castle Rocks, a large jumble of rocks going out to sea. The spot can be recognized by the cottages on either side of the road. There is an informal but well-worn gravel parking area on the landward side of the road. Kit up alongside the road and walk down the steps leading past the cottages to the lawn at the bottom. The entry and exit is over the round boulders to the left of the cluster of rocks. Alternatively, you can walk to the little beach about 70m (230ft) to the left and enter there for a shorter swim.
Condition: There is usually a bit of a surge running except in completely flat conditions.
Average depth: 8m (25ft)
Maximum depth: 12m (40ft)
This is an interesting dive with plenty of relief, big submerged rocks and swim-throughs. Invertebrate life is colourful and abundant and there are many big reef fish secure in the marine reserve. It is worth saving a bit of air

MARINE RESERVE

The area from Bakoven Rock (south of Miller's Point) to Bobbejaanklip (south of Partridge Point), for one nautical mile seawards from the high-water mark, is a marine reserve and no marine animal may be collected or disturbed.

to return to the exit point on a compass course as the terrain is covered in kelp and small round boulders. These often shelter small octopuses, rays or dog sharks can sometimes be seen swimming in the gullies.

19 CASTLE ROCKS

★★★★★★

Location: 34°14,40'S; 18°28,72'E, past Miller's Point, on road from Simon's Town to Cape Point. See map p. 130.
Access: Proceed as for the Pyramid Rock (no. 18) but the entry and exit point is to the right of the cluster of rocks. You have to clamber across the round boulders in the water behind the sandy patch – beware of slipping. The dive site is 50-75m (165-250ft) to the south-east. An alternative entry is from the flattish dark rock on the right hand side of the cluster of rocks, further to the east than the gulley. This entry is slippery and a little tricky but allows for a shorter swim. It is not suitable as an exit point as it involves a 1m (3ft) jump.
Conditions: Sheltered from the north-west winds in winter and usually clear although there can be surge on the outside of the rock. Best dived between May and August.

Average depth: 10m (33ft)
Maximum depth: 15m (50ft)
The dive site is at the big rock south-east of the entry point. As this is a marine sanctuary where fishing or the harvesting of any marine life is prohibited, fauna is prolific on these reefs, with large numbers of fish such as Roman, hottentot, butterfish, galjoen and Janbruin, as well as many small bottom sharks. Octopuses and cuttlefish are also found. The fish are very tame and follow the divers around. The rocks are a macrophotographer's dream, covered with multi-coloured invertebrates, including nudibranchs, starfish, urchins, anemones, big gorgonians and sea-fans, huge sponges, crayfish and basket stars.

This is a favourite training dive and also a great spot for night dives, although you must exercise caution on the slippery rocks, especially at night.

20 OUTER CASTLE

★★★★

Location: 34°14,28'S;18°29,02'E, approximately 750m (½ mile) out to sea from the edge of Castle Rocks (no. 19). See map p. 130.

Illustrated here is the extent to which colour is absorbed underwater, with bright colour visible in the torch light.

Access: Some of the tougher local divers consider this a shore dive, but it involves a very long swim and you must be careful of ski-boats. It is best done as a boat dive from Miller's Point. The rock is a blinder which can be seen breaking at low tide.

Conditions: This site is exposed but is calm at depth or after a north-west wind has blown and flattened the sea.

Average depth: 15m (50ft)

Maximum depth: 22m (72ft)

This is a great dive spot where you may see larger rays, gulley sharks and even yellowtail when they are running. The reef life is very colourful and abundant. There is an air-filled cave at the bottom of the rock and divers sometimes surface in it for a chat. This is fun but keep your regulator to hand as the quality of the air is dubious.

21 WHITTLE ROCK

★★★★★★★★★

Location: 34°14,88'S; 18°33,62'E, right out in the bay. See map p. 130.

Access: From Kalk Bay harbour travel on 150° for 17km (10.5 miles) or, from Miller's Point, on 130° for 9km (5.5 miles). It is marked by a metal buoy. It is worth noting that there are a number of great white sharks in the area so divers should kit up properly in the boat and descend as soon as they hit the water as it is not wise to hang around on the surface.

Conditions: It is usually fairly clear and only has surge if there is a very big ground swell running.

Average depth: whatever you want

Maximum depth: 35m (115ft)

The rock rises to within 3m (10ft) of the surface and covers a large area so the best way to dive it is to look for a likely-looking pinnacle on an echo-sounder or fish-finder. The invertebrate life is very colourful and almost unspoilt as the area is not dived too often. It is an exciting dive and quite a few divers have seen a great white cruising past. Although one should be cautious, they have not interfered with scuba divers in this area.

The rock teems with big fish such as yellowtail, stumpnose and Roman and is thus a favourite spearfishing venue. Caution should be taken when spearfishing here and all fish should be kept in the boat, not on a float line, as the spearfish are likely to attract sharks.

22 PARTRIDGE POINT

★★★★★

Location: 34°15,38'S; 18°28,68'E, just to the north of Smitswinkel Bay on the road to the Cape of Good Hope Nature Reserve. See map p. 130.

WHELKS

Whelks are rather vicious predators. They drill a hole through the shell of their prey, using their specially modified radula (or teeth) and often a dilute acid. They then suck the flesh out of their victim. They prey thus on other molluscs and many even gang up to attack something as big as a crayfish.

Access: Although this is a long way from shore and reaching the entry point involves a long, steep climb, this used to be a very popular shore dive. The land has since changed hands and the path is no longer open to the public, so this spot can only be dived from a boat. From Miller's Point, travel south along the coast until you see a green-roofed stone house on a rocky point. The dive site is at the large rocks a few hundred metres out to sea from the house.

Conditions: This is a fairly sheltered spot and is best dived after a few days of north-westerly winds when the water should be clean.

Average depth: 15m (50ft)

Maximum depth: 20m (65ft)

This site is characterized by magnificent underwater scenery with caverns, overhangs, swim-throughs and a tunnel, almost large enough to drive a bus through. The marine life is abundant and typical of False Bay with colourful sponges, soft corals, crinoids and many molluscs. There is a very friendly colony of seals nearby and they might well come to play, or you could even swim out to them, if you like.

23 BATSATA ROCK

★★★★★★★★★

Location: 34°16,60'S; 18°28,88'E, on the southern end of Smitswinkel Bay. See map p. 130.

Access: By boat launched from Miller's Point or Kalk Bay harbour. Approximately 5km (3 miles) south of Miller's Point and is clearly marked on charts.

Average depth: whatever you want

Maximum depth: 30m (100ft)

Batsata Rock is a large blinder that comes to within approximately 6m (20ft) of the surface. The rock creates dramatic underwater scenery with pinnacles and deep gullies. Fish life is prolific and typical of the False Bay waters, and the rocks are covered with lush and colourful marine growth.

This is an excellent site for a multi-level dive as it slopes gently from 30m (115ft), and there is a large interesting flat surface at 6m (20ft). It is also a very popular spearfishing spot, but beware of sharks.

24 THE WRECKS OF SMITSWINKEL BAY

★ ★ ★ ★ ★

Location: 34°16,08'S; 18°28,55'E, in the middle of Smitswinkel Bay. See map p. 130.

Access: These wrecks are best reached by boat launched from Kalk Bay, Miller's Point or Simon's Town. They are situated approximately 4km (2.5 miles) from Miller's Point. An echo-sounder is essential to locate them and a local skipper or diver may be able to use shore markers to identify which wreck has been picked up by the echo. This can be tricky as they lie quite close together and even many local divers are not sure which wreck is which.

Conditions: It is usually calm as the bay is sheltered and the depth dampens the effect of even quite a large swell.

Average depth: 35m (115ft)

Maximum depth: 40m (130ft)

Five wrecks were scuttled by the navy in the early 1970s to form an artificial reef which has proved to be a success and now teems with a variety of fish and other marine life. These wrecks are the SAS *Transvaal*, and the SAS *Good Hope*, both former navy frigates, the *Rockeater*, a diamond dredger, and two fishing trawlers, the *Princess Elizabeth* and the *Oratava*. The depth, combined with the ghostly appearance of the upright frigates and dredger, makes this a thrilling dive. Because of the depth it is necessary to take some form of artificial light down to the reef to fully appreciate the marvellous colours of the marine life. The wrecks teem with pretty white, red, yellow and mauve soft corals. Sponges, sea-fans and starfish are plentiful, as well as numbers of colourful anemones and nudibranchs.

Cape of Good Hope Nature Reserve

This relatively small reserve is primarily a floral sanctuary but it is blessed with some absolutely beautiful coastal scenery, not least being the 'fairest cape in all the world', Cape Point. There is a daily entrance fee charged at the gate and an extra fee for boats – surfboards constitute a boat in the opinion of the park officials.

MARINE RESERVE

The entire west coast of the Cape of Good Hope Nature Reserve, from Cape Point to Scarborough, 10m (33ft) seawards from the high-water mark, is a marine reserve, with the exception that crayfish may be caught, subject to general regulations, in the area from Hoek van Bobbejaan to Cape Point.

The shore entries are a little rough but the area is very popular for the gathering of perlemoen (abalone) and crayfish. Ask at the gate when you enter the park where this is permitted. This is a truly lovely place to spend the day and maybe fit in a snorkel dive while you're there.

25 BUFFELS BAY

★ ★ ★ ★ ★

Location: 34°18,12'S; 18°27,66'E. See map p. 130.

Access: Buffels Bay is a popular recreation spot within the Reserve and is well signposted. It is about 9km (5.5 miles) from the entrance gate. The best part of the site is identified by the remains of a trawler. There are easy entry and exit points to the reefs directly out to sea.

Conditions: This spot is good for winter diving and is occasionally diveable in summer as it is quite sheltered.

Average depth: 6m (20ft)

Maximum depth: 10m (33ft)

This is a favourite crayfish and perlemoen spot in season and the sizeable fish make this a popular spearfishing site. The remains of the wooden trawler, *Tania*, are scattered over the seabed in shallow water which makes for an interesting dive. Large patches of urchins occur in the kelp forests, creating beautiful and rather surreal underwater vistas.

26 GARDEN OF EDEN

★ ★ ★ ★

Location: 34°21,00'S; 18°29,50'E, on the eastern side of Cape Point. See map p. 130.

Access: Follow the road through the reserve right to the end where there is a café and a gift shop. Go down the steps leading to the toilets below the road, and take the steep footpath leading down. Wear proper walking shoes for the climb, which takes about 15 minutes down and between 20-30 minutes up. The entry and exit points are easy and plentiful.

Conditions: It is sheltered from most of the prevailing winds except for the easterlies. On fine days the sea is sometimes mirror-smooth.

Average depth: 5m (16ft)

Maximum Depth: 10m (33ft)

This lovely and secluded spot is well worth the trip if you can spare a whole day. On good days it offers excellent snorkelling for crayfish, perlemoen and alikreukel (giant periwinkles). While you can scuba dive, it is not really worth the effort of carting the gear down the path. You can be fairly confident of obtaining a full quota here and, when conditions are perfect, a more relaxed and pleasant snorkel dive cannot be wished for.

Cape Peninsula Western Seaboard

The western seaboard must rate as one of the most scenic areas in the country, with spectacular drives along the steep mountain cliffs, leading to superb dive sites which often have excellent visibility in clear, cold water. While some of these sites can only be reached by boat, most are accessible from shore.

It is close enough to town to dive while non-diving companions enjoy the urban pleasures of Cape Town but it also offers many other delights. The busy fishing harbour of Hout Bay is picturesque and interesting, there are many beautiful day walks in the surrounding mountains and horse rides are offered on Long Beach which, living up to its name, stretches from Noordhoek to Kommetjie.

Serious sunbathers can enjoy a preening session on Clifton, South Africa's premier body-watching beach, or spend a much more relaxing day swimming or strolling on Llandudno, Camps Bay or Long Beach. The Clifton/Camps Bay area offers great coffee shops, restaurants and the very popular seafront watering hole, La Med.

Cold-water corals, sea-fans and brightly coloured sponges are typical of the western seaboard dive sites.

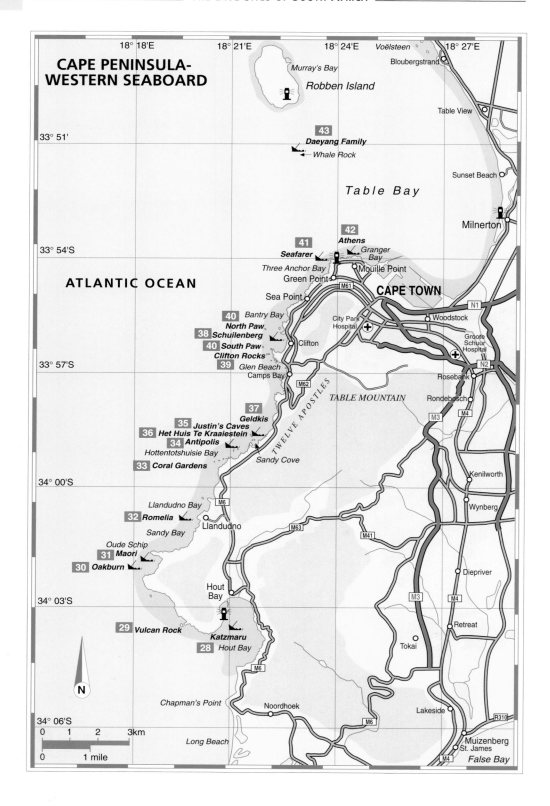

CAPE PENINSULA-
WESTERN SEABOARD

18° 18'E   18° 21'E   18° 24'E   *Voëlsteen*   18° 27'E

Murray's Bay

Robben Island

Bloubergstrand

Table View

33° 51'   **43**
Daeyang Family
← *Whale Rock*

Sunset Beach

Table Bay

Milnerton

42
Athens
33° 54'S   **41**   *Granger*
Seafarer   *Bay*
Three Anchor Bay   Mouille Point
Green Point   **CAPE TOWN**

ATLANTIC OCEAN

M61

Sea Point

N1

Woodstock

City Park
Hospital

40   Bantry Bay
North Paw
38 **Schuilenberg**
40 **South Paw**   Clifton
Clifton Rocks
33° 57'S   **39**   Glen Beach
Camps Bay

M62

Groote
Schuur
Hospital

N2

Rosebank

TABLE MOUNTAIN

Rondebosch

M3   M4

37
Geldkis
35 **Justin's Caves**
36 **Het Huis Te Kraaiestein**
34 **Antipolis**
Hottentotshuisie Bay   Sandy Cove
33 **Coral Gardens**

TWELVE APOSTLES

Kenilworth

34° 00'S

Llandudno Bay   M6
32 **Romelia**
Sandy Bay   Llandudno

Wynberg

M63

M41

Oude Schip
31 **Maori**
30 **Oakburn**

Diepriver

Hout
Bay

M3   M4

Retreat

29 **Vulcan Rock**
Katzmaru
28 *Hout Bay*

34° 03'S

Tokai

M6

N

34° 06'S

Chapman's Point   Noordhoek

Lakeside

R310

0   1   2   3km

0   1 mile

Long Beach

Muizenberg
St. James

M4   *False Bay*

27 THE LUSITANIA (1911)

★★★★

Location: 34°23,40'S; 18°29,65'E, on the eastern side of Bellows Rock which breaks approximately 4km (2.5 miles) off Cape Point.

Access: The closest launch site is Miller's Point. The wreck lies on the eastern side of the blinder which can be seen breaking.

Conditions: The wreck is in a very exposed area and conditions have to be absolutely perfect to dive on it – even moderate swells can cause significant turbulence near Bellows Rock.

Maximum depth: 37m (122ft)

The *Lusitania*, a Portuguese twin-screw passenger liner of 5557 tons, struck Bellows Rock at midnight on 18 April 1911. It only sank two days later when it slipped off the rock, and all but eight of the 800 people aboard survived.

The unfortunate passengers died when a lifeboat capsized. A large amount of steel plating and some bronze fittings remain on the site and may not be removed. The sea life is beautiful and varied with many invertebrates and sometimes large fish.

This is a deep dive and it is essential to navigate away from the rock underwater to avoid the strong surge near the surface. This dive is, therefore, only recommended for very experienced divers.

28 THE KATZMARU (1970s)

★★★

Location: 34°03,20'S; 18°21,20'E, in the middle of the mouth of Hout Bay. See map p. 140.

Access: The boat is launched from Hout Bay harbour from where it is a very short trip to the site.

The icy, nutrient-rich Cape waters encourage a prolific growth of beautifully coloured and textured marine algae.

Young seals are friendly, curious and playful.

Conditions: It is usually calm inside the bay. Despite concerted resistance by local divers, residents and environmental groups, a sewage pipeline has been constructed with the main outfall just metres from this wreck. At the time of writing, discharging had not begun and the wreck was diveable but enquire before taking the plunge.
Average depth: 29m (97ft) on deck
Maximum depth: 32m (106ft) on the sand
The *Katzmaru*, an Oriental trawler that sank in the 1970s in Hout Bay, lies on a stark, sandy bottom and is virtually intact condition. A multitude of fish and other marine life typical of the Atlantic Ocean can be seen here. This is a popular and easily accessible deep wreck often used for advanced training, but it will, unfortunately, be ruined once sewage discharge commences.

29 VULCAN ROCK

★★★★★

Location: 34°04,00'S; 18°18,60'E, a blinder off the Karbonkelberg, to the south-west of Hout Bay. See map p. 140.
Access: The blinder breaks at all except the highest spring tide and can be seen from the sea. It is a short boat trip (about 15-20 minutes) from Hout Bay Harbour. Most of the dive shops and charter boats run trips to this spot in the summer months.
Conditions: It can be very clear but icy cold after a good upwelling. There can be a strong surge if there is a swell running. You should always check conditions carefully before exiting the boat as there is sometimes a 4-5 knot (9.25kph/5.75mph) current, either on the surface or at

depth. Even if there appears to be no current, a drift line of a few hundred metres is strongly recommended.
Average depth: 25m (80ft)
Maximum depth: 40m (130ft)
Vulcan Rock is a large pinnacle rising to 5m (16ft) below the surface. It is covered in colourful marine growth, such as hard and soft cold-water coral, nudibranchs, deep-water cowries and crayfish. Many playful seals are present and fish such as hottentot, galjoen, and other species are plentiful. There is a large tunnel running through the rock at the bottom.

30 THE OAKBURN (1906)

★★

Location: 34°02,20'S; 18°70,00'E, in front of the large round boulder, south of Maori Bay. See map p. 140.
Access: It is a short boat trip from Hout Bay Harbour and is also a popular destination for dive charters.
Conditions: This site can ony be dived on calm days as it is in an exposed position. The wreck is deteriorating and extreme care should be taken before attempting even the shallowest penetration as some sections could be unstable.
Average depth: 20m (65ft)
Maximum depth: 25m (80ft)
The *Oakburn*, a British cargo steamer of 3865 tons, was wrecked in fog on 21 May 1906, on a voyage from New York to Sydney. Two lives were lost. Its cargo included railway lines and equipment, glassware, sewing machines, musical instruments, oil and paper. It lies on a steep slope with the boilers and engine block at the bottom and the bow to the south. Marine life is not particularly colourful, and kelp is plentiful.

31 THE MAORI (1909)

★★★

Location: 34°01,90'S; 18°18,90'E, north of the *Oakburn* (no. 30) approximately 75m (250ft) offshore directly in front of the large, flat cleft rock. See map p. 140.

EXPLORING VULCAN ROCK

Like Whittle Rock (no. 21) in False Bay, the whole area surrounding Vulcan Rock has an interesting relief. Local divers often cruise the area with the echo-sounder on and dive any likely-looking pinnacle, a practice which is highly recommended.

CRAYFISH SANCTUARY

No crayfish (lobster) may be caught for 12 nautical miles out to sea, from Melkbos Point to Die Josie (near Chapman's Peak).

Access: It is only a short trip from Hout Bay harbour and is probably the most popular charter destination in the summer months.

Conditions: The bay is well protected so it is usually calm. In summer, after a few days of south-easterly wind and strong upwelling, it can be crystal clear but icy cold, and the wreck can be seen from the dive boat. Be very careful of sharp, protruding bits of metal, particularly when there is a surge.

Average depth: 20m (65ft)

Maximum depth: 25 m (80ft)

The *Maori*, a British cargo steam ship of 5317 tons, was carrying a cargo of explosives, water piping and crockery from London to New Zealand, when it was wrecked on striking a rock in thick fog and drizzle on 5 August 1909. During the wreck 32 lives were lost.

It lies in the protection of the well-sheltered bay and the waves break over it only in the worst storms. For this reason it has remained remarkably intact and was declared the most well preserved wreck of its vintage by Jacques Cousteau when he visited the site. Local divers have since then blasted some sections, though. The total length of the wreck is approximately 175m (580ft). Marine life is not particularly colourful and is mostly dominated by kelp, fish and crayfish.

32 THE ROMELIA (1977)

★★★★

Location: 34°00,65'S; 18°19,90'E, off Sunset Rocks, Llandudno. See map p. 140.

Access: Take the Llandudno turnoff which is some 8km (5 miles) from the Camps Bay police station (the wreck can be seen from here) and follow the Sandy Bay signs. It is difficult to find parking near the wreck on summer weekends, and you may have to persuade the person controlling the access boom to let you drive in and drop your gear off. It is an easy walk down to the rocks from where a little careful clambering brings you to the water's edge. You can enter off one of the flat rocks or into one of the gullies. It is a swim of approximately 200m (660ft) to the wreck.

Conditions: Like elsewhere on this coast, it is cold and clear after a south-easterly wind has blown. The surge can be very strong on the southern side and there is a strong suction through a hole on the Llandudno (the northern) side of the wreck, so this site should only be dived when the conditions are perfect.

Average depth: 12m (40ft)

Maximum depth: 25m (80ft)

The *Romelia* was a Liberian oil tanker of some 20000 tons that foundered on Sunset Rocks on 29 July 1977 while en route to a Taiwanese breaker's yard in the company of the *Antipolis* (no. 34). Both ships were in tow when the cable snapped in one of Cape Town's spectacular and notorious winter storms.

The stern section, which has since slipped off the rocks, is still fairly intact, but most of the bow was destroyed. The ship has interesting portholes and fittings to swim and peer through. They also make good photo props. Beware of suction through the hull and don't attempt penetration without an experienced buddy and a swim line. The engine room is only partially submerged (although it must be entered underwater) and is particularly interesting when the rusty interior is lit only by sunlight filtering through the turquoise water. Take along a torch to illuminate the mysterious interior.

Colourful invertebrates, crayfish, hottentot and other small fish can be seen living in the dense kelp forests. This dive is not recommended for novice divers.

Kelp forests are typical of the western seaboard.

The wreck of the Romelia off Sunset Rocks is a favourite spot for leisurely summer dives.

33 CORAL GARDENS

★★★★★★★★

   R

Location: 33°59,20'S; 17°23,00'E, south-west of the Hottentots Huisie recreation resort. See map p. 140.

Access: The easiest way of getting to the reefs is by boat, the Municipal slipway in Three Anchor Bay being the nearest launch site. To do a shore dive, turn off to Hottentots Huisie from Victoria Drive (about 5km (3 miles) from Camps Bay). You will need to pay an entrance fee at the gate. The most direct route is to follow the concrete drainage channel on the far side of the parking lot and then keep to the left on the little path. This involves rather a steep scramble and some boulder-hopping to get to the water's edge. It is then a swim of about 100m (330ft) to a long, flattish rock. The dive site is directly behind this rock.

Conditions: It is best dived on calm days as the site is in the path of the prevailing swells and is therefore subject to heavy surge.

Average depth: 10m (33ft)

Maximum depth: 18m (60ft)

This is one of the most beautiful but less well-known sites in the Peninsula. The underwater gardens of hard and soft coral form a kaleidoscope of brilliant pink, yellow, red, orange and purple, complemented by fields of urchins and brightly coloured anemones. The coral may

not be removed and heavy fines are levied on those who attempt to do so. The resort is for day trippers only and camping is not allowed. There are toilets, fresh water and fireplaces available. This is a lovely spot to spend the day, but bear in mind that it is very popular with large family groups and can sometimes be very crowded.

34 THE ANTIPOLIS (1977)

★★

     R

Location: 33°59,00'S; 18°21,45'E, on the rocks off Victoria Road, Oudekraal. See map p. 140.

Access: Park in the region of the White House (you can't miss it, there is only one house on this road) and walk down to the water's edge. Enter anywhere over the slippery, round boulders.

Conditions: It is well protected on the landward side, but there can be surge inside the wreck. Watch out for sharp metal objects.

Average depth: 10m (33ft)

Maximum depth: 12m (40ft)

The *Antipolis* was a derelict Greek oil tanker of almost 25 000 tons built in 1959 and wrecked on 29 July 1977 in the same incident as the *Romelia* (no. 32) while being towed to the breaker's yard. It came to rest in a very stable position on the rocks and was a favourite venue for shipwreck parties until the superstructure was cut off for scrap. The *Antipolis'* engine parts, ladders and portholes can be seen. This is an interesting dive if you are particularly keen on modern wrecks as it gives a sense of the vastness of even a small tanker. However, it is decidedly monochromatic, with the thick kelp exactly the same shade of brown as the rusted steel of the hull. The area does not boast much pretty marine life.

35 JUSTIN'S CAVES

★★★★

    R

Location: 33°58,90'S; 18°20,65'E, a little closer to Camps Bay than the wreck of the *Antipolis* (no. 34). See map p. 140.

Access: To enter, kit up alongside the road and scramble down a steep incline next to the concrete drainage channel to the round boulders at the bottom, or take the long way along the footpath which leads to the entry for Sandy Cove (no. 36) and then veer left. There are two entry points, both of which involve scrambling over round boulders and entering into a gulley. Check both of them

carefully as the relative ease of entry changes with the tide. The swim to the dive site is approximately 150m (500ft). The dive site is amongst the furthest clump of rocks, almost directly in line with the drainage channel, and the cave is under the tallest round rock. Descend in the channel between the two rocks.

Conditions: This is usually dived in summer when the water is clear, but cold. A strong south-easterly chops the sea up quickly and makes the swim back tiring, so it is easier done underwater under these conditions. The broken nature of the sea bed is disorientating, though, so a compass is necessary. The surge is very strong through the caves when a swell is running.

Average depth: 12m (40ft)

Maximum depth: 18m (60ft) on the outer side

Large underwater caverns and breathtaking swim-throughs offer an exciting and colourful dive to both the novice and the experienced diver.

Marine life is prolific and vividly coloured invertebrates, such as nudibranchs, anemones and hard and soft corals, grow on the ceilings and walls of the caverns. A torch is necessary to do justice to the splendour of the caves' interiors. Many large crayfish flourish in the reserve. Hottentot and other small fish are present, as well as small harmless bottom-dwelling sharks. This is a

Diving at Justin's Caves involves a tricky entry over round boulders, and a long swim through kelp.

spectacular night dive but the entry and exit are a little tricky. This is one of the most popular shore dives in the area, particularly in summer.

It is also a very popular spot for picnics (no open fires are allowed here) before, after or even between dives, with the Twelve Apostles forming a magnificent backdrop to a leisurely meal.

36 SANDY COVE: HET HUIS DE KRAAIESTEIN (1698)

★★

     R

Location: 33°58,85'S; 18°21,70'E, opposite the White House. See map p. 140.

Access: Park a little closer to Camps Bay than you would for Justin's Caves (no. 35), although you may not have a choice over weekends. Follow the well-worn footpath and when it seems to disappear into a grassy clearing, step over a rock on your right (half obscured by a bush) after which you will rediscover the path. It leads to a tiny sheltered beach which affords an easy entry and exit. An alternative is the gulley to the left which can be recognized by the iron rails running out to sea.

To find the wreck (which is not easy), swim out keeping to the left of the small cluster of rocks approximately 50m (165ft) out. Once past them, swim to a point about 30m (100ft) behind them and find the small darkish rock with a cleft through the middle and line yourself up so that you can see directly through the cleft. Once you have this line (you're facing the shore), look to your right and you will see a large egg-shaped rock about two-thirds of the way along the large cluster of rocks going out to sea. Keep swimming out to sea until you can see the hole at the left edge of this rock and you will be directly above the wreck site.

Conditions: The area is well sheltered and as a rule is calm and clear in summer.

Average depth: 6m (20ft)

Maximum depth: 15m (50ft) on the outer side of the *Het Huis de Kraaiestein*.

The wreck has broken up completely and all that is left are a few iron cannons, an anchor and a some pieces of wood. All these remnants are entirely overgrown and you will only recognize them by looking for unusually straight lines. This is a favourite training dive in summer and consequently the site could be a bit crowded.

The marine life here is interesting and prolific but not particularly colourful. The kelp cover is thick, many species of invertebrates cover the rocks and hordes of crayfish hide in deep holes. There are some real granddaddies among them as this area is protected, falling within the crayfish sanctuary. It is said that a big basking shark, affectionately called Johnny, often visits the site but divers are not bothered by him (or her). This is a favourite night diving spot, especially in summer .

A rare encounter – a diver swimming with a sunfish.

37 GELDKIS

★★★★

   R

Location: The furthest rock out to see from Sandy Cove. See map p. 140.

Access: Carry on past the *Het Huis de Kraaiestein* (no. 36), and past the two flattish rocks to the furthest clump of rocks. It is a swim of about 400m (¼ mile) in icy cold water, but you can stop at the flat rocks on the way back for a rest and to warm up in the sun.

Conditions: This spot should be dived in perfect conditions as the swim can be very tiring in choppy sea and there can be quite a surge around the blinder in a big sea.

Average depth: 12m (40ft)

Maximum depth: 22m (73ft)

This is a lovely dive on the outer side of the rock or around the blinder, which breaks a few metres out to sea from the rock. There is a cave with a chimney at approximately 15m (50ft) and the reef is quite unspoiled as not too many people brave the long, cold and tiring swim out to this site.

The blinder is beautiful and plays host to anemones of varying pastel colours, many species of nudibranchs, plenty of crayfish. Shy octopuses can be found hiding in crevices and overhangs in the reef .

PORTABLE BC-POCKET FRIDGE

One of the advantages of diving in the icy Cape waters in the middle of summer is that you can put a can of your favourite beverage in your BC pocket. After a long swim and a hard climb back up to the road, an icy cold drink makes up for breathing all that dry air and takes the salt off your tongue.

Since the 15th century, the ships of many nations have sailed past this rugged and extensive coastline. Shipping casualties were frequent and shipwrecks represent an important source of historical information.

Details about how the vessel was built, the daily lives of the crew and passengers, cargo composition and even foods and medicines used aboard the ship provide new historical insights. These clues to the past can only be interpreted if a site is carefully investigated and the exact position of each artefact is accurately recorded.

In order to preserve the rich archaeological heritage which these wrecks represent, a maritime archaeological trust, Save our Shipwrecks (SOS), was founded towards the end of 1994.

The trust's main objective is to educate the diving and non-diving public on the importance of historical wrecks. One of its first projects is the development of a Shipwreck Route in and around the Cape Peninsula. It is intended to have both a land-based and an underwater component and will initially include the following wrecks:

The *Brunswick*, an 18th century wreck which will also form a part of the proposed underwater museum in Simon's Bay, the *Good Hope* (no. 24), as an example of a modern wreck, the *Maori* (no. 31), a rather abused wreck, the *Het Huis de Kraaiesteen* (no. 36), a favourite training dive, the *Seafarer* (no. 41), also a modern wreck, and the *Athens* (no. 42) off Moullie Point.

The initial development is likely to be the drawing up of a site map of the *Het Huis de Kraaiesteen*. This will be sold, together with a short history of the wreck, through dive shops and at the Maritime Museum.

*The Good Hope in 1983 (**above**) showed very little marine growth compared to seven years later (**below**).*

This dive is best done as an outing by swimming out to the site, diving and surfacing with about half your air left and then swimming to the flat rock where you can warm up in the sun for the long swim back. (You may have to shoo a few seals into the water but they usually leave when they see divers approaching.) After warming up it is less tiring to swim a compass course underwater most of the way back to shore and you could possibly see rays, cuttlefish or octopus en route. This site is only for fit, experienced divers and should not be dived in a group of less than four divers.

38 THE SCHUILENBERG (1756)

★★

Location: 33°56,20'S; 18°22,60'E, 30-50m (100-165ft) off Second Beach, Clifton. See map p. 140.
Access: Take the steps leading down to Second Beach, Clifton, keeping to the right. To the right of the steps, 20-30m (65-100ft) out to sea, is a small, round rock known to locals as Cherry Rock. Behind it is another flat rock which does not always protrude above the surface. The wreck site is directly behind the rocks towards the edge of the kelp beds.
Conditions: The sea has to be very flat as the wreck site is in the surf zone and the surge can be tremendous.
Average depth: 7m (23ft)
Maximum depth: 10m (33ft)
The *Schuilenberg* was wrecked on 3 June 1756 during a north-westerly gale, while carrying provisions from Table Bay to False Bay. All that identifies the wreck are three cast-iron cannon that are partly buried in sand. It is not a scenic dive but, because of the ship's age, spotting the cannon alone may be rewarding. Perlemoen may be taken, subject to permit, and the cannon are shallow enough to snorkel on.

A salvage permit has been awarded, but not much work has taken place so far and nothing of value has been found. Nothing may be removed from the wreck (on the off-chance that you might find something).

39 CLIFTON ROCKS

★★★★

Location: 33°56,38'S; 18°22,30'E, 75-100m (250-330ft) off Fourth Beach, Clifton. See map p. 140.
Access: Take the footpath between the bungalows leading to the big rocks on the south end of Fourth Beach. The easiest way to reach the entry point is to circle round to the left to get to the sand at the bottom. From there enter the sea from the rocks facing the cluster of huge boulders out to sea. The dive site is around the boulders

and involves a swim of about 75-100m (250-330ft). You can also swim from the beach if you are happy doing a surf entry (see p. 41).
Conditions: It is sheltered from even the strongest south-easterly winds.
Average depth: 10m (33ft)
Maximum depth: 15m (50ft)
The marine growth on and around the rock is colourful and the dense patches of kelp with masses of urchins give the sensation of diving in a forest. Crayfish are plentiful as this area falls within the sanctuary. Smaller fish such as hottentot are often seen.

As the dive is situated off one of the most popular and scenic beaches in the country, you can combine your dive with a pleasant beach outing. There is no lack of amenities; food and cold drinks are available at the shop and there are showers and toilets on Fourth Beach.

40 NORTH AND SOUTH LION'S PAWS

★★★★

Location: North Paw: 33°55,80'S; 17°21,90'E; South Paw: 33°56,25'S; 17°21,95'E. See map p. 140.
Access: This site is best reached by boat from the Municipal Slipway in Three Anchor Bay.
Conditions: Clear and very cold after a south-easter.
Maximum depth: North Paw 25m (80ft); South Paw 21m (69ft).
With a little imagination, these rocks resemble the paws of the lion of Lion's Head. This site is for the diver looking for something relatively deep, but is still close inshore and within a short distance of the launch sites. The two rock pinnacles are large at their bases, tapering to small islands just above the surface.

The sites are similar in appearance and make for colourful dives as the area is full of marine growth and literally crawling with crayfish. Hottentot are common and fishing boats are often seen in the area.

This beach is a favourite destination for day sailors from Hout Bay Yacht Club or the Royal Cape Yacht Club so, if you are invited for a sail, take your dive gear along.

41 THE SS SOUTH AFRICAN SEAFARER (1966)

★★★★

     R

Location: 33°53,80'S; 18°23,80'E, 50-75m (165-250ft) offshore slightly to the left of the Green Point lighthouse. See map p. 140.
Access: Slightly to the right of the car park behind the lighthouse are steps leading down to the wall. There is a concrete groyne jutting about 50m (165ft) into the sea which can be used as an entry and exit point but involves a difficult climb down and up the vertical face of the groyne. It is much easier to get there by boat launched from the Municipal slipway in Three Anchor Bay.
Conditions: This area was badly polluted when the Green Point sewerage pipeline broke in 1991 but is now safe to dive, although it is not wise to collect seafood in the area. Summer is the best time to dive as the south-easter clears the water.
Average depth: 5m (16ft)
Maximum depth: 8m (25ft)
This 8000 ton Safmarine freighter was wrecked during a north-westerly gale on 1 July 1966. Most of the cargo was lost when it broke up quickly and the sea bed resembles a junkyard, with the huge propeller shaft and countless unidentifiable machine parts lying around. Most of the non-ferrous fittings were removed shortly after the wrecking. All 63 crew members and 12 passengers were rescued by helicopter the following day.

The remains of a Greek cargo vessel, the *George M Livanos* (1947) and a steel screw barquentine, the *Thermopylae* (1899) lie close by. The *Thermopylae* was carrying £10 000 worth of gold specie, most of which was saved at the time.

42 THE RMS ATHENS (1865)

★★

     R

Location: 33°53,85'S; 18°24,57'E. See map p. 140.
Access: Follow Beach Road from Sea Point to Mouille Point past the Green Point lighthouse. Pass Fritz Sonnenberg Road on the right and look for the car park on the left. The wreck lies a little further west; its engine block can be seen approximately 75m (250ft) out to sea. It is easiest to approach by way of the parallel gullies leading to the site. This is a popular surf spot and is known somewhat inaccurately as 'Thermopylae' by local surfers, but don't let this confuse you.

Starfish surrounded by sea cucumbers on a sponge.

Conditions: This area was badly polluted when the Green Point sewerage pipeline broke in 1991 but is now safe to dive, although it is not wise to collect seafood in the area. Because of the shallow depth the surge can be quite strong.
Average depth: 5m (16m)
Maximum depth: 7m (23ft)
A clearly visible engine block marks the site of this mail steamer of the Union Steamship Co., which was wrecked during the great gale of 17 May 1865 with the loss of the whole crew of 29. They tried to steam out of the bay to escape the stormy weather but the heavy seas swamped the boiler fires and the ship drifted to its present site, breaking up rapidly when it hit the reef, with only the engine block to be seen the following day.

A few other wrecks such as the *Piscataqua* (1865) lie on top of the *Athens* and some cast-iron cannon can be found on the sea bed closer inshore.

Perlemoen may be collected in season when the water is unpolluted although this is not recommended. Crayfish are plentiful but the site falls within the crayfish sanctuary. This wreck and the more modern *Seafarer* will become part of the wreck route (see p. 147).

43 THE MV DAEYENG FAMILY (1986)

Location: 33°50,80'S; 18°22,90'E, on Whale Rock, just off Robben Island. See map p. 140.
Access: By boat from Cape Town harbour.
Conditions: Can be hazardous as there is tremendous suction through a gaping hole in the hull.
Average depth: 12m (40ft)
Maximum depth: 15m (50ft)
This wreck is worth diving if you are interested in modern wrecks, as it gives an idea of the enormous size of this moderate-sized ore tanker. It is not an easy dive, though, and is definitely not suitable for novices.

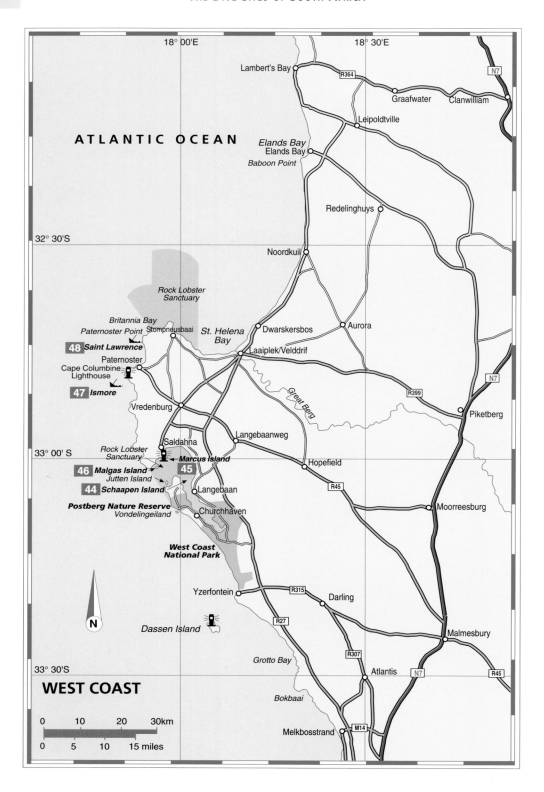

18° 00'E

18° 30'E

Lambert's Bay

R364

N7

Graafwater   Clanwilliam

Leipoldtville

ATLANTIC OCEAN

Elands Bay
Elands Bay
Baboon Point

Redelinghuys

32° 30'S

Noordkuil

Rock Lobster
Sanctuary

Aurora

Britannia Bay
Paternoster Point   Stompneusbaai
48 Saint Lawrence

St. Helena
Bay

Dwarskersbos

Laaiplek/Velddrif

Paternoster
Cape Columbine
Lighthouse
47 Ismore

Great Berg

R399

N7

Vredenburg

Piketberg

Langebaanweg

33° 00' S

Saldahna

Rock Lobster
Sanctuary
46 Malgas Island
        Jutten Island
44 Schaapen Island

Marcus Island
45

Langebaan

Hopefield

R45

Moorreesburg

Postberg Nature Reserve
Vondelingeiland

Churchhaven

West Coast
National Park

N

Yzerfontein

R315

Darling

R27

Dassen Island

R307

Atlantis   N7   R45

33° 30'S

Malmesbury

WEST COAST

Grotto Bay

Bokbaai

0   10   20   30km

0   5   10   15 miles

Melkbosstrand   M14

The West Coast

This wild and lonely stretch of coast is mostly dry and relatively inhospitable. The summer days are hot, but nights are cool. During winter the daytime temperatures are usually moderate with cool to very cold nights. It hardly ever rains. Sea temperatures are low throughout the year and readings range, on average, between 6 and 12°C (43–54°F). When diving here, adequate insulation in the form of a thick wetsuit, or even a dry suit, is necessary to prevent the possible quick onset of hypothermia.

These waters are extremely rich in fish of commercial importance and this is a popular sport angling destination. Spearfishing is not particularly rewarding, though, as the visibility is usually poor, due to the roughness of the sea. Crayfish are legion and many divers travel up here to collect these delicacies. Almost any spot outside of the reserves is worth diving; just look for a reasonably easy entry and start searching in the kelp beds. Don't forget to get a permit first, though.

There are many wrecks of historical significance but they are not well preserved or easy to dive as most of them are in, or just beyond, the very high energy surf zone. The protected waters of Langebaan Lagoon, most of which falls into the West Coast National Park, offer the most worthwhile scuba diving on the this coast.

In spring, one of nature's miracles takes place and this dull brown expanse of parched earth breaks out into a multi-coloured carpet of flowers stretching to the horizon. This is not to be missed. The rest of the year, though, most of this coast is attractive only to the few hardy souls who can appreciate its harsh beauty.

Most of the coast in the area north of Lamberts Bay falls within diamond diving concessions, so recreational diving is not allowed.

Sandy anemones, in various pastel colours, typically clustered together in the shallows.

The West Coast National Park

This sheltered natural harbour remained a low key settlement rather than developing into a major port due to the shortage of fresh water. It has grown recently with the development of the Saldanha Bay iron-ore terminal and is a major processing centre for rock lobster, anchovies, pilchards, fish meal and marine algae.

The small rocky outcrops of Malgas, Marcus, Meeu and Schaapen islands inside the bay all host thousands of birds that flock here during summer, some having undertaken the enormous journey from Siberia. These islands may only be visited by special arrangement with the National Parks Board.

In 1985 the entire Langebaan Lagoon, including the islands, was proclaimed the West Coast National Park in order to protect and maintain the considerable wealth of natural fauna and flora.

The water of Langebaan Lagoon is slightly warmer than that of the outside ocean due to the shallow water, averaging between 10 and 14°C (50-57°F) but the marine life is still typical of the West Coast.

Visibility averages between 3 and 15m (10-50ft). Vast forests of kelp proliferate in the nutrient-rich water and these are the habitat of large black mussel beds on which crayfish thrive. The rocky ocean floor hosts a variety of small, harmless sharks, octopuses and cuttlefish, sea and brittle stars, urchins and anemones.

The fish life consists mainly of small fish, such as hottentot, steentjie, mackerel, and mullet, with bigger varieties like kabeljou and galjoen at certain times of the year. Diving is best done in the morning as the wind comes up most afternoons when divers and non-divers alike can enjoy some excellent windsurfing or dinghy sailing; there are also long walks or horse trails in the area.

Tiny strawberry anemones are common in this region.

MARCUS ISLAND

★

Location: 33°02,70'S; 17°15,20'E. See map p. 150.
Access: By boat approximately 9 km (5.5 miles) from Langebaan, or 7km (4.5 miles) from Club Mykonos. Permission is needed from the Port Captain of Saldanha. Beware of passing boat traffic, including huge bulk ore carriers.
Conditions: The north-western side of the island is the most protected and diving is recommended here.
Average depth: 7m (23ft)
Maximum depth: 12m (40ft)
The reefs around the island are not very colourful and the marine life is dominated by sea cucumbers, dense mussel beds and masses of whelks and crayfish. The fish to be seen in the vicinity are not spectacular, and most are of the smaller varieties.

44 SCHAAPEN ISLAND

★★

Location: 33°05,60'S; 18°01,50'E, about 500m (⅓ mile) from Langebaan and about 5km (3 miles) from Club Mykonos. See map p. 150.
Access: Must be done as a boat dive as divers are not permitted to land on the island.
Conditions: Usually calm and clear.
Average depth: 2m (6ft)
Maximum depth: 8m (25ft)
The ocean floor in the vicinity of the island is rocky and extremly rich in marine growth such as sea anemones, urchins, starfish, cuttlefish and octopuses. A variety of small fish can be seen and it is a good site to dive if you want to learn to identify the more common species. The National Parks Board are presentlly mapping out an official snorkeling trail in this unique area.

46 MALGAS ISLAND

★

Location: 33°03,20'S; 17°55,60'E. See map p. 150.
Access: By boat about 14km (9 miles) from Langebaan, or 10km (6 miles) from Club Mykonos. Permission is needed from the Port Captain of Saldanha harbour, tel. (02281) 4 1726. Though shore dives are not recommended, they can be done if prior permission has been obtained from the National Parks Board. A flag Alpha must be flown as the island lies in the way of harbour traffic.
Conditions: The protected side of Malgas island, near the guano hut and jetty, offers the best diving conditions.
Average depth: 7m (23ft)
Maximum depth: 30m (100ft)
The rocky and kelp-covered bottom around the island is interspersed with wide stretches of sand, covered with

---

TRANSSEXUAL LIMPETS

The slipper limpet *(Crepidula porcellana)* displays an interesting reproductive strategy. They live on other, larger, molluscs and always form stacks. The first larva to settle will automatically become a female. The next larva will settle on top of the first and become a male. Subsequent larvae will settle on top of the pile and become male while those underneath change their sex to female, all being fertilized by the topmost individual.

---

swarms of brittle stars, creating an almost surreal landscape. The marine life is typically west coast with dense seaweed, sponges and redbait, and the fish are of the smaller variety, for example, hottentot The reefs are well stocked with crayfish but Malgas Island falls within the crayfish sanctuary and consequently they may not be removed or disturbed.

Paternoster

This quaint fishing village, with its whitewashed and thatched cottages, is very picturesque and is a popular destination for crayfishing trips. One of the better spots is the rather delightfully named 'Tietiesbaai' in the Cape Columbine Reserve. (Ask a local!)

Very keen wreck divers also trek up here to dive some of the interesting historical wrecks in the area. These are only recommended for real wreck aficionados as the diving is tricky, the wrecks are difficult to find, there is not much to see and what there is is scattered around on the sea bed. Those interested should contact Duncan at Orca Industries (see p. 155).

47 THE SS ISMORE (1899)

★

Location: 32°49,30'S; 17°50,70'E. See map p. 150.
Access: From Paternoster, the boat trip takes approximately 15 minutes, and from St Helena Bay, about 45 minutes, depending on conditions.
Conditions: Usually rough and murky.
Average depth: 10m (33ft)
Maximum depth: 15m (50ft)
A British four-masted steamer of almost 7500 tons carrying troops and horses on its maiden voyage from Liverpool to Table Bay, the *Ismore* was wrecked north of Cape Columbine on 3 December 1899. No human lives were lost, but most of the horses drowned. The wreck lies on a blinder and its broken up boilers can still be seen. There are also large, deformed sheets of steel which

make excellent photography props when the visibility is good. The appearance of the wreck site reminds one of the *Oakburn* (no. 30). Not much remains on the site.

48 SS SAINT LAWRENCE (1876)

★

Location: 32°44,50'S; 17°53,20'E. See map p. 150.
Access: From Paternoster, the boat trip takes approximately 15 minutes, and from St Helena Bay, about 45 minutes, depending on conditions.
Conditions: Usually rough and murky.
Average depth: 8m (25ft)
Maximum depth: 15m (50ft)
The *Saint Lawrence* was an iron steam troopship wrecked on Great Paternoster Point on 8 November 1876 on a voyage to Cape Town with troops and a cargo of nine mountain guns on board. No lives were lost during the wrecking of the ship and the guns were not recovered. The two boilers still remain on the site, together with the propeller and shaft. There is also old ammunition around.

Some garlic butter, a bottle of wine, and this is lunch.

HOW TO GET THERE

By road, train and air: Cape Town is served by an international airport and is well serviced by train and bus from Johannesburg, Durban and the east coast. The eastern shore of False Bay is about an hour's drive away; take the N2 and then the Gordon's Bay turn-off. The West Coast stretches north of Cape Town and is reached by following the R27 coastal road.

WHERE TO STAY

METROPOLITAN CAPE TOWN
Although this area comprises three different diving regions, it is small enough for divers to stay anywhere in the city and still have access to dive sites. Contact the **Cape Town Visitors' Accommodation and Services**, P O Box 6969, Roggebaai 8012, tel. (021) 685 7878, fax (021) 685 7889, an agency for privately owned accommodation in the Cape Peninsula and coastal districts, which will be able to give you good advice on where to stay. Probably the most comfortable and elegant hotel in town is the luxurious five-star **Mount Nelson**, tel. (021) 23 1000, where guests will certainly be pampered. The **Breakwater Lodge**, tel. (021) 406 1911, is built around a renovated jail but the rooms are comfortable. It offers reasonably priced accommodation right in the very fashionable V & A Waterfront. The **Gardens Centre Holiday Flats** in Mill Street, Gardens, tel. (021) 461 5827, has centrally situated, fully furnished, equipped and serviced flats. Those on a much tighter budget will find many very reasonably priced backpackers hostels from which to choose. **Zebra Crossing**, 82 New Church St, tel. (021) 22 1265, and **Cloudbreak**, 219 Upper Buitenkant St, Vredehoek, tel. (021) 461 6892, are two of the many. Enquire at the Hostelling International desk (see p, 155) or consult *BUG* (see p. 21) for more.

FALSE BAY EASTERN SHORE
The three-star **Van Riebeeck Hotel** in Gordon's Bay, tel. (024) 561 441, is on Beach Road right opposite the main swimming beach. The **Hendon Park Holiday Resort,** also in Gordon's Bay,

tel. (024) 56 2321/71, is very big and offers camping, caravan stands and self-catering chalets right on the seafront.

FALSE BAY WESTERN SHORE
Strange as it may sound, there are no hotels on this coast, but there are a number of pleasant bed and breakfast establishments. **Castle Hill**, 37 Gatesville Rd, Kalk Bay, tel. (021) 788 2554, has a magnificent view of the bay and offers comfortable and elegant accommodation in three *en suite* rooms and two rooms with private, but separate, bathrooms. **Bosky Dell on Boulders Beach**, 5 Grant Ave, The Boulders, Simon's Town, tel. (021) 786 3906 or 23 1818, is situated on one of the prettiest and most sheltered beaches along this coast. It offers comfortable accommodation in the main house or in three self-contained appartments. The **Blue Lantern Holiday Cabins**, Main Road, Froggy Pond, also in Simon's Town, has 12 self-contained and fully equipped cabins which sleep two to six people. They are about 2km (1.25 miles) from the centre of Simon's Town and are close to the sea. Tel. (021) 786 2113 for more details. **The Breakers** in Main Road, St James, tel. (021) 788 1902, is a comfortable guest house overlooking False Bay. The **Seaside Cottages**, almost on Fish Hoek beach, are self-contained, fully equipped cottages. To book, contact P O Box 22286, Fish Hoek 7975, tel. (021) 782 5128. Those on a very tight budget can opt for the **Abe Bailey Youth Hostel**, 11 Maynard Road, Muizenberg, tel. (021) 788 2301.

WESTERN PENINSULA
The Bay Hotel, tel. (021) 438 4444, fax (021) 438 4455 / 33, offers five-star luxury right opposite Camps Bay Beach on Victoria Drive. **Monkey Valley Beach Nature Resort**, tel. (021) 789 1143, Mountain Road, Noordhoek, is set in a magnificent Milkwood forest overlooking Noordhoek Beach. An RCI-affiliated time-share resort, accommodation is provided in attractive wooden chalets. **Flora Bay Resort** on Chapmans Peak Drive in Hout Bay, are self-contained flats, maisonettes and bungalows on the mountainside with magnificent views overlooking the bay, tel. (021) 790 1650 or fax (021) 790 1650. Also in Hout Bay

is the **Hout Bay Beach House** in Royal Avenue, tel. (021) 790 4228.

WEST COAST
Club Mykonos, tel. (02287) 2101 is a RCI-affiliated time-share Mediterranean-style resort on Langebaan Lagoon. A comfortable and unusual accommodation option is to hire a *Leisureliner* or keelboat from Club Mykonos. There is a **Municipal Camp Site** in the town, tel. (02287) 2 2115 / 6 / 7 and the **Langebaan Lodge**, tel. (02287) 2 2144, offers accommodation in comfortable chalets.
  The **Paternoster Hotel**, tel. (02285) 703, is an unpretentious sea-side country hotel. The **Tietiesbaai Camping Resort** in the Cape Columbine Nature Reserve, tel. (02285) 718, offers beach-front camping.

WHERE TO EAT

METROPOLITAN CAPE TOWN
There are many restaurants in this area, mostly clustered together in the V & A Waterfront, Main Road Sea Point, Rondebosch or Lower Main Road, Observatory. For something a little out of the ordinary and with a local flavour, try one of the following: **Africa Cafe**, Lower Main Road, Observatory, tel. (021) 47 9553, offers cuisine from the whole continent. **Biesmiellah**, tel (021)23 0850, is situated in the historic Bo-Kaap and offers traditional Malay cooking. Booking is essential and no alcohol is allowed. **Kaapse Tafel** offers traditional Cape cuisine in an elegant setting, tel (021) 23 1651. At the top end of the market, **Buitenverwachting**, tel. (021)794 3522, serves superb food in a splendid setting on a wine farm in the Constantia Valley. Excellent and reasonably priced pub lunches can be had at **Foresters Arms**, Newlands Avenue, Newlands, tel. (021) 689 5949, while **Quay 4** and **The Ferrymans** are just two of the many pubs in the V & A Waterfront which serve delicious pub fare. The **Dias Tavern Pizzeria**, 15 Harrington Street, Cape Town, tel. (021) 45 7547, serves Portuguese fare and seafood in a vibrant atmosphere. They often have live music in the evenings, as does the ever popular **Hard Rock Restaurant**, located at 28 Main Road, Rondebosch, tel. (021) 689 1211.

FALSE BAY EASTERN SHORE
The Gazebo, tel. (024) 56 2676, is right on Beach Road in Gordon's Bay. It is light and airy and very popular. **Port Gordon** in the Gordonia Building, also in Beach road, tel. (024) 56 2299, is somewhat more upmarket. It is an intimate restaurant with an innovative menu featuring vegetarian dishes, seafood and grills.

FALSE BAY WESTERN SHORE
The **Natale Labia Museum Coffee Shop**, on Main Road, Muizenberg, tel. (021) 788 4106, is conveniently situated for an after-dive light meal and offers wonderful breakfasts, teas and lunches. It's closed on Mondays. **Gaylords Eastern Cafe**, also in Main Road Muizenberg, tel. (021) 788 5470 to book, offers marvellous northern Indian curries, including a number of seafood and vegetarian options. In Kalk Bay, the **Brass Bell**, on the station and overlooking the sea, is best known for its seafood and informal Sunday afternoon open-air fish barbeques, accompanied by mellow jazz music, tel. (021) 788 5456. **Seaforth Restaurant**, on Seaforth Beach, Simon's Town, serves excellent Italian and seafood meals. The restaurant has a fantastic sea view and a cosy atmosphere. Tel. (021) 786 1659 to book.

WESTERN PENINSULA
This coast is much more fashionable than the eastern side of the peninsula. **La Med Restaurant and Tapas Bar**, at the Glenn Country Club, tel. (021) 438 5600, is a popular watering hole with wonderful sea views. Paraglider and hang-glider pilots drop in from time to time. **Blues**, Victoria Road, Camps Bay, tel. (021) 438 2040 to book, has a lovely view of Camps Bay beach. It serves delicious, well presented Californian cuisine, and i's the ideal place for a sundowner. The **Chapmans Peak Hotel**, Main Rd, Hout Bay, tel. (021) 790 1036, is well known for it's speciality in seafood. It has a cosy restaurant or you can enjoy lunch on the balcony with a magnificent view of Hout Bay and the mountain.

WEST COAST
Muisbosskerm is a must for anyone keen on seafood. It offers a very informal *al fresco* seafood buffet on the beach, tel. (027) 43 1017. Booking is essential.

FALSE BAY EASTERN SHORE
Ocean Divers International, tel. (024) 56 2952, offer courses, air fills and gear rental and sales. They take charters to the local dive sites.

METROPOLITAN CAPE TOWN
Orca Industries, Claremont Medical Centre, Main Road, Claremont 7700, tel. (021) 61 9673, offer all diving related services and can organize wreck diving excursions to the West Coast.
Two Ocean Divers, Victoria Drive, Camps Bay, tel. (021) 438 9317, and **Underwater World** and their subsidiary **Two Oceans Diving Academy**, Zero House, Wicht Close, Cape Town 8001, tel. (021) 461 5500 or 461 8290, also offer all services. **Iain's Scuba School**, P O Box 1331, Sea Point 8060, tel. (021) 439 9322, based at Atlantic Underwater Club, offer charters and courses ranging from beginner's to nitrox and skippers courses. **Aquasport**, SA Adventure Centre, 48A Strand Street, Cape Town 8001, tel. (021) 419 1835 and **Flipper Services**, P O Box 26839, Hout Bay 7872, tel. (021) 790 7500 offer courses and charters. **Blueprint Diving**, have a branch in Cape Town, Shop 5, Quay Five, V & A Waterfront, tel. (021) 418 5806, and offer all services.
Underwater Video Services will make a professional video of your dives in Cape Town or anywhere else in the region, tel. Charles Maxwell at (021) 75 4100 for more information.

METROPOLITAN CAPE TOWN
There is so much to do and see here, but a cable-car trip up **Table Mountain,** a drive to **Cape Point** and a visit to the **V & A Waterfront** are a must. Don't miss a visit to the Two Oceans Aquarium in the Waterfront. The Cape is well known for its excellent and relatively inexpensive wines. Wine-tasting trips can be undertaken independently or as a guided tour.
A rather novel way of exploring the winelands is by canoe. Contact **Felix Unite River Adventures**, tel. (021) 762 6935, or on horseback, tel. **Wine Valley Horse Trails**, tel. (021) 981 6331, or in a

hot-air balloon, contact **Wineland Ballooning**, tel. (02211) 4138, to book.

WEST COAST
The flowers in spring are wonderful and the **Cederberg Mountains** offer magnificent wilderness hiking, tel. (027) 482 2812, to book.

National Parks Board, P O Box 787 Pretoria 0001, tel. (012) 343 1991 or P O Box 7400, Roggebaai 8012, tel (021) 22 2810.
National Hiking Way Board, Private Bag X447, Pretoria 0001, tel. (012) 310 3839 (for booking hiking trails).
Western Cape Nature Conservation, tel. (021) 948 7490, fax (021) 948 8640.
Captour, in the Tourist Rendezvous Building near the station in Adderley Street, Cape Town 8001, tel. (021) 418 5214, provides information about the whole Cape and organizes bookings.
The Tourist Rendezvous, same address as Captour, tel. (021) 418 5222, carry information on the whole country.
Hostelling International South Africa, tel. (021) 419 1853, also in the Tourist Rendezvous Building, offers information for budget travellers.
West Coast Publicity Association, tel. (022281) 4 2088 / 58, for detailed information on this area.

Recompression facilities are available at the SAS *Simonsberg*, tel. (021) 787 4682, or contact IMM (see below).
Institute for Maritime Medicine (IMM), tel. (021) 786 2920 or (after hours) (021) 787 3821.
There are a number of **hospitals** in the south-western Cape:
Groote Schuur, Cape Town tel. (021) 404 9111
Somerset Hospital, Green Point tel. (021) 402 6911
Victoria Hospital, Wynberg tel. (021) 797 8131
Constantiaberg Medi-Clinic, tel. (021) 799 2911
DivEvac Emergency Number: (011) 403 7080 or toll-free (0800) 02 0111
General Emergency Number: 10 111
Ambulance: 10 177

INLAND DIVE SITES

Most of the diving in southern Africa is carried out in the oceans, but there are many divers who do their qualifying dive courses inland. Fortunately, there are some exciting and worthwhile dive sites in the interior, so if you find yourself inland, the following dives should give you an opportunity to get wet and the chance to experience diving with a difference. Inland dives are mostly very deep and may contain caves or overhangs, so plan your dives carefully and, preferably, dive with a knowledgeable local. The water is often clearer than that of the average sea dive and there are none of the usual hazards like kelp or heavy surge, but these sites have their own peculiar hazards.

The dives outlined here are all at altitude and adjustments must always be made. If you intend driving to Johannesburg after the dive, please note that Johannesburg's altitude is some 2000m (6600ft) above sea level. It is important to note that you should not dive for at least 24 hours after arriving from sea level, and don't forget to allow sufficient surface interval before changing altitude in any way.

Apart from these more accessible and popular dive sites described here, there are others that offer an incredible dive experience, but these are either very deep or situated deep in caves, and do not fit into the sport diving category. If you are particularly interested in this type of diving, contact either the South African Speleological Association, P O Box 4812, Cape Town 8000, or the Cave Diving Club of South Africa, P O Box 2411, Cresta 2118; they will be able to provide you with more information.

There are also many diveable dams in the interior and though the visibility may not be what ocean, cave and lake divers are used to, they do offer the chance to get wet. Many dam dives require permits and it is recommended that interested divers contact the Department of Water Affairs and Nature Conservation. Diveable dams include the Ebenezer Dam, Tzaneen Dam, Klaserie Dam, Ohrigstad Dam, Blyde Dam and Jonkmansspruit, near Hoedspruit in the Eastern Transvaal.

*Although some sunlight penetrates the water (**above**), it becomes darker with depth and a torch is thus essential. Surrounded by weathered rock formations, Wondergat (**left**) contains a cave extending to unknown depths.*

1 WONDERGAT

★★

Location: Within the triangle formed by Lichtenburg, Zeerust and Mafikeng in the North-West.

Access: The roads are in good condition and the entire journey should not take much more than three-and-a-half hours from Johannesburg. The Lichtenberg Sub-Aqua Club have built steps down to the water's edge, making entries and exits fairly easy.

Conditions: Can be dived at any time of the year and visibility is best in winter, but summer is the most popular season, when daytime surface temperatures often get rise to the mid-thirties. Visibility is usually between 10 and 20m (33-65ft) and the water temperature about 14-18°C (57-65°F). The bottom is covered in thick silt, which can be easily stirred up, reducing visibility to zero. Wondergat is 1500m (5000ft) above sea level.

There are many overhangs and a deep cave. This must be considered a hazardous dive and should not be attempted by novices. Many divers have lost their lives here due to inadequate training or dive planning.

Average depth: Anything from 8-40m (25-130ft) at the entrance to the cave, but can vary as much as 15m (50ft) between dry and wet seasons as the water level changes.

Maximum depth: Wondergat has been dived to 70m (230ft) at the furthest accessible reaches of the cave. The cave extends to unknown depths.

The surface of the pool is approximately 75x100m (250x330ft) and it is surrounded by weathered rock formations. From the surface the water appears black and forbidding but it takes on a greenish-grey colour below, with some sunlight reflecting off the rocky walls. It becomes darker with depth and it is essential to take a torch below 30m (100ft).

In the shallows, small freshwater fish can be found and barbel swarm around some of the smaller, shallower caverns. Crabs are also found and freshwater shrimps are easily spotted at night.

At approximately 40m (130ft), the ominous mouth of the large cave looms. It tilts down at an angle of approximately 30° and is about 50m (165ft) long. The bottom is covered in thick silt and care must be taken not to disturb it as this will reduce visibility to zero. The cave should be entered only by experienced cave divers with a swim line.

One of the more interesting dives here is 'Wagon Wheels', a large, flat, horizontal overhang with big and small circular formations. Local divers practise 'moon-walking' here. Take off your fins, handing them to your buddy, while remaining safely under the overhang inflate your BC (buoyancy compensator) to achieve positive buoyancy. You can then walk upside down on the 'crater-pocked surface', experiencing something very close to weightlessness. This is quite a disorientating feeling and is only recommended for very experienced divers.

Wondergat may be linked to the Sterkfontein Caves in the western Transvaal, about 200km (125 miles) away, an eerie and exciting prospect.

Badgat's placid surface conceals a warren of underground tunnels (campsite and access steps in the background).

Many inland dive sites require specialized equipment and extremely detailed pre- and post-dive planning.

BADGAT

★★

Location: On the farm Sterkspruit, approximately 25km (15 miles) from Badplaas in the Eastern Transvaal.

Access: Contact the farm owner, Lourens Swanepoel, tel. (01344) 41077, for directions to the farm. It is advisable to dive this site with knowledgeable local divers. A fee must be paid for each person in the party and divers must sign an indemnity form. Concrete and steel steps lead down to the water's edge.

Conditions: Warmest in summer, with temperatures ranging from 18°C (65°F) at depth to 24°C (75°F) at the surface. In winter it can be as low as 14°C (57°F) at the surface and 10°C (50°F) at depth. Average visibility is 5-8m (16-25ft), improving with depth. It is about 1100m (3600ft) above sea level. The trip back to Johannesburg requires travelling over a mountain pass of about 2500m (8000ft) so pre- and post-dive planning is essential.

Maximum depth: 55m (180ft) in the main hole, varying with the seasons, but some of the shafts are very deep indeed. The hole is a 180x120m (600x400ft) oval-shaped, disused open-cast asbestos mine that was flooded in 1985. It was previously known as The Badplaas Chrysolite Asbestos Mine.

There are a number of overhangs, caves and mine shafts leading off the main hole between about 9 and 25m (30 and 80ft). The caves can be very disorientating and the shafts lead to vertical shafts which, in turn, lead to more horizontal shafts, veritably a warren of disused, sometimes unstable, passages. Only experienced cave divers should consider entering any of these holes as they

can appear deceptively benevolent from the entrance. When doing a night dive, or diving in low visibility, a SMB must be used to prevent accidentally entering one of the caves or shafts. To date, the only fatality in this spot was caused in this way. Other than algae, there is not much water life. The visibility is surprisingly good and improves with depth where no algae grows.

3 BASS LAKE

★★

Location: Henley on Klip, approximately 40km (25 miles) from Johannesburg.

Access: You must pay an entrance fee at the gate. Access to the water is a simple walk down a shallow slope.

Conditions: The water is usually clean. Summer visibility ranges from 6-10m (20-33ft) and in winter it can be over 20m (65ft). There is often a thermocline at about 10m (33ft). It is just under 1500m (5000ft) above sea level.

Average depth: Whatever you want as there are convenient ledges going down in stages.

Maximum depth: 24m (80ft)

This disused quarry is a very popular inland training venue and is also used for scuba-orienteering competitions. This is a fun and sociable dive venue. Divers often make a day's outing of it, or even camp overnight.

Local divers have turned the quarry into an underwater amusement park. There are training grids at 6 and 9m (20 and 30ft), a bus, a home-made submarine (it did work!), an aeroplane and two cars underwater. Topside there is a small shop offering air fills and equipment sales.

Inland dives are usually very deep, many contain caves, and the water is often clearer than that of the sea.

HOW TO GET THERE

WONDERGAT

Take the R24 from Johannesburg through Krugersdorp and Ventersdorp to Lichtenburg and then to Mafikeng. Turn right at the 'Mafikeng/Buhrmansdrif' signpost, approximately 24km (15 miles) from Mafikeng. Turn right again after 6km (4 miles) to Slurry/Molopo-Oog and right again onto a little dirt road after 4,2km (2.5 miles) exactly. It is a few hundred metres to the gate where an entrance fee is levied. The total distance from Johannesburg is about 286km (172 miles).

BADGAT

Directions can be obtained from Lourens and Maryke Swanepoel, tel. (01344) 41077, who own the farm.

BASS LAKE

Take the R26 south from Johannesburg, go left at the Blesbok offramp and, after about 2km (1.25 miles), turn left at the stop street. Carry on (the road becomes a dirt road) until you reach the gate where an entrance fee is levied.

WHERE TO STAY

WONDERGAT

There is a camp site at Wondergat with ablution blocks, but not much else. Close by on the outskirts of Mmabatho and Mafikeng is the **Mmabatho Sun**, P O Box 600, Mafikeng 8670, tel. (0140) 89 1111, a comfortable Sun International Hotel. **Cookes Lake Holiday Resort**, Private Bag X2078, Mmabatho, 8681, tel. (0140) 81 2601, is situated on the shores of Cookes Lake, 1km (2/8 mile) from Mafikeng, and has caravan stand with full ablutions.

BADGAT

Camping is available on Badgat farm itself, offering comfortable sites with clean ablutions. In Badplaas, 25km (15 miles) away, is **Aventura Badplaas**, P O Box 720, Groenkloof 0027, tel. (012) 346 2288. This resort is built around a mineral bath at the foot of the Hlumuhllumu Mountains which offers hotel and self-catering accommodation, as well as caravan and tent sites with full ablutions.

BASS LAKE

You may camp at the lake, but you have to pay for the whole weekend on arrival. There are flush toilets and cold-water showers available.

WHERE TO EAT

WONDERGAT

The nearest shops and restaurants are in Mafikeng. It is wise to bring all your own supplies.

BADGAT

There is a small farm shop which sells basic supplies, firewood and ice. Otherwise bring your own provisions.

BASS LAKE

The little dive shop, which, at time of writing, is due to expand, sells substantial snacks and cold drinks. It is a good idea to bring your own supplies.

DIVE FACILITIES

Recommended training facilities and dive outlets in the Gauteng area are:
Bass Lake Scuba, tel. (016) 66 0133 or (083) 250 4385, have a shop at Bass Lake. It offers air fills, and sells, services and hires equipment. A full cylinder testing facility is planned.
Blueprint Diving, tel. (011) 432 2573, has a concession at Sodwana Bay.
Ocean Divers International, Pretoria, tel. (012) 342 1782 / 3, does regular trips to Wondergat.
BOING, (Breathers of Oxygen, Inert and Nitrox Gases), tel. Drew Grey (011) 320 8443, or Mike Bailey, tel. (011) 636 7952, consists of a group of divers who regularly do mixed gas dives and often visit Badgat. Suitably experienced divers can contact them for information .
Aquadisiacs, 1st floor, Library Centre, Fir Drive, Northcliff, tel. (011) 476 6287.
Bud & Cathy's Scuba Academy, 22 Wagenaar Road, Edenglen, Edenvale, tel. (011) 609 6924.
The Dive & Watersports Shop, 376 Jan Smuts Avenue, Craighall, tel. (011) 326 3213.
The Dive Shop, Lower Floor, L47, Sandton City, tel. (011) 884 6115.
Africa Coastal Diving, Shop 17, Giftacres, Garden City, Lynnwood Avenue, Pretoria, tel. (012) 807 1930.

Scuba City, cnr. Bond & Vale streets, Ferndale, Randburg, tel. (011) 789 5693.
Delta Diving, 4 Village Centre, 47 Esselen Street, Sunnyside, Pretoria, tel. (012) 341 2066.

REGIONAL HIGHLIGHTS

LICHTENBURG

Lichtenburg's **nature reserve** which serves as a breeding centre for the National Zoological Gardens. It is home to 35 species of mammal: among its more exotic species are the scimitar oryx, pygmy hippo, Indian water-buffalo, Hartmann's mountain zebra and Pere David and axis deer. The reserve also has a cheetah enclosure and a large variety of waterbird. Tel. (01441) 2 2818 for more details or to book a camp site.

INFORMATION AND BOOKING

National Parks Board, P O Box 787, Pretoria, 0001, tel. (012) 343 1991, or P O Box 7400, Roggebaai 8012, tel. (021) 22 2810.
National Hiking Way Board, Private Bag X447, Pretoria 0001, tel. (012) 310 3839 (for booking hiking trails).

EMERGENCY NUMBERS

Recompression facilities are available at the **Institute for Aviation Medicine** (IAM), tel. (012) 664 5954. The **South African Police Services Task Force** has a chamber on a low-bed trailer. It is usually in Pretoria but it is sometimes at Wondergat, Badgat or wherever they happen to be diving. Tel. toll-free 0800 11 07 08 and ask for code 7276. They will contact the chamber whereever it is and the operator will phone you back.
DivEvac Emergency Number: (011) 403 7080 or toll-free 0800 02 01 11
General Emergency Number: 10 111
Ambulance: 10 177

WONDERGAT

The nearest **hospital** is at Mafikeng, 30km (20 miles) away, tel. (0140) 81 2043. There is also a hospital at Lichtenburg; turn right at the first intersection into Lichtenburg from Wondergat. The hospital is a few hundred metres further on, on the left, tel. (01441) 2 3041.

THE MARINE ENVIRONMENT

Marine Conservation in South Africa

The underwater environment off the coast of South Africa is one of the richest and most diverse in the world, ranging from the coral reefs of Maputaland to the icy-cold kelp forests of the Cape. The transitional areas between these extremes contain many endemic species.

Much of the marine life found in these habitats is being commercially exploited, utilized in a subsistence fashion or, in some cases, even recklessly plundered. Although pristine areas still remain, many regions are quite visibly degraded as a result of these and other pressures.

Many marine organisms, including corals and other reef invertebrates, shellfish, reef fish and even pelagic fish, are slow-growing; if injured or removed they may require years to recover or be replaced.

Hazards to the Marine Environment
In the natural course of events, storm-driven waves may cause destruction of reefs, a process which is particularly common in coral reefs in the cyclone belt, and the silt load from flooding rivers may smother, and sometimes even totally destroy, reefs near their mouths. Many human activities are similarly destructive, especially pollution, blast fishing and the indiscriminate collection of shells and corals to sell as marine curios.

Overfishing, too, is a deadly hazard to reef environments, and has already led to perilously declining populations of target species in some areas. This, like any environmental imbalance, can cause grave damage; for example, decreasing the populations of herbivorous fish can lead to an explosive increase in the algae on which those species feed, which may cause corals and other invertebrates on the reef to be smothered or overgrown.

Some areas are also being damaged by pollution, especially where reefs occur close to large centres of human population. Corals and other reef creatures are sensitive to dirty, sediment-laden water, and are at risk of being smothered when silt settles on the ocean floor. Sewerage, nutrients from agricultural fertilizers and other organic or inorganic materials washed into the sea, may

encourage the growth of one or more species of fauna or flora over others, thus potentially altering the delicate balance of offshore reefs.

Areas particularly at risk in South Africa include one of the most beautiful subtropical reefs in the country, the Aliwal Shoal, which is subject to industrial effluent from the SAICCOR pulp plant. Although many surveys have been conducted and the authorities insist that this effluent has no detrimental effect on the reef, divers and marine scientists are concerned that this will not prove to be the case. Areas around large urban concentrations are subject to sewerage outfall, despite the outcry of concerned conservationists, civic rights organizations, scientists and recreational users of the marine environment.

Divers and the Marine Environment
Although, as divers, we simply wish to enjoy ourselves and are, as a rule, conscious of conservation issues and take steps to reduce any deleterious effects of our presence, tourism and development in general have created many problems for the underwater environment. Harbours, jetties and sea walls are, on occasion, built so close to reefs – sometimes even on top of them – that the environment is drastically altered, and populations of reef organisms plummet. Hotels, seaside homes and resorts are often built on dunes, thereby necessitating stabilization, and thus destroying the natural cycle of beach erosion and build-up.

Visiting boats often damage the underwater environment through inadvertent grounding or careless or unconcerned anchoring, and divers themselves, once they get in the water, may cause damage as they move about on the reef.

Although divers, as well as many dive operators and resort management teams, have been at the forefront of the move to protect reefs and marine ecosystems, we all need somewhere to eat and sleep and, no matter how hard we try, we will have an impact on the environments through which we pass. We should try, however, to minimize the negative and maximize the positive impact.

Sodwana Bay is widely accepted as being the mecca of diving in South Africa. Beautiful thistle soft coral (left) provides a colourful backdrop for a shoal of goldies.

Ecotourism

Growing awareness of environmental issues has given rise to the still somewhat nebulous concept of 'ecotourism'. The main underlying principle is often summarized as 'take nothing but photographs, leave nothing but footprints' which, in the diving context can be translated to 'take nothing but photographs, leave nothing but bubbles'. This definition is not complete, though, as it is inevitable that we will make an impact on the environments in which we live and dive. A much more constructive way to think of ecotourism is in terms of managing tourism, and the tourists themselves, in such a way as to make the industry ecologically, financially, socially and politically sustainable.

In order to achieve this end, try to spend your money with local dive operators and support local businesses, especially small ones. Avoid spending money with operators who do not have some commitment to the area and the local community.

Local Communities

If the people who live in an area, many of whom may represent generations-old local families, do not benefit directly from tourism, they will have no incentive to care for the environment. On the contrary, they will see the benefits of their home territory going to outsiders and will resent arbitrary restrictions on their utilization of local resources. Put simply, you cannot tell a local fisherman with a family to feed that he should not catch certain species of fish, or even turtles, if he has no income. He will, and rightly so, perceive that he is being asked to let his family go hungry so that the rich tourists can look at the fish. Clearly, this is not a sustainable situation.

Individuals

In such discussions of ecotourism we are looking at the larger scale. It is all too easy to forget that 'tourists' and 'divers' are not amorphous groups but collections of individuals, with individual responsibilities and capable of making individual decisions. Keeping reefs ecologically sustainable depends as much on each one of us as it does on the dive and resort operators.

Conservation as a Way of Life

A vacation to a pristine environment (and that's what every dive is) should serve to remind us of the need for conservation in our daily lives. Conservation is an attitude which we can nurture by approaching everyday decisions in a thoughtful way. Concerned divers should, therefore, consider the effect their day-to-day lifestyle has on the marine environment, even if they live thousands of miles from the sea.

Energy

A major threat to the marine environment in South Africa is spillage from oil tankers, as a large proportion of the world's oil is transported around the Cape. In winter, these tankers may encounter violent storms and, if

wrecked, spill thousands of tons of crude oil into the ocean to the severe detriment of seabirds and other marine life. Consider, therefore, your everyday use of the limited energy resources of our planet.

Plastic

Another major threat to marine environments worldwide, is the indiscriminate use of plastic packaging. Very often this is not properly disposed of or, even if it is, the refuse disposal authorities in many cities in the world do not take sufficient care that dumps are sited where refuse cannot be blown away. Any litter or refuse which is not properly disposed of is quite likely to end up in the storm-water drain system. This will take it to the nearest river and hence to the sea. Turtles, one of the most popular and endangered inhabitants of tropical reefs, are at great risk of being killed by plastic litter. They mistake floating plastic for jellyfish and eat it. Please, therefore, be aware of your use of packaging and vote with your wallet by refusing to buy overpackaged products, and, where possible, avoid the use of plastic carrier-bags. Make recycling a habit and campaign for recycling centres in your community.

Seafood

Remember, too, that the frozen fish so neatly packaged in the supermarket, pet food, the fish meal to feed battery chickens, and the shellfish in that fancy restaurant, all came from the sea.

Many of the methods of commercial fishing operators are suspect, to say the least. Gill nets are probably the most well known culprits; these invisible nets float in the open ocean, stretching for miles (yes, miles). All marine life, including non-target species such as turtles, dolphins and small whales, get caught in these 'walls of death', struggle for a while and then, exhausted, drown. Some large-scale shrimp fishing boats indiscriminately destroy whole sections of the ocean floor and fishing companies will gladly deplete a productive fishing ground knowing that, if they don't, a rival company will. The same goes for shellfish such as lobster (crayfish), perlemoen (abalone), clams and oysters.

No-one would suggest that you cease to consume the products of the sea but, if you are truly concerned about the environment in which you dive, be a concerned and informed consumer. Try to put pressure on suppliers of marine products to disclose the source and means of capture of the organisms they process and market. Many people are already putting pressure on companies who operate gill nets by eating only 'dolphin-friendly' tuna; their example is to be lauded and followed. One can only hope that some control is maintained over the use of such labels, and you have the right to query such use.

And finally ...

This may all sound rather extreme but you don't have to rush out and join Greenpeace. Just be aware that your actions, every day, not just when you dive, count.

Some Tips on Responsible Diving

Here are just some of the ways in which you, as a diver, can help preserve the reefs that have given you so much:

• Try not to touch living marine organisms with either your body or your diving equipment. Be particularly careful to control your fins, as their size and the force of kicking can damage the reef. Don't use deep fin-strokes near the reef because the surge of water can disturb delicate organisms. It may not look elegant but, when you are close to the reef, especially in a gulley, it is best to keep your feet still and propel yourself along by making small swimming strokes with your hands until you are clear of the reef.

• Look behind you to see if your console is dragging across the reef and, if it is, hold it in your hand or tuck it into your BC or weight belt.

• Learn the skills of good buoyancy control – divers descending too rapidly or crashing into the living reef while trying to adjust their buoyancy may cause irreparable harm. Make sure you are properly weighted and learn to achieve neutral buoyancy.

• If you haven't dived for a while, practise your skills, especially buoyancy control, in a pool or in a relatively barren area which is devoid of delicate organisms, such as a sandy spot near the reefs.

• Avoid kicking up sand. Clouds of sand settling on the reef can smother corals and other invertebrates. Snorkellers should be careful not to kick up sand when treading water in shallow reef areas.

• Never stand on corals, however robust they may seem. Living polyps are easily injured by even the slightest touch. Never pose for pictures by standing inside giant basket sponges or barrel sponges. Even the apparently robust local orange 'wall' sponges can be harmed by careless contact.

• If you are out of control and about to collide with the reef, steady yourself with your fingertips on exposed rock, a part of the reef which is already dead, or on one of the more robust algaes (the more common kelp in the Cape is particularly rugged).

• Unless you are sufficiently experienced to ensure that you don't injure the reef inhabitants, don't dive when there is strong surge.

• If you need to adjust your mask or any other part of your diving equipment, try to do so in a sandy area well away from the reef.

• Don't collect or buy shells, corals or any other marine souvenirs, and be very particular about where, when and from whom you buy seafood or any marine products.

• On any excursion, whether it is with an operator or privately organized, make sure you take your garbage back for proper disposal on land, and please remember to pick up any litter that you may find.

• Take great care in underwater caverns and caves. Avoid crowding into the cave, and don't stay there too long; your air bubbles collect in pockets on the roof of the cave, and delicate creatures living there could possibly 'drown in air'.

• Don't feed fish. It may seem harmless but it can upset their normal feeding patterns, provoke aggressive behaviour and be unhealthy for them if you give them food that is not part of their normal diet.

• Don't move marine organisms around to photograph or play with them. In particular, don't hitch rides on turtles: it causes them considerable stress. When observing marine animals, take into account that they may be resting, feeding or breeding and that your presence may disturb them; this is particularly important in the case of larger animals such as sharks – the 'raggies' at Aliwal Shoal are a prime example.

• When booking a live-aboard dive trip or a stay at a resort, ask about the company's environmental policy regarding waste management, relationship with the local community (particularly in rural areas), anchoring, and usage of energy and fresh water. Boycott dive boats that cause unnecessary anchor damage, have bad oil leaks, or discharge untreated sewerage near reefs, and do not support operators who exploit the local environment and community without returning any benefit. (Yes, you are entitled to ask them if they repatriate profits to a foreign country, who they employ, what they pay them and how the local community benefits from their operation.)

• Try to be conservative in your use of water and power as these resources are in short supply in South Africa.

• If you spearfish or hunt any seafood, make sure you are familiar with all local fish and game regulations and obtain any necessary licensing. Prove your expertise in spearfishing by killing exactly the right size, number and species of fish for the next meal. Any more is wasteful, destructive and counter-productive.

• Most important, enjoy your dive and, yes, take only photographs and leave only bubbles!

HEALTH AND SAFETY FOR DIVERS

The information in this section is intended as a guide only. It is no substitute for thorough training or professional medical advice. The information is based on currently accepted health and safety information but it is certainly not meant to be a replacement for a comprehensive manual on the subject. We strongly advise that the reader obtains a recognized manual on diving safety and medicine before embarking on a trip.

Please note that:

• Divers who have suffered a diving-related injury, no matter how minor, should consult a doctor, preferably a specialist in diving medicine, as soon as possible after the symptom or injury occurs.

• If you are the victim of a diving injury do not hesitate to reveal your symptoms, no matter how minor they seem to be. Mild symptoms can later develop into a major illness with life-threatening consequence. It is better to be honest with yourself and live to dive another day.

• No matter how confident you are in formulating your own diagnosis, remember that unless you are a trained medical practiner, you are not a doctor.

• Always err on the conservative side when considering your ailment; if you discover your illness is only minor, the worst that can happen is that both you and the doctor will be relieved.

GENERAL FIRST AID PRINCIPLES

The basic principles of first aid include:
• DOING NO HARM
• SUSTAINING LIFE
• PREVENTING DETERIORATION
• PROMOTING RECOVERY

SAFETY

In the event of any illness or injury, a simple sequence of patient assessment and management can be followed. The sequence first involves assessment and definition of any life-threatening conditions, followed by management of the problems found. The first things to check are commonly known as the ABCs, i.e.:

A – for AIRWAY (with care of the neck)
B – for BREATHING
C – for CIRCULATION
D – for DECREASED level of consciousness
E – for EXPOSURE

Ensure both the patients and your own safety by removing yourselves from the threatening environment (usually the water). Make sure that whatever your actions, they in no way further endanger the patient or yourself.

NEVER ASSUME THAT THE PATIENT IS DEAD.

A. AIRWAY

1. With attention to the neck, is there a neck injury?
2. Is the mouth and nose free of obstruction? Any noisy breathing is a sign of airway obstruction.

B. BREATHING

1. Look at the chest to see if it is rising and falling.
2. Listen for air movement at the nose and mouth.
3. Feel for the movement of air against your cheek.

C. CIRCULATION

Feel for a pulse next to the windpipe (carotid artery).

D. DECREASED LEVEL OF CONSCIOUSNESS

Does the patient respond to any of the following procedures (AVPU)?:

A – Awake, aware, spontaneous speech
V – Verbal stimuli: Wake up!
P – Painful stimuli: Pinch him
U – Unresponsive

E. EXPOSURE

The patient must be adequately exposed in order to examine him properly, so remove clothes as necessary.

NOW, SEND FOR HELP.

If you think the patient's condition is serious following your assessment, you need to send or call for help from the emergency medical services (ambulance, paramedics). Whoever you send to get help should return to confirm that help is indeed on its way.

RECOVERY POSITION

If the patient is unconscious but breathing normally, there is a risk of vomiting and subsequent choking. It is therefore critical that the patient be placed on his side in the recovery position.

1. Kneel next to the patient's chest on his left.
2. Try to maintain the head in line with the trunk.
3. Place the patient's right hand under his head with the palm forwards.
4. Cross the left leg over the right leg at the ankle.
5. Fold the left arm over the chest
6. Grasp the left hip and pull the patient over onto his side with your right hand, while supporting the patient's right cheek with the left hand.
7. Now flex the patient's left knee to 90 degrees.
8. Flex the patient's left arm to 90 degrees and place the forearm flat on the ground.
9. The patient is now in the recovery position.

CARDIOPULMONARY RESUSCITATION (CPR)

Cardiopulmonary resuscitation is required when a patient is found to have no pulse. It consists of techniques to:

• VENTILATE THE PATIENT'S LUNGS
(expired air resuscitation)
• PUMP THE PATIENT'S HEART
(external cardiac compression)

Once you have checked the ABC's and found the patient to have no breathing and pulse, you need to **do** the ABC's.

A. AIRWAY

1. Gently extend the head (head tilt) and lift the chin with two fingers (chin lift). This will clear the tongue away from the back of the throat and open the airway.
2. If you suspect a foreign body in the airway, sweep your finger across the back of the tongue from one side to the other, if one is found remove it.

Do not attempt this in a conscious or semi-conscious patient as they will either bite your finger off or cause them to vomit.

B. BREATHING

If the patient is not breathing you need to give expired air resuscitation, in other words you need to breath into the patient's lungs.

1. Pinch the patients nose closed.
2. Place your mouth, open, fully over the patients mouth, making as good a seal as possible.
3. Exhale into the patient's mouth hard enough to cause the patients chest to rise!
4. If the patient's chest fails to rise you need to adjust the position of the airway. The 16% of oxygen in your expired air is adequate to sustain life.
5. Initially you need to give two full, slow breaths.

6. If the patient is found to have a pulse in the next step continue breathing for the patient once every five seconds, checking for a pulse after every 10 breaths.
7. If the patient begins breathing on his own you can turn him into the recovery position.

C. CIRCULATION

After giving the two breaths as above you now need to give external cardiac compression.

1. Kneel next to the patient's chest.
2. Measure two finger breadths above the notch where the ribs meet the lower end of the breastbone.
3. Place the heel of your left hand just above your two fingers in the centre of the breastbone.
4. Place the heel of your right hand on your left hand.
5. Straighten your elbows.
6. Place your shoulders perpendicularly above the patients breastbone.
7. Compress the breastbone 4-5cm (1.5-2in) to a rhythm of one, two, three...
8. Give 15 compressions.

Continue giving cycles of two breaths and 15 compressions, checking for a pulse after every five cycles.

The aim of CPR is to keep the patient alive until more sophisticated help arrives in the form of paramedics or a doctor with the necessary equipment. Make sure that you and your buddy are trained in CPR. It could mean the difference between life and death.

DIVING DISEASES AND ILLNESSES

ACUTE DECOMPRESSION ILLNESS

Acute decompression illness means any illness arising out of the decompression of a diver, in other words, by the diver moving from an area of high ambient pressure to an area of lower pressure. It is divided into two groups:

• **DECOMPRESSION SICKNESS**
• **BAROTRAUMA WITH ARTERIAL GAS EMBOLISM**

It is not important for the diver or first aider to differentiate between these two conditions because both are serious and both require the same emergency treatment. The important thing is to recognize acute decompression sickness and to initiate emergency treatment. The differences between decompression sickness and barotrauma are described below:

• DECOMPRESSION SICKNESS

Decompression sickness, or the 'bends', arises following inadequate decompression by the diver. Exposure to higher ambient pressure under water causes nitrogen to dissolve in increasing amounts in the body tissues.

If this pressure is released gradually during correct and adequate decompression procedures, the nitrogen escapes naturally into the blood and is exhaled through the lungs. If this release of pressure is too rapid the nitrogen cannot escape quickly enough and physical nitrogen bubbles form in the tissues. The symptoms and signs of the disease are related to the tissues in which these bubbles form and the disease is described by the tissue affected, e.g. joint bend.

Symptoms and signs of decompression sickness include:
- Nausea and vomiting
- Dizziness
- Malaise and loss of appetite
- Weakness
- Joint pains or aching
- Paralysis
- Numbness
- Itching of skin or rashes
- Incontinence
- Shortness of breath

• BAROTRAUMA WITH ARTERIAL GAS EMBOLISM
Barotrauma refers to the damage that occurs when the tissue surrounding a gaseous space is injured following a change in the volume of air in that space. An arterial gas embolism refers to a gas bubble that moves in a blood vessel usually leading to obstruction of that blood vessel or a vessel further downstream.

Barotrauma can therefore occur to any tissue that surrounds a gas filled space:

• ears	middle ear squeeze	burst ear drum
• sinuses	sinus squeeze	sinus pain, nosebleeds
• lungs	lung squeeze	burst lung
• face	mask squeeze	swollen, bloodshot eyes
• teeth	tooth squeeze	toothache

A burst lung is the most serious of these and can result in arterial gas embolism. It occurs following a rapid ascent during which the diver does not exhale adequately. The rising pressure of expanding air in the lungs bursts the delicate alveoli, or lung sacs, and forces air into the blood vessels that carry blood back to the heart and ultimately the brain. In the brain these bubbles of air block blood vessels and obstruct the supply of blood and oxygen to the brain, resulting in brain damage.

The symptoms and signs of lung barotrauma and arterial gas embolism include:
- Shortness of breath
- Chest pain
- Unconsciousness or altered level of consciousness
- Weakness, incoordination and paralysis
- Blurred vision, loss of balance

Treatment
1. ABC's (see Safety, p. 168) and CPR (p. 167) as needed.
2. Position the patient in the recovery position (p. 167) with no tilt or raising of the legs.

3. Administer 100% oxygen by mask (or demand valve).
4. Keep the patient warm.
5. Remove to the nearest hospital as soon as possible. The hospital or emergency services will arrange the recompression treatment required.

CARBON DIOXIDE OR MONOXIDE POISONING
Carbon dioxide poisoning can occur as a result of:

- skip breathing – diver holds his breath on Scuba
- heavy exercise on Scuba
- malfunctioning rebreather systems

Carbon monoxide poisoning occurs as a result of:

- exhaust gases being pumped into cylinders
- hookah systems air intake too close to exhaust fumes

Symptoms and signs would be:
- Headache
- Blue colour of the skin
- Shortness of breath
- Decreased level of consciousness or loss of consciousness

Treatment
1. Safety, ABC's as necessary.
2. CPR (p. 169) if required.
3. 100% oxygen through a mask or demand valve.
4. Remove to nearest hospital.

HEAD INJURY
All head injuries should at all times be regarded as potentially serious.

Treatment
The diver should come to the surface, any wound should be disinfected, and there should be no more diving until a doctor has been consulted.

If the diver is unconscious, the emergency services should be contacted; if breathing and/or pulse has stopped, CPR (p. 169) should be administered.

If the diver is breathing and has a pulse, check for bleeding and other injuries and treat for shock (p. 169); if wounds permit, put sufferer into recovery position (p. 167) with no elevation of the legs and administer 100% oxygen. Keep him or her warm and comfortable, and monitor pulse and respiration constantly.

DO NOT administer fluids to unconscious or semi-conscious divers.

HYPERTHERMIA (increased body temperature)
A rise in body temperature results from a combination of overheating, normally due to exercise, and inadequate fluid intake. The diver will progress through heat exhaustion to heat stroke with eventual collapse.

Heat stroke is an emergency and if the diver is not cooled and rehydrated he will die.

Treatment
Remove the diver from the hot environment and remove all clothes. Sponge with a damp cloth and fan either manually or with an electric fan. If unconscious place the patient in the recovery position and monitor the ABC's. Always seek advanced medical help.

HYPOTHERMIA
Normal internal body temperature is just under 37°C (98.4°F). If for any reason it is pushed much below this – usually, in diving, through inadequate protective clothing – progressively more serious symptoms may occur, with death as the ultimate endpoint.
• A drop of 1°C (2°F) leads to shivering and discomfort.
• A 2°C (3.5°F) drop induces the body's self-heating mechanisms to react; blood flow to the peripheries is reduced and shivering becomes extreme.
• A 3°C (5°F) drop leads to amnesia, confusion, disorientation, heartbeat and breathing irregularities, and possibly rigor.

Treatment
Prevent further heat loss by wrapping him in a space blanket, surrounding the diver with you and your buddies' bodies, and cover the diver's head and neck with a woolly hat, warm towels or anything else suitable. In sheltered warmth, re-dress the diver in warm, dry clothing and then put him in a space blanket. If the diver is conscious and coherent, a warm shower or bath and a warm, sweet drink should be enough; otherwise call the emergency services and treat for shock (this page) while deploying the other warming measures noted.

NEAR DROWNING
Near drowning refers to a situation where the diver has inhaled some water. He may be conscious or unconscious. Water in the lungs interferes with the normal transport of oxygen from the lungs into the blood and near drowning victims are therefore often hypoxic.

Treatment
Remove the diver from the water and check the ABC's. Depending on your findings, commence EAR (see Breathing under CPR, p. 167) or CPR where appropriate, beginning with EAR in the water if necessary. If possible, administer oxygen by mask or demand valve. All near drowning victims can develop secondary drowning, a condition where fluid oozes into the lungs causing the diver to drown in his own secretions, so all near drowning victims should be observed for 24 hours in a hospital.

NITROGEN NARCOSIS
The air we breathe is about 80% nitrogen; breathing the standard mixture under compression, as divers do, can lead to symptoms very much like those of drunkenness – the condition is popularly called 'rapture of the deep'. Some divers experience nitrogen narcosis at depths of 30-40m (100-130ft). Up to a depth of about 60m (200ft)

– that is, beyond the legal maximum depth for sport diving in the UK, RSA and USA – the symptoms need not (but may) be serious; beyond about 80m (260ft) the diver is likely to become unconscious. The onset of symptoms can be sudden and unheralded. The condition itself is not harmful; dangers arise through secondary effects, notably the diver doing something foolish.

Treatment
The sole treatment required is to return immediately to a shallower depth.

OXYGEN TOXICITY (Poisoning)
Oxygen, if breathed at a partial pressure of greater than 1.5 atmospheres, can be poisonous to the lung and brain tissues.

• Lung toxicity is a more chronic event and is not commonly seen in sports divers.
• Brain toxicity is common and manifests when breathing pure (100%) oxygen at depths greater than 7msw (metres of sea water) or air deeper than 90msw.

The advent of Nitrox diving (increased oxygen percentage in the breathing mixture) will inevitably increase the incidence of brain oxygen toxicity.
  The clinical presentation of oxygen toxicity is sudden and unpredictable with unconsciousness and seizures which can be catastrophic under water.

The management revolves around prevention:
• Don't dive on 100% oxygen.
• Don't dive deeper than recommended for a particular Nitrox Mix.
• Don't dive deeper than 70m on air.

Treatment
Convulsions cannot be treated underwater. Bring the diver to the surface and connect him to a gas mixture with the correct oxygen content. Prevent the convulsing diver from self-inflicting injuries by *guiding*, not *inhibiting*, his movements. If possible, put a knotted handkerchief in the diver's mouth to prevent tongue-biting; do *not* prise the mouth open, but wait for an opportunity to present itself.
  The diver should be taken to a recompression chamber and a doctor, and kept under observation for at least 24 hours – oxygen poisoning inevitably inflicts neurological damage.

SHOCK
Shock refers not to the emotional trauma of a frightening experience but to a physiological state in the body resulting from poor blood and oxygen delivery to the tissues. As a result of oxygen and blood deprivation the tissues cannot perform their functions. There are many causes of shock, the most common being loss of blood or hypovolaemic shock.

Treatment

Treatment is directed at restoring blood and oxygen delivery to the tissues, therefore maintain the ABC's and administer 100% oxygen. Control all external bleeding by direct pressure, pressure on pressure points and elevation of the affected limb. A tourniquet should only be used as a last resort and then only on the arms and legs.

Unconscious, shocked victims should be placed on their side with the legs elevated.

DIVING RESCUE

The question is always asked as to what to do if you find your buddy or another diver unconscious underwater. Fortunately this is a rare occurrence as most diving incidents and accidents happen on the surface. The short answer to the question is that incidents and accidents should be avoided as far as possible by the following:

• Thorough training both initially and continuously in personal diving, rescue and emergency care skills.
• Maintaining good physical and mental fitness for diving and avoiding substances like alcohol and drugs that compromise that fitness.
• Equipment maintenance with regular servicing and checks to ensure reliable function. Familiarizing yourself with new equipment in the pool before using it in the sea. Diving with equipment appropriate to the complexity of the dive. Wearing appropriate thermal protection.
• Thorough predive checks of equipment.
• Attention to buoyancy ensuring that you are not over- or underweight and that buoyancy control mechanisms are functioning normally.
• Detailed attention to thorough dive planning no matter how apparently routine the dive. Dive planning is an exercise in accident prevention.

If you find yourself in a situation where a diver requires active rescue, the situation can be managed in the following sequence:

1. DIVER RECOVERY
2. DIVER RESUSCITATION
3. DIVER EVACUATION

Diver recovery involves freeing the diver from any entrapment underwater and then providing buoyancy and lift to get them to the surface without further injury. The emphasis in getting the diver to the surface is on control of the ascent. The diver must be brought to the surface in a controlled manner to avoid the possibility of barotrauma and air embolism.

To provide positive buoyancy, it may be necessary to release the weight belt, inflate the victim's buoyancy compensator or inflate your own buoyancy compensator. A position behind the diver should be taken up with your right hand under the chin keeping the airway open and the other hand on the victim's BC inflator/deflator hose. Swim upward at a controlled, moderate pace, being

conscious of your own exhalation and a need not to become exhausted. Once on the surface, resuscitation should be begun in the water with expired air resuscitation while the diver is towed to the nearest boat or land where CPR can begin. Resuscitation is continued while preparations are made to evacuate the injured diver.

Treatment would include:
• EAR or CPR (p. 167) as necessary with or without the assistance of medical equipment.
• 100% oxygen by mask, through a bag, valve, mask or demand valve.
• Keeping the diver warm.
• Maintaining hydration by intravenous therapy if skills and equipment are available.

Evacuation of the diver is by the quickest available means to the nearest resuscitation facility (hospital trauma unit), the options being by sea, land or air, or a combination of the three. The recompression treatment that may be required is arranged from the resuscitation facility once the diver has been adequately assessed.

Ignorance is your greatest enemy in a rescue situation and time and money spent on dive rescue training is an investment in life. Approach your nearest agency for traning in rescue and before going for a dive, find out what rescue facilities are available in the area of the dive and how they are contactable in an emergency.

MARINE-RELATED AILMENTS

Apart from the specific diving-related illnesses, the commonest ailments divers are inflicted with include cuts and abrasions, coral cuts and stings, swimmers ear, sea sickness, jellyfish stings and sunburn.

CUTS AND ABRASIONS

Divers should wear appropriate protection against abrasions. The prominent areas, hands, knees, elbows and feet, are the most common areas affected. The danger with abrasions is that they become infected and all wounds should be thoroughly rinsed with water and an antiseptic, like hibitane in alcohol, as soon as possible after the injury occurs. Infection may progress to a stage where antibiotics are needed. Spreading inflamed areas should prompt the diver to seek medical advice.

SWIMMER'S EAR

Swimmer's ear is an infection of the external ear canal resulting from constantly wet ears. The infection is often a combination of a fungal and bacterial one.

Treatment

Prevent this condition by always thoroughly drying the ears after diving and, if you are susceptible to the condition, inserting alcohol or acetic acid drops after diving, is the best measure. Never stick anything into your ear (including ear buds) as this will damage the normal lining and predispose the ear towards infection. Once infected, the best possible treatment is by stopping diving/swimming for a few days and seeking medical advice. If you are prone to swimmer's ear and are likely to be in a remote area, carry antibiotic drops with you as recommended by your diving physician.

SEA OR MOTION SICKNESS
Motion sickness can be an annoying complication of a diving holiday involving boat dives. If you are susceptible to motion sickness seek medical advice prior to diving.

Treatment
To prevent sea sickness only eat light meals before going to sea and avoid alcohol the night before. Normally a combination of metaclopamide (maxolon) and an antihistaminic (Valoid) or similar drugs offer a simple preventative solution. A cautionary note must be made that the antihistamine can make you drowsy which may impair your ability to think and act while diving. Divers on antihistamines should limit their diving depth to less than 3m (100ft). A sea sick diver should not attempt to dive.

SUNBURN
The sun in South Africa is particularly harsh.

Treatment
Divers are advised to wear appropriate wide-brimmed hats and clothing. High-protection-factor sun creams are recommended.

TROPICAL DISEASES
Visitors to Africa are advised to have had tetanus, yellow fever, typhoid, polio, tuberculosis and Hepatitis B vaccinations. Malaria is another serious problem from Northern KwaZulu-Natal northwards. Specialist advice on the correct anti-malarial prophylactics can be obtained from the Department of Pharmacology at the University of Cape Town, or from your doctor or pharmacy.

MARINE ANIMALS THAT BITE

SHARKS
Sharks rarely attack divers but should always be treated with respect. Attacks are usually associated with the spearing of fish and the resultant vibrations released into the water. The great white, common in South African waters, is an exception to the rule. It has an unpredictable nature and should be avoided. Leave the water if a great white makes an appearance. Seals are the normal prey of the great white and theories have it that divers are often mistaken as such.

Grey nurse (spotted ragged-tooth), Zambezi, bronze whaler, tiger, cat-, reef-, basking and whale sharks are commonly spotted in South African waters. If a shark displays agitated behaviour, such as arching of the back and ventral pointing of the pectoral fins this may be a sign of impending attack and the diver should leave the water.

Treatment
Injuries are normally severe and involve severe blood loss resulting in shock. Blood loss control is the main objective. Control bleeding by applying direct pressure to wounds, pressure on pressure points, and by elevating the affected limb. Tourniquets may be used on limbs above an amputation. Preferably use a wide rubber bandage as a tourniquet. The diver should be stabilized as far as possible with the available medical help before being transported to hospital.

MORAY EELS
Probably more divers are bitten by morays than by all other sea creatures added together – usually through putting their hands into holes to collect shells or lobsters, remove anchors or hide baitfish. Often a moray refuses to let go, so, unless you can persuade it to do so with your knife, you make the wound worse by tearing your flesh as you pull the fish off.

Treatment
Thorough cleaning and usually stitching. The bites always go septic, so antibiotics and antitetanus shots are recommended.

TRIGGERFISH
Large triggerfish – usually males guarding eggs in 'nests' – are particularly aggressive, and will attack divers who swim too close. Their teeth are very strong, and can go through rubber fins and draw blood through a 4mm ($\frac{1}{6}$ inch) wetsuit.

Treatment
Clean the wound and treat it with antiseptic cream.

MARINE ANIMALS THAT STING

Scorpion-, lion- and stonefish are the most common fish and venomous. Many venomous sea creatures are bottom-dwellers, hiding among coral or resting on or burrowing into sand. If you need to move along the sea bottom, do so in a shuffle, so that you push such creatures out of the way and minimise your risk of stepping directly onto sharp, venomous spines, many of which can pierce rubber fins. Antivenins require specialist medical supervision, do not work for all species and need refrigerated storage, so are rarely available when required. Most of the venoms are high-molecular-weight proteins that break down under heat.

Immerse the limb in hot water (e.g. use the cooling water from an outboard motor, if no other supply is available) at 50°C (120°f) for about 2 hours, or until the pain stops. Several injections around the wound of local anaesthetic (e.g. procain hydrochloride) if available, will ease the pain. This is known as the **hot water treatment**. Younger or weaker victims may need CPR. Remember that venoms may still be active in fish that have been dead even for 48 hours.

CONE SHELLS

Live cone shells should never be handled. The animal has a mobile tube-like organ that shoots a poison dart. The result is initial numbness, followed by local muscular paralysis, which may extend to respiratory paralysis and heart failure.

Treatment
Apply a broad ligature between the wound and the body. CPR (p. 167) and supportive care may be needed.

FIRE CORAL

Fire orals are not true corals but members of the class Hydrozoa, i.e. they are more closely related to the sting-ing hydroids. Some people react violently from the slightest brush with them, and the resulting blisters may be 15cm (6in) across.

Treatment
Apply vinegar / acetic acid.

JELLYFISH

Most jellyfishes sting, but few are dangerous. As a gener-al rule, those with longest tentacles tend to have the most painful stings. The box jellyfish, or sea wasp, and blue bottle are the commonest stingers encountered.

Blue bottle and sea wasp stings can be treated with vinegar or alcohol applied locally. Divers commonly develop allergies to these stings and those sentitized should always carry a supply of antihistamines and, if necessary, their injection of adrenalin.

LIONFISH / TURKEYFISH / FIREFISH

These are slow-moving except when swallowing prey. They hang around on reefs and wrecks and pack a heavy sting in their beautiful spines.

Treatment
Use the hot water treatment (see p. 171).

SCORPIONFISH

Other scorpionfish are less camouflaged and less danger-ous than the stonefish but are more common and quite dangerous.

Treatment
As for **Stonefish** (see next column this page).

SEA URCHIN

The spines of sea urchins can be poisonous. Even if they are not, they can puncture the skin – even through gloves – and break off, leaving painful wounds that can often go septic.

Treatment
For bad cases give the hot water treatment (see p. 171); this also softens the spines, helping the body reject them. Soothing creams or a magnesium-sulphate compress will help reduce the pain, as will the application of the flesh of papaya fruit. Septic wounds require antibiotics. Alcohol applied after the heat might prove useful.

STINGING PLANKTON

You cannot see stinging plankton, and so cannot take evasive measures. If there are reports of any in the area keep as much of your body covered as possible.

Treatment
Apply vinegar / acetic acid locally.

STINGRAYS

Stingrays vary from a few centimetres to several metres across. The sting consists of one or more spines on top of the tail; though these point backwards, they can sting in any direction. The rays thrash out and sting when trod-den on or caught. Wounds may be large and severely lacerated.

Treatment
Clean the wound and remove any spines. Give the hot water treatment and local anaesthetic if available; follow up with antibiotics and antitetanus.

STONEFISH

Stonefish are the most feared, best camouflaged and most dangerous of the scorpionfish family. The venom is contained in the spines of the dorsal fin, which is raised when the fish is agitated.

Treatment
There is usually intense pain and swelling. Clean the wound, give the hot water treatment (p. 173) and follow up with antibiotic and antitetanus.

MARINE ANIMALS THAT SHOCK

The onefin electric ray is common in South Africa and is normally found on sandy bottoms. Contact with the ray will result in a powerful shock which could unsettle the diver sufficiently to cause an accident.

MARINE ANIMALS THAT ARE POISONOUS TO EAT

Eating shellfish can result in gastroenteritis, allergic reac-tions or paralytic shellfish poisoning. Avoid eating any-thing but fresh shellfish. If considering eating mussels, first find out from the locals if it is safe or if there has been a red tide recently.

Ciguatera poisoning can result from eating reef and game fish contaminated by a dinoflagellate. Obtain local advice on which fish are safe to eat. Pufferfish and sun-fish are not edible and ingestion of their flesh can result in death. Scromboid poisoning results from eating mack-erel and tuna that have been allowed to lie in the sun. Avoid all but the freshest fish.

UNDERWATER PHOTOGRAPHY AND VIDEO

It is almost impossible to describe to non-divers the incredible beauty of the underwater environment. The best we can do is to take photographs and videos which will also serve to preserve our precious memories for our own pleasure. Neither of these skills is easy, though, and the aspiring photographer or videographer has to be a competent diver, first, and then learn the complexities of photographic equipment and the behaviour of light underwater. You will need perseverance – and a bit of luck – to get really good results but, if you're prepared to persist with this challenging skill, you may well develop a passion that will last for a lifetime of diving.

Buddies

Try to dive with a buddy who understands the photographic process and is prepared to just tag along, allow for your idiosyncracies, model if necessary, find subjects and generally look after you. If you are doing a shore dive, kit up, get in the water and let your buddy, without fins or tank, hand you your camera from the shallows. When exiting, do the opposite. Wait for him or her to exit, take off tank and fins and then hand it up. Explain to your buddy before the dive that she or he is to stay behind and above you or you may find yourself peering at the reef through a cloud of bubbles or silt.

Power Supplies

Even though torch batteries may fit into your strobe or video camera, buy only camera batteries as they will give you better results. Rechargeable Ni-Cad (nickel-cadmium) batteries are an excellent choice but make sure that you have a sufficient supply so that you can use one set and have a spare while recharging. It might be worth your while, depending on your travel plans, to bring along a charger that can work off the cigarette lighter of a car. Although memory-free batteries are advertised, most still have memory problems. To ensure long life of your Ni-Cads, deep charge them at least every fourth or fifth charge (let them go completely flat and then charge them up to full) and never store them absolutely flat.

The little flat 1.5 or 3 volt batteries that power your camera (the camera, not the flash) are so difficult to get hold of in out-of-the-way places and take up very little room, so it is wise to stock-pile a good supply.

General Hints

• If you have not operated your camera with gloves, practise before the dive. You may find that it is easier to dive without gloves, but this can be chilly, especially in the Cape waters.

• Your mask keeps your eyes distant from the viewfinder. Buy the smallest-volume mask you can wear.

• Refraction makes objects appear one-third closer and larger than in air. Reflex focusing and visual estimates of distances are unaffected but, if you measure a distance, compensate by reducing the resultant figure by one-third when setting the lens focus.

Maintainance

• Follow all the manufacturers' instructions regarding post- and pre-dive preparation, paying particular attention to keeping the sealing surfaces clean and grit-free and the 'O' rings clean, supple and greased.

• Use only silicone grease (never spray and **never** petroleum jelly) and replace flattened 'O' rings with new plump ones. If possible, store 'O' rings off the camera to prevent their becoming flattened.

• When changing film or tape between dives, ensure that the outside of your camera is completely dry first. It is important to open the camera with the back facing down so that any stray drops of water will fall away from the camera, not into it.

• Never leave your camera lying on its back in the sun without covering the lens, even for a few minutes.

• If you cannot get your camera into fresh water soon after a dive, wrap it in your wetsuit and try to keep it wet. If the seawater is allowed to dry, it will be more difficult to remove salt particles.

• Very few South African dive boats, or even resorts, have dedicated camera tanks or cleaning tables. You may want to purchase a sealable bucket (like those used for cleaning babies' nappies) for this purpose.

Taking photographs and videos provides special memories of the incredible beauty of the underwater environment.

Still Photography

Underwater photographs are mementos to be treasured. They can be blown up to adorn walls, made into greeting cards or even, if they are of sufficiently high quality, sold for publication. One of the major advantages of still photography over video is that each shot is a single entity. Even if most of the photographs are fuzzy blurs, one good shot is well worth the cost of the film and the developing and printing.

Choosing a Camera
When starting out, your major choice will be whether to buy a relatively cheap camera with which you can play around, or to go for an expensive, professional system. You choice will depend on your budget and ambitions.

There are several waterproof automatic cameras on the market. These range from throwaways (usually manufactured by film companies) to quite sophisticated autofocus and auto-exposure cameras which may operate down to five, or even 10, metres (16-33ft). As well as buying waterproof disposable cameras, you can obtain a relatively inexpensive perspex housing for the standard, non-waterproof Fuji disposable camera.

If all you want is a few mementos, these simple cameras will give you acceptable results in clear, shallow water with colour print film.

For serious underwater photography, you have two options. The first is to splash out on a purpose-built waterproof camera; the second is to buy a waterproof housing for a SLR (single-lens reflex) or land camera, should you already own one or plan to purchase one. Each system has both advantages and disadvantages.

Dedicated Underwater Cameras
The submersible camera used by most professionals is the Nikonos, a 35mm non-reflex camera. The newer models (IV-A and V) have a TTL (through-the-lens) automatic exposure system and the Nikonos V has TTL flash exposure. The older models have no built-in exposure meters but are, nevertheless, excellent, rugged cameras that give good results. You can often buy one of these second-hand for a very good price but will need to acquire a hand-held submersible light meter.

This system, with its specially designed Nikonos lenses, gives sharper results underwater than any housed system, an advantage which (except in the case of very skilled photographers) is usually offset by the lack of reflex focusing. Another disadvantage of this system is the lack of through-the-lens composition. You have to use a little guesswork in composing pictures and you may easily cut off part of a subject. The Nikonos, except with some of the dedicated underwater lenses, also makes an excellent, rugged, weatherproof land camera, with the above-mentioned limitations. Nikon have recently introduced the RS-AF, a fully waterproof reflex camera with autofocus and dedicated lenses and flash-

gun, but it is extremely heavy and expensive. If and when the price comes down, this may prove to be a good buy for use as a dedicated underwater camera but it is very clumsy on land.

The most popular rival to the Nikonos is the smaller, lighter and less expensive Sea and Sea range. They have recently brought out the first amphibious camera on which you can change lenses underwater. Ask a dealer who specializes in underwater cameras to discuss these and other models with you before making this significant financial investment.

Waterproof Housings
Specially constructed housings are available for all the popular brands of reflex cameras and even for some of the simpler, preset cameras. These may be made from metal, perspex or flexible plastic, each of which has advantages and disadvantages. Metal housings are strong, reliable, work well at depth and last a long time if properly maintained; they are heavier to carry, but are buoyant in water. Their higher cost is justified if your camera is expensive and deserves the extra protection.

Perspex housings are slightly less robust and need careful handling both in and out of the water. They are lightweight, which is convenient on land, but may be buoyant in water so you may have to weight them. They are far less costly and, if properly maintained, should give long service.

Flexible plastic housings are cheaper still. They have an optical quality glass port, which fits over the lens of the camera and built in 'gloves' so that you can operate the controls directly. These are easier to use, but compress at depth so only give good results in reasonably shallow water.

Lenses and Accessories
Whatever system you use, unless it is a very simple one, you will have a range of lenses from which to choose. Except for the new Sea and Sea system, all lenses must be changed topside. This means you'll have to choose a lens before you enter the water. If you are using a housing, the chances are that it will be designed for only one lens. The most useful choice in this case would be a wide angle (24mm), or a short zoom such as a 28-70mm, with macro facility.

For the Nikonos, the most versatile lens is a 35mm one which can be used on land or underwater, both as is as is and with either extension tubes or a close-up unit to facilitate macro photography.

A longer lens, such as the 80mm, practically a telephoto, is difficult to use and is almost useless in local conditions except with macro which will enable you to photograph even (and only) the tiniest reef creatures.

Wider angle lenses, such as the 28mm, 20mm or 15mm, give excellent results underwater as they minimize backscatter and light loss by allowing you to get much closer to your subject. They are, unfortunately, not amphibious and so are useless on land. They are also very expensive, with the price increasing dramatically with decreasing focal length. The problem of composing photographs with the Nikonos can be somewhat simplified by the use of parallax viewfinders. These fit on top of the camera and compensate for the difference between what you see and what the lens 'sees'. These range in price significantly, with the more affordable option being a single viewfinder with different screens for different lenses.

As a general rule, you can use a longer lens in cleaner water, and macrophotography, with extension tubes or a close-up unit, is the only possibility in very poor visibility. Extension tubes and close-up units have the same effect, that of allowing you to get really close to your subject and fill your viewfinder with a small area. The close-up unit has one major advantage over extension tubes – it can be removed underwater, so allowing non-macro photography on the same dive.

Lighting
The amount of available light underwater decreases with depth and different wavelengths of light are absorbed by water at different rates, or depths. The first to be absorbed is red, thus giving the underwater environment a bluish cast. If you have more skill and ingenuity than funds, this can be used to great advantage in natural light photography. Think of your photographs more as black and white than colour; concentrate on contrast, shadows and silhouettes and you will get superb shots, often capturing the atmosphere of the site.

In very clean water with plenty of light, you can compensate for the colour imbalance by using a yellow filter, specially designed for underwater use. This will cut down the amount of available light so, if you are using a hand-held light meter, you will need to compensate about half a stop.

The most satisfactory system, though, is to use artificial light, usually in the form of synchronised strobes. This solution is, like most aspects of underwater photography, not without its problems. The most obvious is that of backscatter; suspended particles in the water reflect the light of the strobe and show up as bright white spots in the photograph. This can be quite creative but is usually a nuisance. In order to minimize this, position your strobe as far from the camera as you can; most modern strobes are sold with brackets and arms to achieve this but you will still get some backscatter. The use of a slave strobe can help to solve this problem by adding another light source and, at the same time, even out the lighting and eliminate shadows. The slave is programmed to flash in response to the flash of the primary strobe. The Nikonos V allows TTL flash exposure metering.

Film
You will obtain best results with colour positive (slide transparency) film of 50 or 100 ASA. If you are not too sure of your ability to obtain correct exposures, use a colour negative (print) film, as it is more forgiving.

Regardless of the type of film you use, buy it from a reputable photographic store. Check the expiry date and store it in a cool, dark place (preferably a refrigerator). When travelling, keep it in a well insulated camera or film bag. Try to get your films processed as soon as possible as they are at their least stable when they have been exposed but not yet processed, so be particularly careful to keep them cool after exposure.

On the Shoot
Take care in choosing a buddy who will look after you as photographers are notoriously bad buddies, always peering through a viewfinder at the reef and taking no notice of their buddies, air consumption or dive time.

Subjects
What you photograph depends on your personal interests but there are a few generalizations which may help you decide where to start.

Macrophotography is the easiest to get right, particularly with a TTL flash and a framer as the lens-to-subject and flash-to-subject distances are fixed and the effects of silting in the water are minimized. Expose a test film at a variety of exposures; the best result tells you the exposure to use in future for this particular setting and film.

Some fish are strongly territorial and therefore predictable; this is why, for example, there are so many excellent shots of clownfish. Manta rays are curious and will keep coming back if you react quietly and do not chase them. Angelfish and Chaetodons (butterflyfish) swim off when you first enter their territory but, if you remain quiet, they will usually return and allow you to photograph them. Hottentots are attracted to the whine of a flash and will often gather around you, usually too close to photograph but you might get some excellent macro portraits. The klipvis is the local favourite in the Cape as it is very common, totally calm if not unduly harassed and has beautiful colouring.

Don't forget the wonderful potential of marine algae; some of the red seaweeds have the most exquisite textures and the huge kelps form beautiful patterns against water-filtered sunlight.

Diver and wreck photography are the most difficult and require wide-angle lenses. You will need to instruct your model in the mechanics of photography so that he or she can best utilize the surrounding reef life and you will need to use a flash if you want the diver's face to be well exposed. You will get the best results on wrecks if you concentrate on small features – it is almost impossible to photograph a whole frigate underwater.

Underwater night photography can be very rewarding. Many interesting creatures, such as squid, cuttlefish and some sharks, are predominantly nocturnal, most invertebrates extend their feeding polyps at night and some fish are more approachable because they are half-asleep. However, focusing quickly in dim light is difficult, and many subjects retreat into the darkness as soon as they are lit up, so you need to preset your controls.

Video

Some divers prefer to take videos rather than stills. It is, as a rule, easier to obtain good results and is considered by many to be a more interesting and dynamic medium through which to share the underwater environment with friends and family.

Choosing a Camera
Besides the choice of video format, there are two basic choices to make: between a housed or a dedicated underwater camera. There are a few excellent dedicated cameras on the market and they have the advantage of being reasonably small and easy to manoeuvre, with the controls well laid out. If you already own a video camera, you may opt to acquire a housing. You may find one on the market or may have to have one made or modified. A disadvantage of this system is that the controls may be difficult to handle. There are companies who specialize in this; you can find their addresses in dive magazines.

The choice of format depends, to a large extent, on what you plan to do with your footage. If you intend it only for domestic use, you could use a standard VHS camera. These are rather big, though, so a better choice would be 8mm or VHS compact. If you feel you might like to use your tapes for promotional, teaching or semi-public purposes, super VHS or Hi-8 would be a better, but slightly more costly, alternative as you will be able to make better quality copies. With any of these systems, you can edit directly onto your home VCR.

If you have higher aspirations or ambitions of being a professional underwater videographer, go straight to beta-cam and start building up a professional system. You'll spend a lot more money but you will have the capability of producing broadcast-quality footage.

Lighting
You can get away without artificial lighting, although only in very good conditions, as you can set the colour balance on your video camera to compensate, to a certain extent, for the blue cast. You will, of course, obtain much better results if you use artificial light.

Specially designed underwater lights are reasonably compact, neutrally buoyant and easy for a competent assistant to handle underwater.

Planning your Shoot
Unlike still photography, it is not usually satisfying to get just one good shot or one good sequence on video; you will probably want to be able to produce a 'programme' of at least five or ten minutes, even if it is just for home use. To this end, you will need to do some basic scripting – at least in your head.

Work out a vague story line and ensure that you have footage which can support your script. Plan to film divers while they are kitting up, relaxing before and after the dive, and entering and exiting the water. Don't forget to get footage of the dive boat, scenic topside shots and close-ups of your companions. Before you enter the water, plan the direction of movement of all the shots in which the divers appear.

On the Shoot
• Avoid diving with inexperienced divers as you will want a buddy who can hold equipment, such as lights, for you and who can keep track of dive time and depth as you are bound to be preoccupied.

• Try to keep the direction of movement of divers constant (unless, of course, you are aiming for a special or humorous effect). Brief your models thoroughly, ensuring that they understand your requirements, and work out signals to communicate what you want them to do.

• Avoid the temptation to overuse the zoom – rather take the same shot twice, once on wide-angle and once on telephoto – you can do some creative editing later. If you don't switch the camera off between these shots, you can use the zoom section as well.

• As soon as you see something interesting, start the camera and then move into the shot as it is very difficult to edit in the first few seconds of any individual shot. For the same reason, leave the camera running a few seconds after you have taken the shot. This will make your life a lot easier at the editing stage.

• Take 'cutaway' shots. These are sneaky little shots of arbitrary images, for example, divers' faces, small fish, fin strokes through the water.

Editing
This really is the fun part. You can be as serious or as frivolous as you like but a standard script would include pre-dive shots, entry, underwater footage, including divers and marine life, exit and post-dive shots. This is where you will be grateful for those arbitrary little sequences you filmed.

If you add two shots together and they tend to 'jump' or otherwise not look quite right, experiment with adding a cutaway shot. You can even alternate short sequences of two long shots. This is your chance to have fun; if you don't like it, just wipe the tape and start again. What a medium!

Sound
Your underwater shots, if they have sound at all, will just have bubbles. You can add a voice-over, or commentary, or even music. If you are producing this masterpiece for purely domestic viewing, add whatever you like.

If, however, you plan to use the video for marketing or teaching purposes, check the copyright status of any music you plan to use. You can start your enquiries at a local video or music production company – they will tell you who to contact.

Index